The Blair Agenda

edited by
Mark Perryman

Lawrence & Wishart
London
In Association with Signs of the Times

Lawrence & Wishart Limited
99A Wallis Road
London E9 5LN

First published 1996
Reprinted 1996
Collection Copyright © Mark Perryman 1996
Each Essay © the individual author

The authors have asserted their right under the Copyright,
Designs and Patents Act, 1988, to be identified
as authors of this work.

British Library Cataloguing in Publication Data
A catalogue record for this book is available from
the British Library.

ISBN 0 85315 843 6

Photoset in North Wales by
Derek Doyle & Associates, Mold, Flintshire.
Printed and bound in Great Britain by
Redwood Books, Trowbridge.

HE BLAIR AGENDA

Contents

v

CONTENTS

Acknowledgements

The essays in this collection were informed, and shaped by, the Autumn 1994 and Spring 1995 seminars organised by the London-based discussion group *Signs of the Times*. Entitled 'Coming up for Air: A Seminar Series to Review the Blair Agenda' and, 'Faultlines: Seminars for a New Millennium', they are part of an ongoing programme of open-minded, committed intellectual work that *Signs of the Times* has sought to pioneer since early 1992 (for further details on publications and events see page 253).

As a group we describe this process as 'remaking the political', a process which wouldn't be possible without those who help to organise the group's activities: Geoff Andrews, Andrew Blake, Kevin Davey, Jeremy Gilbert, Stefan Howald, Andy Jones, Steve Pile, Herbert Pimlott, Karen Triggs, Wendy Wheeler and Alan White. Special thanks to Geoff Andrews for helping with the commissioning and editing of the chapters by Leighton Andrews and Anne Showstack Sassoon.

Our seminars continue to be held amidst the splendid surroundings of *Anna's Place*, London's premier Swedish restaurant, where good food is served six days a week, and on a Monday evening we provide good ideas instead of the customary culinary fare. A great debt of thanks is due to Anna Hegarty for her generous and continuing hospitality. Each summer we also host a conference. Themes to date have ranged over the legacy of Michel Foucault's work, via the complexities of postmodern political and cultural theories and the rise of a new urban politics. We are very grateful to the Barry Amiel and Norman Melburn Trust for their financial support in enabling these conferences to be such a success, and thanks are also due to *New Statesman* for sponsoring these events.

The editing, production and publication of this book would not have been possible without the dedication and professional skills of the staff at Lawrence & Wishart. More than just a book publisher, Lawrence & Wishart have done a great deal to support the development of the kind of politics that *Signs of the Times* seeks to champion. The enthusiasm of our commissioning editor, Sally Davison has once again helped us to guide an idea into a publishing reality, many thanks indeed. Gareth Smyth was a most able copy-editor in the latter stages of producing this book. Jan Brown designed the book's cover to her usual high standards of visual impact and clean-cut classicism.

On a personal note, Anne Coddington continues to feed me with love and ideas, while Tottenham Hotspur add the occasional dash of hope that there may yet be light at the end of at least one of life's long tunnels.

Mark Perryman, July 1996

Notes on Contributors

Leighton Andrews was active in Liberal and Liberal Democrat party politics for nearly twenty years. From 1993 he has been Head of Public Affairs at the BBC, having previously worked as a leading consultant on parliamentary and media relations since the mid-1980s.

Kevin Davey helped set up the *Signs of the Times* group in 1992 and has worked on organising the group's seminars ever since. A former chair of both The Socialist Society and The Socialist Movement he has also been employed as a researcher for a number of Labour MPs. A regular contributor to *New Statesman*, *New Times*, and *Tribune*, his book on changing forms of Englishness will be published by Lawrence & Wishart in late 1997.

Nina Fishman teaches history and industrial relations at the University of Westminster. The author of *The British Communist Party and the Trade Unions, 1933–45* (Scolar Press, 1995), a frequent contributor to *New Times*, she is also a member of the council of the Electoral Reform Society.

Andrew Gamble is Professor of Politics at the University of Sheffield. The author of a wide range of books and articles on Thatcherism, his latest book is *Hayek: The Iron Cage of Liberty* (Polity, 1996). He is presently researching the politics of ownership, and has written for a number of publications on this subject, including *New Left Review* and *Renewal*.

Gerry Hassan is the Press Officer for a Scottish voluntary sector organisation. He writes on the politics of devolution for the Scottish press, in particular *The Herald* and *The Scotsman*, and has also written for *New Statesman*, *New Times*, *Renewal* and *Tribune*. At present he is completing his PHD thesis, 'Scottish Labour and Devolution, 1974–97'.

Mark Perryman convenes the *Signs of the Times* seminar and conference organising groups. A freelance marketing consultant he advises a wide range of magazines and organisations on circulation, promotional and membership-services matters. A contributor to *New Statesman* and *Parliamentary Brief*, he is also the editor of *Altered States: Postmodernism, Politics and Culture* (Lawrence & Wishart, 1994).

Anne Showstack Sassoon is Professor of Politics, and the Director of the European Research Centre, at Kingston University. Chairperson of the Social Justice Group, she has written widely on Gramsci, women and the state, equality and difference, and changes in the voluntary sector in both Britain and Hungary.

Gareth Smyth co-edited the book *Turning Japanese: Britain with a Permanent Party of Government* (Lawrence & Wishart, 1994). He currently writes about British and international politics for *GQ*, *Financial Times*, *New Statesman*, *New Times* and a number of other publications.

Martin Summers is a former researcher for Michael Portillo MP, and research associate at The Institute of Economic Affairs. He now works as policy-adviser for ProShare, an organisation established to promote a greater understanding of the benefits of share-ownership.

Wendy Wheeler has been closely involved with the *Signs of the Times* group since its inception. A Senior Lecturer in English Literature and Critical Theory at the University of North London, she is in the process of writing a book on images of mourning in the contemporary English novel.

Helen Wilkinson is a project director at Demos, the radical independent cross-party think tank. her work for Demos includes the reports *No Turning Back: Generations and the Genderquake* and *Freedom's Children: Work, Relationships and Politics for 18–34 year olds in Britain Today*. Her book *The Age of Androgyny* is due to be published by HarperCollins in 1997.

INTRODUCTION:
COMING UP FOR AIR
Mark Perryman

For some there's always a single, easy, political answer to every defeat and setback. In a long and ponderous critique of Neil Kinnock's time as Labour leader Mike Marquese and Richard Heffernan ring out the new with the old refrain, 'Given time, resources and a united commitment from the leadership and the rank and file, Labour can win the next election on a socialist programme ... That is the only way the Party can both win and then go on to exercise power in the interests of the people who vote for it ... There is no alternative to the Labour Party'.[1] Those who are inspired and guided in their political actions by homilies of this ilk have had very little in the way of satisfaction since John Smith's untimely death in 1994. Of course the tide had already turned decisively against the most factional elements of Labour's left a long time before Tony Blair was a gleam in our eye, most notably with Neil Kinnock's firebrand assault on the Militant Tendency at the 1985 Bournemouth party conference. But it is Blair who is the ultimate inheritor of all the portents of change, and it is his particular combination of qualities that has enabled him to refashion Labour, finally, into an effective party for government.

But is this refashioning, popularly dubbed 'modernisation', modern enough? Is there the depth to sustain the vision and grapple with the momentous changes that are sweeping economy and society towards the millennium? As Kevin Davey points out, in a critical contribution to this collection, the consequences of Labour's failure to successfully provide the answers to these questions are severe indeed, potentially threatening 'the (continuing) viability of the Labour Party as a formation by which the interests and aspirations of a major section of the British polity are negotiated and expanded'.[2] It is the consequences of failure to win office at the fifth time of asking, to make the winning of that office actually mean something, and finally to win a second term, that make the 'Blair moment' so important. There is therefore a depressing predictability in the left's bewildering desire to shoot itself in its intellectual foot with every ringing doubt about the Blair agenda.

There seems to be a wilful inability to distinguish the potential that Blair has undoubtedly unleashed for radical and momentous social change from the self-evident fact that as yet it is far too early to say in what particular direction that change may take us. Pessimism of the intellect is a noble, if at times depressing art, but self-fulfilling prophecies are something anyone serious about politics should avoid like the plague. As Anne Showstack Sassoon recounts in her careful survey of the long-term implications of Labour's Commission on Social Justice that appears in this book's central section, the left has a long heritage on which to draw in learning the value of compromise. 'Whereas Lenin was most concerned to establish doctrinal correctness and party discipline, Gramsci was much more worried about political isolation when a party loses touch with reality and when unity becomes merely mechanical'.[3]

CHIPS OFF OLD BLOCKS

In the wake of Labour's 1992 defeat one self-fulfilling prophecy seemed to be one-party government, or the Japanisation of British politics. While there were few who went so far as to argue that Labour was now inherently unelectable[4] there were respected commentators who doubted the new Labour leader, John Smith, in his capacity to deliver the kind of changes the party needed to equip itself properly for victory. Martin Jacques was one who offered Smith some friendly advice on the eve of him becoming party leader in July 1992:

> Think long term. Labour's problems are so acute that there can be no salvation in the quick fix or one more heave. The party needs to open its windows and let in some fresh air. It needs to open up a dialogue with other political forces. Even more importantly, it must find a way of talking to and learning from the most dynamic and interesting groups in society. Set in motion a set of chemical reactions that might lead to a very different Labour Party, or in effect, a new party. Finally, Labour has to come to terms with the new society, this requires a wholesale transformation in Labour's politics.[5]

Within two years John Smith was dead, though he left his party in a state of recovery few would have predicted when he assumed the leadership and with the beginnings of a new style of inner-party democracy thanks to his victory on One Member One Vote. However, against Jacques's checklist the work had hardly begun.

Tony Blair was another with a checklist against which to judge Labour's progress and he was one of the first from within the party to urge a drastic change of pace in the process of change. A 1991 article in *Marxism Today* sketched out just how far Blair thought the party still needed to travel.

> We should accept the lessons of our history and build on them, not be intimidated or shackled by them. We must fashion a modern view of society which recognises the vested interest of both market and state and articulates a new over-arching concept of the public interest standing up for the individual against those vested interests. This requires a new political settlement between individual and society, a bargain between the two which determines rights and obligations on both sides. The notion of a modern view of society as the driving force behind the freedom of the individual is in truth the implicit governing philosophy of today's Labour Party. It will benefit us greatly now, both internally and with the public, if we spell it out with confidence.[6]

It was highly appropriate that this inveterate opponent of dogma, in both its social-democratic and marxist versions, should set out his views in the deeply heretical *Marxism Today*. However there was something disingenuous in what he was arguing. The centring of individualism within the philosophy of Labour's socialism had hardly begun in 1991; it certainly wasn't the party's 'governing philosophy' though it is Blair's singular achievement to have made it so. This is clearly one of the policy benchmarks against which Blair judges his party; it affects everything he says and does. This is an achievement that not only connects with the bipolar popular will that elected four successive Tory governments yet remained deeply committed to welfarist ideals in its social attitudes; but also with an earlier socialist tradition that predated the misplaced trajectories of Leninism and Fabianism.

Andrew Gamble's opening chapter offers this estimation of the scale of the shift in Labour's ideology that Blair has secured, 'New Labour represents the acceptance that socialism has to reconnect with the radical egalitarian individualism of the enlightenment from which it was born.'[7] Not only is it rare to find these historical antecedents to today's new Labour being recovered, but it is also regularly claimed that the championing of individualism is out of touch with tomorrow's political generation.[8] In fact the picture is far more complicated: the high profile of direct action politics certainly foregrounds an impatience with a parliamentary political system that is seen as outmoded, out of touch and incapable of responding to the urgency of impending environmental disaster. The 'politics of the deed' has a well-deserved resonance that is unlikely to be matched by the cut and thrust of a besuited session of Parliament. However this self-same political generation that is finding new and dynamic forms of political action being practised by a minority of its most active representatives can also relate to the values and virtues of an individualism rescued from the strictures of conservatism.

As Carol Samms reported in her working paper for Demos, 'It has become a universal that the group of 18–29 years realise that they wish to be strong individuals in a group. There is a net perception that you have to individually look after yourself, because the state may not be able to, and the demise of some of the more conventional social fabrics and structures means that it is your responsibility'. Samms goes on to distinguish between a concept of self and a determination of self-identity and a secondary concept of personal responsibility that is matched by an awareness of the limits of individual action.[9] In this sense Blair's moving of Labour's 'governing philosophy' onto the terrain he first mapped out in the early 1990s is an essential precursor for a party that is preparing for the future.

THE KISS OF LIFE

When individualism is accompanied by self-identity, personal responsibility and a consciousness of the impact of one's actions on others, then we are starting to engage with the basis for a truly pluralistic politics. After the stunning by-election victory by the Liberal Democrats at Newbury in 1993 Blair went further than most in proclaiming the need for dialogue and co-operation between the opposition parties: 'The dialogue of ideas with those outside the Labour party will and should go on'. His parenthesis was, however, depressingly familiar 'But inevitably the debate will centre on Labour ... All roads to change must come through the Labour Party.'[10] Clearly Labour does now dominate our political horizon, but why can't Labour politicians not only recognise, but welcome, contributions likely to be made in policy debates, strategic analysis, campaigning for and building popular coalitions, by those well outside the ambit of party politics, let alone Labour Party membership. Such a politics isn't weak, it is in fact strong and powerful, committed to pluralism as a central value and guiding tenet.

As David Marquand, one of the most consistent proponents of a pluralist politics, put it:

> The left has to embrace pluralism. It has to root out the whole notion of the hegemonic mass party, embodying a single truth and struggling to remake society in accordance with that truth. It has to accept that there are many truths, conflicting goods and diverse interests. Instead of the politics of top-down change, imposed by the central state, it has to practise a politics of bottom-up negotiation.[11]

For all of the revisionism and modernisation, the 'Blair agenda' remains divorced from the message of pluralism. It lacks a dimension that would open up its avowed populism to negotiating the intricacies of the genuinely popular coalition-building that Marquand is surely referring to – negotiations that should be seen as a vital prerequisite to securing majority support through the difficult mid-term years prior to seeking a second period in office. Arch-moderniser Tony Wright MP unwittingly revealed one reason why new Labour has failed to stimulate such a pluralisation of our politics, 'The scene is set for that long awaited realignment on the left, except that it will take the form of the reintegration of honest social democrats into the Labour Party'.[12] For even the most enlightened of Labour's pluralists the temptation to retreat into the security of the party mantle is just too strong. Parties have their place within the politics of pluralism, of course, for without them governments cannot be elected, but the most effective harbingers of a politics of change are still most likely to be found in the much broader realm of civil society.

THE SOFT CENTRE

Kevin Davey in his contribution to this collection also questions the viability of new Labour, doubting that it can become 'a sustainable political formation', describing it as 'technical, temporary and pragmatic.'[13] His thesis is that the formation is simply an electoral expedient, an important enough contingency but not enough in itself. The contrast with the deeply ideological nature of the Thatcherite project is an obvious one, and it is perhaps ironic that when Tony Blair has paid some very public dues to Thatcherism he has provoked the ire of the self-same critics who perpetually ask 'Where's the beef?'

What is needed is an ideological underpinning of new Labour that would give it something to counter Kevin Davey's well-founded fear of impermanence. Stuart Hall was one of the first to realise that through its ideological formation and practice Thatcherism was anything but impermanent. His assessment of Thatcherism tells us much of what new Labour still has to achieve to secure its place in history:

> Ideological transformations and political restructuring ... works on the ground of already constituted social practices ... It wins space there by constantly drawing on these elements which have secured over time a traditional resonance and left their traces in popular inventories ... It changes the field of struggle by changing the place, the position, the relative weight of the condensations within any one discourse and constructing them according to an alternative logic.[14]

Stuart Hall sought a politics that had an attachment to popular culture, that could reshape that culture from within and in so doing would change the nature of the political terrain. The aim was to fashion a new balance of political forces and this was the only basis on which a new politics could be founded. Leftist intellectuals were appalled. Hall was accused of an over-indulgent approach to Thatcherism, of prioritising ideology at the expense of political economy, and worst of all: 'Neglecting to prioritise issues around a unifying theme which identifies the movement as socialist. The left needs to develop a new socialist general will within which conflicting economic-corporate interests can be negotiated'.[15] The idea that socialism itself might be problematic was clearly beyond the pale, and as long as this remains the case leftism will continue to act as a conservative brake on radical renewal.

THINKING DEEP

One of the consequences of the collapse of marxism as a system of belief is the effective erosion of an organised and rigorous critique of society, one that actively seeks to make connections between critical thought and political action. In recognising the end of marxism one needs at the same time to reassert the place for intellectual work. There remain of course those for whom marxism is still their uncomplicated creed: for them the world remains unchanged, with Tony Blair simply the latest in a long line of revisionists prepared to sell their soul for an illusory power. The conclusions for those like the Socialist Workers Party's (SWP) Paul Foot are obvious.

> Parliamentary democracy is not strong enough to control the increasingly multinational capitalist monopolies ... the only power which can control and overturn these monopolies is the power of the working class ... socialists must come together and organise where that power lies, based on the most implacable opposition to the monopolies, their state and their class ... the only party which can do any of this is the SWP.[16]

Sticking to their principles, Paul Foot and his like remain locked into an ideological time-warp: they have their holy grail of class struggle and guiding light, party, and nothing is going to shift them. The beliefs can remain the same, it's just the world that lets them down, time after time.

If marxism is no longer capable of providing the intellectual depth that we need to develop a strategic analysis of where the Blair agenda could take us, what will? One looks in vain to the political parties and their satellite organisations for serious, sustained political thought. This isn't simply to decry the 'soundbite' – we do after all live in a media age. Rather it is to question how we might revive the art of political conversation: debate that doesn't revolve around entrenched positions; thinking that doesn't exist simply in an ahistorical time-warp; ideas that don't relegate culture to our mental back-pages. Britain is notorious for its anti-intellectualism. Those that have challenged this tradition have always existed at the margins, though the best-selling performances of recent books by Will Hutton and Eric Hobsbawm do suggest that there may be some subterranean cultural change afoot.

Intellectual work remains trapped within a closed-off world of obscurantist journals and a conference circuit that serves a strictly limited clientele. The idea of intellectualism existing in a public arena remains, literally, metropolitan at best, foreign or alien at worst. A politics that is both practical and intellectual requires a reworking of priorities, as Suzanne Moore put it in a well-argued critique of how the left has a very restrictive vision of the radical: 'The bottom line ... must surely be that it somehow challenges power and power is both institutional and political, cultural and personal. Traditionally much of the left has had vested interests in tackling the first two at the expense of the last two.'[17]

GOODBYE TO ALL THAT?

The moment of opportunity of ending umpteen years of Tory misrule should not be lightly squandered. It is too easy to sit back and relish the cosily fashionable rubbishing of the popular potential that this victory represents. When John Pilger writes 'The new Tories like Blair embody a variation of the same class-based hierarchy ... his (Blair's) genteel viciousness towards the most vulnerable will probably mark his place in modern British social history,'[18] he reveals a dangerous disregard for the actuality of change. Getting your retaliation in first is a recipe for flourishing rhetoric: it is of little or no use politically. Instead we need to find a way of retaining our critical faculties, encouraging the most progressive aspects of the Blair agenda, nurturing the enthusiasm that the dumping of this most *ancien* of *ancien regimes* could inspire and acknowledging, in the words of a deeply realistic editorial from one of Tony Blair's most inveterate critics, that 'After Clause Four anyone ... who refuses to recognise that, for the foreseeable future, Blair is the only show in town, is living in a dream-world.'[19]

How this balance will be maintained remains to be seen. It will shift inevitably as policy proposals become transformed into acts of government but avoiding rushing from the extremities of wide-eyed expectation to wild-eyed denunciation should be the rule. It will be a rocky ride, as even one of Tony Blair's enthusiastic press admirers recognised: 'Labour people fear that the only thing which seems to matter is to avoid giving the Tories something to attack with. This feeling is more widespread now than ever. If Blair continues to think otherwise then he is uncharacteristically out of touch.'[20] The director of the think-tank Demos, Geoff Mulgan, gave a more long-term view of how rocky this ride might become: 'The strength is that the Labour leadership is less tied down by debts to key interest groups and ideological positions. But this lack of anchorage means it also has a very narrow base of support, both within the party and the country at large. This could very rapidly turn people against it if enthusiasm turns to disappointment.'[21]

THE REVISION THING

Blair's commitment to modernisation is reminiscent of earlier attempts to modernise the British state. Nina Fishman gives a historical background to this process by highlighting in her chapter, which opens this book's second section, the efforts of both Harold Wilson and Edward Heath at modernising the British state. 'Both Prime Ministers were committed to enacting important structural reforms, and on the whole they embarked on their attempts with support from their cabinets. But they encountered dense, interlocking webs of relationships and connections which were conservative, intensely protective of vested interests, and inward looking'.[22] It is hugely significant that throughout the 1970s the socialist left remained implacably opposed to these projects of reform: the principles that lay behind this opposition were full of good intentions but, as Fishman puts it, 'The cumulative effect of the left however was to reinforce the conservatism so powerfully present in every part of British society.'[23] There were dissident voices that opposed this socialist conservatism but they remained marginal, dismissed with the telling rebuke of *revisionism*.[24] The accusation of revisionism reveals far more about the accuser than the accused. It is testimony to socialism's nearly fatal fear of the new, its dismissal of the case for revising values and principles that become fossilised and out of touch. This is a culture that is fearful of the uncertain, retreating into old certainties in order to reassert the inevitability of Labour's forward march. In an interesting survey of the experience of intellectuals in the Labour Party Radhika Desai concludes with this tribute to Labour's own revisionists:

> Overall coherence is crucial in making ... a hegemonic doctrine capable of both challenging other doctrines and organising social forces and the numerous functionaries needed to sustain it administratively and politically. The significance of the revisionists lies in their effort, however flawed, and however lacking in radicalism, to do this for the Labour Party.[25]

Lacking in radicalism they certainly were, but for the most part ahead of their time on crucial issues ranging from Europe to proportional representation. It used to be said that while there is only an inch between the Conservative and Labour parties it is in that inch that we exist. Today's equivalent might be that inch between radicalism and revisionism. Labour's drift towards the electorally fruitful pastures of the centre-right could all too easily tempt it into a timidity that will ill-serve new Labour's modernising ambitions. It is this caution that has historically discouraged the emergence of a successful current of ideas and actions inspired by a radical-revisionist project. The hegemony of the Blair agenda within the Labour Party is creating the ideal circumstances for a much broader reassertion of this previously marginalised, and on occasion incoherent, group of radical-revisionist ideas to gain some real purchase and purpose. It is an opportunity that few should want to dismiss lightly.[26]

SOCIALISM WITHOUT A SOUL

Central to any radical-revisionist politics that is a part of an evolving coalition around the Blair agenda for government must be a realisation that politics does not centre exclusively on parliament. This undoubtedly sets up a tension with Labour, even its most 'new' of forms. New Labour in this crucial sense remains irredeemably old, ill-suited for the new millennium as anything apart from a party of government. This is an important enough role but there is a growing realisation that if politics is to be remade this is not enough. As the pioneering late 1980s Communist Party document *Manifesto for New Times* put it:

> The traditional role of political parties is being disrupted by the extension of politics into civil society and the new forms of expression being thrown up around the issues of new times. The old, rigid divisions of power and function between the personal and the political, the state and civil society, parliamentary politics and extra-parliamentary activity, no longer apply.[27]

For all the growth in membership, the democratisation of party structures and the policy changes, new Labour remains a political party of the most traditional of designs. It has little or no sense of culture. New Labour's 'house journal' *Renewal* in no less than twelve editions failed to produce a single article on any aspect of culture. This disavowal of culture was depressingly repeated by an autumn 1995 editorial in the official 'Young Labour' magazine *Regeneration*, 'This summer also saw the battle of the bands – Blur and Oasis – and whether or not their war of words should be likened to the Beatles and the Stones. Here at *Regeneration* we are not old enough to remember the latter and not sad enough to care about the former!'[28] Such an arrogant dismissal of popular culture sits ill at ease with a party that is seeking to renew itself.

In her contribution to this collection Wendy Wheeler urges us not to underestimate the weakness that this reveals; what she encourages us to assert in its place is 'an understanding that politics requires a language of the imagination'. And Wheeler puts this weakness down not to individuals but rather to a tradition: 'The Labour Party's idealists have too often been ... materialists with little or no time for a non-didactic politics of pleasure'.[29] Apart from a healthy liking for football – no doubt encouraged by his Burnley-supporting Press Secretary Alistair Campbell – and a fortysomething's fondness for heavy rock, we know little of Tony Blair's cultural preferences. His rhetoric, however, is replete with a symbolic, poetic meaning that suggests he has ambitions that outstrip the merely utilitarian. This will be an essential prerequisite in the years ahead, as his biographer John Rentoul advises: 'It is certainly true that one of the more significant qualities of a national leader is the ability to tell a country stories about itself which make sense of what a leader and a party are trying to achieve.'[30]

AFTER THE MASSES

Tony Blair's experience in building his Sedgefield constituency party into a mass, community-based organisation is tellingly recalled by Gareth Smyth in his contribution to our second section, which deals with Blair's relationship to the Labour Party. This Sedgefield model party that Blair has offered up to Labour, with John Prescott in busy tow complete with 'Red Rose Roadshow', has helped to revive the party's drive for members. 'Massive but passive' is too glib a put-down for this growth. The turnout in One-Member-One-Vote ballots, however low, still far outstrips in democratic credentials the old-style party management committees that were the playthings of factionalisers from left and right.

In an early outline of his model of modernisation Tony Blair gave due credence to rebuilding the party: 'The process of what is called modernisation is in reality the application of enduring, lasting principles for a new generation, not just by creating a modern party organisation, but by inspiring a programme for a modern society, economy and constitution.'[31] But this credence remains muddled – what are these members for? Are they simply there to make the party more representative? If so, their very act of joining a political party instantaneously makes them unrepresentative of the vast majority of Labour voters. Are they there to support the party financially? Membership will certainly aid this, but Labour's existing experience of direct-response marketing suggests that it hardly needs members to raise funds untainted by trade union benefactors. If the members are there to help Labour win elections then there certainly is a purpose to their membership, and a highly effective one, according to the research of Patrick Seyd and Paul Whiteley.[32] But electoral activity has traditionally been perceived by the Labour Party as a straightforward task of distributing the candidate's election address followed by a cursory canvass. There is no sign yet of a deeper commitment to a communitarian politics that would move the party organisation onto an uncharted terrain of local cultures and differentiated power structures. Lacking a commitment to this new style of organisation, or a similar type suited to other non-geographical communities of gender, race, age and sexuality, Labour's membership growth appears dangerously ephemeral. After all what organisation wouldn't grow with a leader who has the profile, popularity and rhetorical flourish of Tony Blair? This isn't a criticism of Blair – politics desperately needs leadership – but it is to question whether in itself this will save the Labour Party from its well-documented long-term decline.

This current collection of essays is largely born out of a contention that the party form is at an end as an adequate vehicle for any political project that seeks more than the most effective of election-winning machines. The experience of Ross Perot and Silvio Berlusconi suggests that even this one remaining role may be shortlived, a process that will surely be accelerated by any progress towards electoral reform. Sarah Benton has summed up this conundrum:

> The old relationship of homogeneous state and class, which created the mass political party of reform, no longer exists. But the very fragmentation of society creates a need for political leadership. The creation of a political form that can provide that leadership, as well as the promotion of civil political activity, independent of the state, are the two overriding needs.[33]

New Labour falls well short of answering the second of these needs, and as such remains fundamentally flawed. The rapidly growing disenchantment with the entire lexicon of traditional party politics is nowhere sharper than among the young. Tom Hodgkinson sums up the politics of this new generation as united around 'protests against intrusive government ... geared around improving life at an everyday level rather than thinking in the long term; showing distrust of the democratic process'. And he adds: 'It is neither left nor right, but individualistic and in favour of free expression, most likely to value freedom over security'.[34] Promoting a culture of civil political activity independent of the state is not only a pressing need for today but also represents the politics of tomorrow.

INGERLAND, WHOSE INGERLAND?

Tony Blair's project is not only to redefine the role of the state in society, but to remodel the very basis of the nation state within whose borders we currently live. There is little doubt that Scotland will be granted devolution, and the effect this will have on nascent demands for similar legislation pertaining to Wales is hard to predict. The Irish peace process, we must hope, will continue in some form, and with a healthier parliamentary bulwark against the Unionists, the painfully slow negotiations may well get the fillip they so desperately need. Britain's place in Europe is also likely to be more assured, less a source of the kind of nightmarish tensions witnessed in the last five years. But to carry through this ambitious agenda of change will be no mean feat. Leighton Andrews' chapter in our third section offers this estimation of the scale of the task: 'winning an election is one thing but winning a second and turning around deeply-imbued cultural beliefs quite another.'[35] These are beliefs full of contradictory impulses: one person's Middle England will be warm beer and cricket on the village green, another's will be hauling oneself up a Newbury tree to stop a bulldozer or sitting down on an Essex village road to stop the veal calf export trade.

Blair's 'Young Country' is in most senses a vision of one nation under a most social-democratic of grooves. It is perhaps no accident that Tony Blair's first year as party leader was accompanied by a movement in popular music that gloried under the banner of 'Britpop'. There is a widely-felt search for an authentic Britishness, that is neither American nor European, reviving the coherence of community, seeking a unity of cultures. But in an age of difference, local and global tensions will unsettle this search, calling into question its authenticity and potential. England's very own border country, Scotland, will place these tensions in an unforgiving spotlight. The putative proposals for devolution will act as a catalyst for a period of constitutional unpredictability the like of which we haven't witnessed since the granting of women's suffrage. The body politic appears to be woefully unprepared for this moment, a situation that is exacerbated by the myth of a political consensus in Scotland that will deliver a new regime eager to do business with Blair in London. The outcome of devolution remains, impossible to predict but the results will certainly deliver change that affects us all, as Gerry Hassan notes in his contribution to this book's closing section, 'Scotland changes Britain, as Britain changes and influences Scotland.'[36] Nationhood makes concrete our desires, it expands and sometimes explodes our range of emotional intensities. Scotland will be enacting that process at precisely the same time that a revanchist Tory Party is likely to be mining what it sees as a potentially rich seam of anti-European xenophobic support and unadulterated populist racism. Avoiding the disastrous consequences of mishandling this potent mix will be one of the most delicate manoeuvres for the Blair government and there will be few who will forgive those who get it wrong.

ALTERNATIVE EDENS

The consequences of a Blair government getting it wrong are already being set in political stone. Andrew Gamble has described it in predictably cogent terms:

> There would be a deliberate renewal of the Thatcherite project, focussed particularly on authoritarian populism. The regrouped Conservative Party would be poised to take advantage of any plunge in the popularity of Blair's government, and in particular any disillusion with the government's capability to manage the economy, the relationship with Europe and new social policies. There will be a resurgence of support for conviction conservatism and the Conservatives will sweep back to government.[37]

These predictions are dire enough – though it can't be stressed too heavily that they are anything but self-fulfilling – but the collapse of the Blair agenda would also sound the end of a certain type of faith in the capabilities of the democratic process. Part of that fracturing is no bad thing: the politics of the deed that fuels environmental protest, the look to community-based self help and the recovery of alternative traditions of organising outside the state are all indicators of a politics that has plugged into the end of politics as we once knew it. To take this to a cynical end-point where the collective potential for change and progress is robbed of any sense of hope or clarity is, however, the death-knell of democracy. It would be matched by marginalisation and division on a scale previously unimaginable; the privatisation of public life would be complete and the ethics of citizenry robbed of any sense of legitimacy.

We are very close to falling over the edge of planet democracy. Our western standard of living is ecologically unsustainable. The information technology revolution has the capacity to infringe massively upon civil liberties. Multinational industrialism at the end of the twentieth century is eroding the potential for individual enterprise at a local, regional or national level. The most extreme forms of inequality are opening up, nationally and globally. We are witnessing both the growth of a xenophobic brand of nationalism and the rapid rise of migration, a lethal mix. And with the decline in traditional belief systems a moral vacuum is emerging. This is the millennial terrain on which Tony Blair and his colleagues will be tip-toeing as they ponder over their red boxes in Whitehall. For Martin Summers, whose manifesto for a libertarian spin-doctoring of Blair's agenda appears towards the end of this collection, there is one answer to this frightening scenario of failure – the disaggregation of democracy. On this measure, for Summers, Blair falls well short, 'Labour's programme would change the architecture of the system ... but not its culture nor the dominance of traditional party-political activity.'[38] There is clearly a pressing need to reconnect the political system with the people – any failure to meet expectations on this front after such a long period of one-party government cannot have anything but the most serious of democratic consequences. There now exists the capacity, will and wealth, after all, for entire communities to opt out of civic life and to leave the rest to fend for themselves. 'Bladerunner' politics won't leave very much space for radical-democratic utopias; disaggregation would on the other hand accept the glaring inadequacies of national politics and create more manageable units of representation and administration than those currently on offer. With the old divide of left versus right losing what remained of its popular validity, democratic debate will increasingly hinge on a new polarity, the libertarian versus the authoritarian. Disaggregation will further unsettle our consciences and those who prefer to indulge themselves in the fixed positions of dogma and fundamentalism will struggle to play a part.

The final contribution to this collection, by Helen Wilkinson, offers up seven maxims that in some sense represent our resources for hope as Blair begins the difficult task of preparing Britain for a youthful start to the twenty-first century. To throw off the old, Wilkinson advises Blair to be ruthlessly radical; to take culture seriously; to define what it means to be British; to operate inclusively in all that you do; to seek inter-generational equity; to give tomorrow's generation a specific stake in the economy and to develop models of social cohesion.[39] These are maxims that differ greatly from the grand narratives that fuelled the great social movements at the turn of the twentieth century. Yet as one looks back at the twin balance sheets of social democracy and communism there are a lot of ruins, tarnished ideals and broken reputations. There are also commitments, and hopes for a better tomorrow, that have stood the test of time. The trick lies in ensuring that the endurance of our ambitions doesn't bear down upon us with a fixity of position that traps us in a world that we have lost. Tony Blair remains the supreme arbiter of the fluid in British politics. Whether it will wash remains the unanswered question.

REFERENCES

1 Richard Heffernan and Mike Marquese, *Defeat From The Jaws of Victory: Inside Kinnock's Labour Party*, Verso, London 1992, p4.
2 Kevin Davey in this collection, p.100.
3 Anne Showstack Sassoon in this collection, p153.
4 For a measured selection of views on the post-1992 prospects of one-party government see Helen Margetts and Gareth Smyth (eds), *Turning Japanese: Britain with a Permanent Party of Government*, Lawrence & Wishart, London 1994.
5 Martin Jacques, 'What A Pity' in *The Sunday Times*, 12 July 1992.
6 Tony Blair, 'Forging A New Agenda' in *Marxism Today*, October 1991, p32.
7 Andrew Gamble in this collection, p36.
8 For a brief, partisan, picture of the disjunction between new Labour and the 'do-it-yourself' politics of a new generation of activists see Camilla Berens, 'Generation X' in *New Statesman & Society*, 3 February 1993.
9 See Carol Samms, *Global Generation X: Their Values and Attitudes in Different Countries*, Demos, London 1995.
10 Tony Blair, 'The Right Way To Find A Left Alternative', in the *Observer*,

9 May 1993.

11 David Marquand, 'Labour's New Model Army', in the *Guardian*, 26 May 1993.

12 Tony Wright, 'Building A New Hegemony', in *Whatever Next?*, Guardian/Samizdat Publications, London 1994.

13 Kevin Davey, *op.cit.*, p79.

14 Stuart Hall, 'The Great Moving Right Show', in Stuart Hall and Martin Jacques (eds), *The Politics of Thatcherism*, Lawrence & Wishart, London 1983, p39.

15 Bob Jessop, Ken Bonnett, Simon Bromley, Tom Ling, *Thatcherism*, Polity, Cambridge 1988, p124.

16 Paul Foot, 'When will the Blair Bubble Burst?', in *International Socialism*, Issue 67, Summer 1995, p16.

17 Suzanne Moore, 'Hello! And Goodbye Radicals', in the *Guardian*, 16 November 1995.

18 John Pilger, 'Hail to the New Tories', in *New Staesman & Society*, 5 May 1995.

19 Editorial in *New Statesman & Society*, 28 April 1995.

20 Martin Kettle, 'The Party is Jumpy', in the *Guardian*, 22 July 1995.

21 Geoff Mulgan, *New Labour, New Enough?*, Signs of the Times Discussion Paper, London 1994.

22 Nina Fishman in this collection, p49.

23 Nina Fishman, *op.cit.*, p50.

24 See for example, Tom Nairn, *The Break Up of Britain*, Verso, London 1981; Mike Prior and David Purdy, *Out of the Ghetto*, Spokesman, Nottingham 1979.

25 Radhika Desai, *Intellectuals and Socialism*, Lawrence & Wishart, London 1994, p193.

26 For an interesting outline of how intellectuals could have an important role helping a new Labour government see, David Marquand and Tony Wright, 'Engaging the Eggheads' in the *Guardian*, 11 December 1995.

27 Communist Party of Great Britain, *Manifesto for New Times*, London 1990, p53.

28 Editorial, 'Don't Look Back in Anger', in *Regeneration*, Autumn 1995.

29 Wendy Wheeler in this collection, p116.

30 John Rentoul, *Tony Blair*, Little, Brown & Co, London 1995, p403.

31 Tony Blair, 'Why Modernisation Matters', in *Renewal*, October 1993, p10.

32 See Patrick Seyd and Paul Whiteley, *Labour's Grass Roots: The Politics Of Party Membership*, Oxford University Press, Oxford 1992, pp174-200.

33 Sarah Benton, 'The Party is Over', in *Marxism Today*, March 1989, p37.

34 Tom Hodgkinson, 'The Party is Dead, Let's Get on with the Party', in the *Guardian*, 7 June 1995.

35 Leighton Andrews in this collection, p129.

36 Gerry Hassan in this collection, p198.

37 Andrew Gamble, *New Labour, New Enough?*, Signs of the Times Discussion Paper, London 1994.

38 Martin Summers in this collection, p203.

39 Helen Wilkinson in this collection, pp.244-251.

Section One: Margaret Thatcher and the Remaking of British Politics

THE LEGACY OF THATCHERISM
Andrew Gamble

The legacy of Thatcherism is not easy to determine. There have been many conflicting assessments of it, ranging from those who have seen it as marking a revolutionary break from the past,[1] to those who deny it any significant long-term impact at all.[2] Part of the problem arises because Thatcherism cannot be dissected dispassionately. It remains part of contemporary political argument, and still arouses fierce controversy within all the political parties.

A second difficulty is that there is no general agreement as to what Thatcherism was. Was it the particular opinions and political style of one very dominant forceful political leader, Margaret Thatcher? Was it a particular approach to government? Was it a coherent political and economic programme of policy, which established the parameters for a new consensus? Or was it the manifestation of a shift in popular opinion? Sorting out the evidence, claims and counter claims will no doubt keep historians busy for a very long time. The area of disagreement may be narrowed down, but fundamental differences of interpretation will never be eliminated. Thatcher is always likely to be one of those historical figures, like Napoleon, over whom people take sides. She will still excite commitment and opposition long after she has passed from the scene. Her name will be invoked to praise and to condemn policies and political regimes. Thatcherite will never be a neutral term.

Assessing the impact of Thatcherism in terms of the impact of Margaret Thatcher would be hard enough. But the term came to denote more than simply the personality, style and opinions of Margaret Thatcher, important though these undoubtedly were to the construction of Thatcherism, and the meaning which it came to have.[3]

But once the term is widened to embrace the activities of New Right intellectuals in the think-tanks, in the media, and in the Conservative Party, then the difficulty of defining Thatcherism is compounded. On close inspection the unity and coherence of Thatcherism dissolves. It was a contradictory and complex phenomenon, open to a wide variation of interpretations.

Despite the complexity, however, this does not mean that we have to abandon the concept of Thatcherism. The very ubiquity of its use indicates how indispensable it has become. Perception of the Thatcher era as a significant period of transition in British politics is increasing rather than diminishing.[4] This significance is seen in the political, economic, and ideological changes that took place in this period. There can be dispute about the causes of change, to what extent Thatcherism reflected the changes rather than acted as the catalyst for them, but no-one can dispute that change took place. Since becoming leader of the Labour Party in 1994 Tony Blair has acknowledged both the desirability and the irreversibility of many of the changes which took place in the Thatcher era.

To understand the present phase of British politics, the disarray of the Conservatives and the rise of new Labour, an understanding of the Thatcher period and its complex legacy is essential. One key strand of this legacy is the debate about Britain's place in the international economic and political system.

THE EXTERNAL LEGACY

The impact of Thatcherism on Britain's role and identity in the world has been profoundly ambivalent, and has created deep conflicts within the Conservative Party. Thatcher reversed the emphasis established by her immediate Conservative predecessors, Macmillan, Heath, and Home, and gave higher priority to the Atlantic alliance and the relationship with the United States than to the developing relationship with the European Union. Thatcher accepted some key steps towards greater integration, in particular the signing of the Single European Act in 1986 which introduced majority voting in the Council of Ministers for some issues and established the objective of a single market. But she became increasingly concerned about the strengthening momentum towards a federal union, and the threat which that posed to parliamentary sovereignty.

During the 1980s the Thatcher Government sought to rebuild a close relationship with the United States. The pretext was the new cold war with the Soviet Union. By this means the Thatcher government revived what had been one of the mainstays of Britain's role in the post-war world. The Atlantic relationship had provided at that time some compensation for the loss of empire. Britain had retained a significant world role by being at the heart of the NATO alliance, maintaining a special defence and security relationship with the United States, preserving sterling as an international currency, and protecting the global operations and foreign investments of the City of London and British transnational companies.

The former basis of the Anglo-American relationship, the leading role of the United States in guaranteeing the conditions for world order, was however under challenge from the 1970s. As the United States' power has declined so the European Union as an emerging regional association has become more pronounced.[5] The Thatcher government reflected the ambivalence of a large part of British political opinion, both Labour and Conservative, towards European integration. The British government's preference was for the EU to be a free trade area with a minimum of powers handed to supranational agencies to police the single market, to enforce common regulations across the Union, or to be responsible for common programmes of expenditure.

British reluctance to be at the heart of Europe has been interpreted as a nostalgic and defensive attempt to preserve what is left of Britain's independent great power status, which the project of an ever closer European Union might destroy, but also as a realistic assessment of the impossibility of the European enterprise, and the advantages to Britain of remaining a free trade country outside whatever internal and external protectionism the EU adopts.[6]

By the end of her premiership Thatcher had come down decisively in favour of a project of a revived Anglo-America axis as an alternative to the pursuit of deeper integration in the European Union. But the collapse of Soviet Communism was to make this even less plausible. The economic case for Britain to have a close relationship with the EU strengthened considerably during Thatcher's period as Prime Minister. But the legacy of Thatcherism on this crucial issue for the future of British politics was confused, and the Thatcherites themselves were increasingly split on the issue. Thatcher left a very divided party to her successor, and John Major has been preoccupied throughout his premiership with holding the party together. The gulf between the supporters and opponents of further integration has become so wide that it has affected the ability of the Conservatives to present themselves as a strong and united party of government. The divisions raise the spectre of a split in the party. Bitter civil war over its leadership and future direction could result from a period in opposition.

THE POLITICAL LEGACY

The most significant political legacy of Thatcherism was that it restored the Conservative Party to a position of dominance in British politics but it did so by transforming the Conservative Party in ways which were to create severe tensions for the party in the future. Thatcherism makes little sense unless it is understood as a political project of the Conservative leadership to re-establish the credentials of the party as a governing party and to rebuild its electoral support after the failures and setbacks of 1970–4. Thatcher was not a popular choice as Leader as far as the Conservative political establishment was concerned, but she was able to unite the party behind her in the bid to oust the Labour government.

The recovery of the Conservatives from a weak position in 1974 (35 per cent was the lowest percentage the Conservatives had won at any general election this century) to a record-breaking sequence of four general election victories in 1979, 1983, 1987, and 1992 secured Thatcher's leadership through the 1980s, and created the political space for the emergence of more radical and long-term policies of institutional and organisational reform in the third term. What it also did was to underline the enduring electoral strength of the Conservatives in British politics. The election victories in themselves were more impressive in terms of parliamentary majorities than in terms of share of the vote, which remained stuck at 43 per cent, but given the low level of the Labour vote in 1983 and 1987 these were decisive victories, which for a time made Conservative supremacy appear unchallengeable. The possibility of a dominant party system along the lines of Italy and Japan was raised.[7]

It was certainly the hope of the Thatcherites that a party system which gave the Conservatives a monopoly on government would be part of their legacy. They wanted the changes they were introducing to become permanent, and they feared that a future Labour government would reverse many of their measures. The old Tory dictum, that whoever is in office the Conservative Party is always in power, was not shared by the Thatcherites. Since they viewed politics in ideological terms, the consequences of losing power were much more serious for them. The need to stay in office in order to maintain the momentum of policy change therefore became a priority.

One of the important political legacies of Thatcherism, therefore, was that it altered perceptions of the party system. The expectation of a regular alternation of the parties in government, which had been broadly realised since 1945, was challenged by the success of the Conservatives. After the 1987 victory the possibility emerged that British politics was entering a new phase in which the opposition parties would be permanently marginalised. The statecraft of the Thatcher government was directed to that end. Part of the calculation behind many of the policies adopted by the government was electoral; they included council house sales and the widening of share ownership through the privatisation issues, the withdrawal of powers from local government, attempts to politicise the civil service, and to fill the governing bodies of the new organisations of the quango state with Conservative sympathisers.

The constitutional position, however, was not altered in the Thatcher years. The Thatcher government proved highly orthodox and conservative in its approach to constitutional issues. It declared its full confidence in the powers and authority of the Westminster Parliament and strongly opposed any measures of constitutional reform – including devolution of powers to regional assemblies, replacement of the simple plurality electoral system by any measure of proportional representation, and introduction of a Bill of Rights, or measures to secure more open and accountable government. Some of these constitutional changes, such as the creation of a Scottish Parliament, which would have been coupled with the reduction of the number of Scottish seats in the Westminster Parliament, would have further entrenched Conservative dominance, but they were never seriously considered. Thatcher decided that the preservation of the Union and the principle of the unitary British state was to be an absolute priority for the party.

The success of the Conservative Party in winning general elections after 1979 and the vigour with which the Thatcher government utilised the powers of the British constitution seriously weakened the legitimacy of the British constitution in the eyes of the opposition parties, and led to strong movements for reform.[8] One of the most important political legacies of Thatcherism was that it significantly weakened Labour's attachment to the constitutional system and the attachment of the Scots to the Union. The strong centralist style of government favoured by the Thatcherites was nothing new. It faithfully expressed the bias of the British constitution. But coupled with the refusal to make concessions to opposition and the weakening of the expectation that the government would alternate, it helped fuel a strong reaction against the over-centralisation and the arbitrary power exercised by the executive through the Westminster Parliament.

The embrace by the opposition parties of various constitutional reform ideas made the Conservatives even more fearful of losing office. Proportional representation in particular threatened to marginalise the party by installing a permanent Centre-Left coalition. The problem for the Thatcher government was that although in general no Parliament was able to bind its successor, this was not true in the case of constitutional measures such as proportional representation, since once enacted they would change the basis on which future Parliaments were elected. The only means for Conservatives of resisting constitutional changes to which they were opposed, however, was to form the kind of understanding with the main opposition party which the Conservatives had enjoyed with Labour ever since the 1920s. Each party endorsed the degree of autonomy enjoyed by the executive in the expectation that they would be able to exercise it. The disappearance of that expectation in the 1980s created a new situation. The Conservatives needed Labour as a support both for the Union and for the old constitutional state, but this need conflicted with their conduct in government and their ideological agenda.

The constitutional legacy of Thatcherism was the re-establishment of the dominance of the Conservatives in British politics, but it was achieved in such a way that the stability of the system which had served Conservative interests so well for so long was undermined. For a time it seemed that the opposition parties would become firmly committed to a major constitutional reform, so raising the stakes for the Conservatives if they ever lost office. But Labour's establishment of a commanding lead in the polls after 1992 and the rise of new Labour has led to waning interest within the party leadership in either electoral reform or regional government, except in Scotland. The lure of government in the unreformed British state is once again exerting its magnetism. Labour may once again choose not to attempt radical constitutional reform but be content to govern within the constraints of the *ancien regime*.

THE ECONOMIC LEGACY

The economic legacy of Thatcherism lies firstly in the impact of the policies adopted by the Thatcherite government to reverse economic decline, and to restructure the British economy; and secondly in the new conventional wisdom the Thatcher government sought to establish in economic discourse.[9] The ending of the long post-war boom in the world economy in the early 1970s was followed by a period of economic and political reconstruction, during which new technologies and new methods of organisation appeared, amidst a decisive shift away from mass production and manufacturing industry.

The Thatcher government came into office pledged to reverse the long period of relative economic decline of the British economy. The apparent failure of successive governments to manage the economy and the public finances had caused a collapse of confidence in and support for both leading political parties.[10] The distinctive Thatcherite economic programme was one result. It put the emphasis on monetary policies designed to reduce inflation and contain public expenditure, and supply side policies aimed at deregulating industry, privatising state enterprises, and removing obstacles to the workings of markets, particularly restrictive union practices and high taxes.

Economic policy is the area in which the objectives of the Thatcher government were most clearly set out, but there is considerable disagreement over how successful the Thatcher government was in realising them. Some economists have argued that there was considerable success in re-orienting the British economy towards competition, profitability and enterprise.[11] Although the shake-out was severe, and the cost in unemployment and bankruptcies heavy, many of the subsidised, overstaffed, and inefficient parts of the economy were removed, the trade unions were substantially weakened, and the underlying profitability of industry was improved. According to this view the economic legacy of the Thatcher government was that it restored the conditions for a successful capitalist economy on the lines of the Anglo-American model, with its emphasis on maximum deregulation and competition.

The contrasting view[12] of the Thatcherite legacy is that although there was short-term success for Thatcherite policies in the boom which reached its peak in 1987-88, it quickly collapsed in a mountain of public sector debt, rising inflation, and record trade deficits. The policies adopted by the Thatcher government liquidated much inefficient capacity, but also destroyed many important companies and industries that could have been made profitable. As a result there was a significant shrinking of the industrial base, and an increased reliance on the services sector, particularly the financial sector. The main structural weaknesses of the British economy, particularly in training, investment, research and development, infrastructure, and management, were not addressed. From this viewpoint the Thatcher government did not remedy the long-term structural weaknesses of the British economy, and in some respects weakened its long-term competitiveness, by blocking off so decisively any move towards the different kind of capitalism practised in Germany or Japan, with their institutional support for long-term investment, training and research. To the extent that there has been an alternative economic project in recent years it has been focused on the creation of a British developmental state.[13] New Labour has been influenced by these ideas but only partially.

The main economic legacy of Thatcherism however probably lay less in whether or not it had succeeded in overcoming economic decline, but in the terms of the economic discourse which accompanied its policies. These reflected some of the wider changes which were taking place in Britain's relationship with the world economy, but they were given a particular twist by Thatcherism. Most important was the shift from a discourse which was still dominated by conceptions of national economic management and national protectionism to one which accepted a free and open global economy as the context for economic policy-making. The complete lifting of foreign exchange controls in 1979 was an important symbol of this shift because it made government policy more dependent on maintaining the confidence of the financial markets. A loss of confidence could spark huge capital flows and the rapid depreciation of a currency.

The change also showed itself in Britain in the shift towards a deregulated industrial relations system, and the dismantling of the various tripartite institutions which had formed the basis for the experiments with various forms of corporatist regulation. This redefining of the scope of government responsibility for economic outcomes extended to employment. The control of inflation re-emerged as the Government's top priority, even though the Thatcher government had a poor record on controlling inflation, compared to many other members of the European Community in the 1980s.

The monetarist emphasis in macro-economic policy was important for political rather than technical reasons. It signalled the changed political balance which allowed the Thatcher government to disclaim responsibility for many of the matters, such as full employment and economic growth, which had been taken for granted by governments since the 1940s. It also allowed it to focus attention on the tax burden and the burden of public spending. The Thatcher government successfully established a low-tax discourse as the dominant discourse in economic debate, making it extremely risky for any party to recommend raising taxes or pledge itself to raising public spending without specifying how its pledges would be paid for. This was an old tactic, used to great effect for example in the 1959 general election, but it received new force in the 1980s, and it was accompanied by Thatcherite questioning of the legitimacy and the value of the public sector and public services. The relentless attack upon statist solutions and the celebration of the individual as consumer, contributed a new economic morality in which the lower the taxes which were imposed the better. The Conservatives failed in practice to reduce the burden of taxation – income tax went down but many indirect taxes, including VAT, went up – but they did restructure spending in the public sector, and created a new public mood of hostility towards welfare dependents, typified by the tabloid campaigns against 'scroungers'. This mood was further strengthened by the steps taken to sell the nationalised industries to private shareholders and companies, and to create internal markets in health and education. Assumptions about universal welfare provision and public service as the framework within which economic policy was to be discussed were abandoned. In its more radical moments the government was prepared to question the privileges and cartel arrangements of many different professional groups – teachers, doctors, nurses, lawyers, academics, police. Some of these confrontations it backed away from, but others it pursued, and one of its lasting legacies was the change it introduced within the public services. This was most marked in the introduction of the techniques of what became known as the new public management, with its emphasis on performance indicators, devolution of financial management, and internal markets. It was particularly notable in the civil service itself. The Next Steps Initiative, launched in 1988 following the publication of the Ibbs Report, aimed to restructure the civil service into a small policy-advising core while transferring the executive functions of government to separate agencies, headed by chief executives responsible for budgets and performance. Such agencies included by 1995 the Benefits Agency, the Prison Service, and the Employment Service.

CONSERVATISM AFTER THATCHER

Thatcher resigned in 1990, but the trauma of that event has left a long shadow. Despite winning the general election in 1992 the party has still not come to terms with the end of the Thatcher era. One of the most important legacies of Thatcherism has been the changes that were wrought within the Conservative Party. The party became accustomed to a level of factional conflict and ideological dispute which in the past it had tended to avoid.

John Major's famous unguarded remarks to Michael Brunson after he had won the confidence motion in the House of Commons in July 1993 were revealing about the post-Thatcher Conservative Party. He spoke of a section of the party still hankering after a 'golden age that never was' and commented on the extent of the divisions within the parliamentary party, including the three 'bastards' in the Cabinet.[14]

Major's problem ever since he became Leader was that he was elected as the candidate of the Right but was also supported by all those who feared that if Michael Heseltine won he could not unite the party. Major therefore began with both the public endorsement of Thatcher and the support of the most prominent Thatcherites. His victory made her sacrifice in stepping down and not contesting the second ballot worthwhile. It guaranteed, as she thought, continuity of policy, and eliminated the risk if Heseltine had been elected that key elements of the Thatcherite programme might have been reversed. Some changes, such as the abandonment of the poll tax, were inevitable, but under Major it was thought they would be kept to a minimum.

Yet after Major defeated John Redwood in July 1995 in the election he had called to put a final end to speculation about his leadership, he reconstructed his Cabinet in a manner which recalled the pre-Thatcher Conservative Party. Not only was there a new and influential position for Michael Heseltine as Deputy Prime Minister, chairing several key Cabinet committees and with a wide roving brief for policy co-ordination, but both the Foreign Office and the Treasury were in the hands of One Nation Conservatives, and the Treasury team, for the first time since Thatcher entered Downing Street in 1979, did not contain a single committed Thatcherite. John Redwood had departed from the Cabinet, and while Michael Portillo and Peter Lilley remained, they were not given significant promotion, and the new representatives of the Thatcherite tendency in the Cabinet had been consigned to the portfolios of Wales (William Hague) and Scotland (Michael Forsyth). Five years after the departure of Thatcher it seemed that the One Nation wing of the party was regaining its nerve and reasserting the authority it had once enjoyed.

Eighty-nine MPs however voted for John Redwood, and the majority of the Conservative press, including *The Times*, the *Daily Telegraph*, the *Daily Mail*, and the *Sun*, all urged the party to drop Major. Opposition to his continued leadership also came from many Conservative columnists, such as Boris Johnson in the *Spectator*, and William Rees-Mogg in *The Times*. The significance of such widespread hostility in the Conservative press – only the *Daily Express* and the *Daily Star* were loyal in 1995 – is hard to estimate. It clearly did not persuade a majority of Conservative MPs to abandon Major. But it is evidence of his greatly reduced authority within the party, and the way in which opinion is moving against the kind of position that John Major represents.

The point of crisis for John Major's leadership was finally reached in 1995 after a period of exceptional internal strife within the party and a succession of domestic and external reverses. After its triumph in April 1992 the Major government had been plunged into a trough of unpopularity unique in modern times. After the forced exit of sterling from the ERM in September 1992 the Government trailed the Labour Party by more than twenty percentage points in all the main opinion polls for the next three years. The longest period this had ever happened before had been seven months. A succession of humiliating reverses in by-elections, local elections, and European elections repeatedly underlined how unpopular the Conservatives had become.

The main reason for the unpopularity was that the Government had lost its reputation for economic competence. This was in part a legacy from Thatcherism. The boom of the late 1980s was too rapid and led directly to the rekindling of inflation, followed by the deep and very long recession of the early 1990s. The housing market collapsed, plunging many families into negative equity; living standards were hit;

and the Government was forced to raise taxes in order to keep the public finances under control. In 1992 the reputation of the Conservatives for economic competence was still high enough to persuade many voters, despite being hurt by the recession, to trust them again, rather than risk a Labour government. The fiasco of the ERM withdrawal in September 1992 was made worse by the realisation that the Government had kept interest rates higher than they need have been in order to keep sterling within the ERM, and so deepened the recession. This event did more than any other to destroy confidence in the Conservatives. The Government had still not recovered by the summer of 1995.

THE CRISIS OF LEGITIMACY

Even without the ERM debacle the Major government would have suffered some unpopularity because of the effects of the mismanagement of the economy in the late 1980s. For a large part of the core Thatcherite vote the economic miracle vanished after 1989. What made it much harder for Major to deal with however was that he was also faced by two other legacies from the Thatcher period – firstly a rising tide of sleaze and corruption, and secondly deep divisions over a central aspect of policy, relationships with the European Union.

The sleaze and corruption were magnified as a consequence of the Conservatives having been in office for so long. A few ministers in every government are always likely to get into trouble and be forced to resign, but a tidal wave of misbehaviour engulfed the Conservative government after 1992. The most serious allegations against ministers were those which related to government defence contracts in the 1980s,[15] but there was also deep disquiet about the recruitment of ex-ministers to work for companies, which in the case of public utilities were often those for whom they had a direct policy responsibility when in government. The impression of a government whose members had become so used to office and its trappings that they had become arrogant and careless of normal standards of public decency and public service became irresistible. Many commentators saw the roots of this attitude in the encouragement of individual enrichment in the 1980s and the undermining of an ethos of public service in so many organisations. Major himself tried to strike a very different note, as in his 'Back to Basics' campaign, and he was personally uncompromised by the scandals. But his administration at times appeared in danger of being overwhelmed. The 'Back to Basics' campaign excited widespread ridicule because of a succession of revelations about the private lives of particular Conservative MPs and ministers, and by public incredulity when it was revealed that some MPs were charging fees to lobbyists for asking parliamentary questions. The Cash for Questions row, although the sums themselves were trivial, appeared to symbolise the decline in public standards under the Conservatives.

The other lasting legacy of Thatcherism was the division over relationships with the European Union. There had always been a small section of the parliamentary party which had opposed the applications to join the Common Market,[16] but the leadership had remained united in its conviction that this was the realistic course of action for Britain and had to be accepted. The Conservatives became identified as the European party in British politics and it was the Labour Party which was deeply divided over the issue. One of Thatcherism's most important legacies for the Conservative Party and for British politics was that by the middle of the 1990s the Conservatives had ceased to be the European party. The pro-European wing of the party, which still comprised most of the leadership, had become isolated, and clear majorities on the backbenches had become hostile to further moves towards integration.[17] Leading Thatcherites outside the Government including Thatcher herself, Norman Tebbit, and Cecil Parkinson, were vocal in their criticism of the Government and of the direction of European policy.

One of the difficulties in handling the internal conflict on Europe for John Major was that since the start of his premiership he had closely identified himself with a pro-European policy. Together with Douglas Hurd, then Foreign Secretary, he had finally persuaded Thatcher, in September 1990, that Britain must join the ERM. When he became Prime Minister in November he took charge of the negotiations which led to the conclusion of the Maastricht Treaty in December 1991. He proclaimed that his ambition was for Britain to be at the heart of Europe. But this ambition was already undermined at Maastricht when in deference to opinion in the party he negotiated opt-outs for Britain from crucial clauses of the Treaty, on economic and monetary union and on the social chapter. These opt-outs were not enough to appease the anti-European wing of the party, who did not want Britain to sign the Maastricht Treaty at all. But it also dismayed the pro-European wing who argued that Britain could not play a full part in European debates about the future shape of Europe if it kept seeking opt-outs.

The division of opinion over Maastricht set the tone for subsequent developments. A significant group of Euro-rebels challenged the Government and fought the ratification process through Parliament. A long and wearisome struggle ensued. The size of the rebellion was at times substantial, although the number of MPs who were prepared to defy the Whip and vote against the Government was only a small part of those who indicated, for example by signing parliamentary Early Day Motions, that they were sceptical or hostile to further moves to European integration.[18] The small majority which Major had secured at the 1992 election meant that the open and repeated defiance of well-organised backbench rebels posed severe problems of party management. Knowing that the rebels represented a much larger section of opinion in the party made the situation potentially much more serious. It dictated a strategy of appeasement and constant shifting of position in order to try and hold the party together.

Major's performance in managing the internal divisions was skilful, but necessarily made him appear indecisive and weak, especially in comparison with the conviction leadership style of Thatcher. It also offered no prospect of ending the deep divide in the party. The split between the factions became more polarised, particularly over the issue of the possibility of Britain ever joining a single currency.

THE FUTURE OF THE CONSERVATIVE PARTY

The extent of division on this question of Europe is unprecedented in the modern Conservative Party, and is a direct legacy of the way in which the party was led by Thatcher. By breaking the consensus the party leadership had previously established over Europe she re-opened the question of Britain's place in the world. In pursuing the logic of this line of argument she focused on the question of national sovereignty and the preservation of Britain's national identity. This was the same logic which had animated Enoch Powell.[19] Thatcher has never gone as far as Powell who openly called for Britain's withdrawal from the EU, but it is the logic of her position if the rest of the Community continue to support moves towards a federal union, and the creation of supranational institutions which are no longer controlled by nation states.

The issue poses a stark choice for the future direction of the Conservative Party. The debate is about Europe, but not only about

Europe. The party is deeply divided over Europe but it is also deeply divided over its immediate past. Some look back nostalgically to the Thatcherite era and long to recreate it and build on it.[20] Others regard that period as having brought superficial short-term success at the expense of gravely weakening the party's long-term prospects, hollowing out Tory England, and destroying the party's links with the institutions and interests which for so long placed it at the centre of British public life, equipping it with an ability to articulate not only the requirements of the state but also the needs and aspirations of the people.[21]

The anti-European wing of the party has become increasingly confident. It claims that it speaks for the majority of the parliamentary party and the majority of the constituency activists. Although John Redwood did not win enough votes to seriously trouble John Major, there is evidence that opinion is continuing to move in his direction and that the attitudes of the party are increasingly anti-European. Anti-European sentiments command the Conservative press, both broadsheets and tabloids. But the anti-European tide has so far failed to win a majority in the Cabinet. Key portfolios – Foreign Affairs, the Treasury, and the DTI – remain in the hands of the pro-European wing.

In the 1995 leadership election the anti-European wing was divided on tactics. The most vociferous element – the Eurorebels – had been pressing for a leadership election and Major's removal because he would not rule out the possibility of a single currency. Their activities prompted Major's pre-emptive strike. But another group, mainly composed of the hard core Thatcherites, was fearful that if Major was forced out the leadership would be seized by a pro-European candidate such as Heseltine. They preferred to back Major in the belief that time is on their side, the party is steadily consolidating behind an anti-European position, and because if the party loses the next election under Major's leadership it is the anti-European wing which is best placed to win the leadership election.[22] Then the reconstruction and purging of the party can go ahead in earnest, undistracted by the short-term need either to maintain unity or to win the election.

The calculations of the pro- and anti-European factions determined the outcome of the leadership election. Major was confirmed in the leadership, in the process winning both authority and time. But this is leadership with no alibis. Its One Nation flavour means that it has one last opportunity. To stay in control of the Conservative Party it must win the next election. If the party goes down to defeat under John Major, the backlash in the party when it goes into opposition is likely to favour the anti-Europeans. The Major government is likely to be viewed within the party in a similar light as the Heath government was in 1975, as a failed administration. The electoral need to provide effective opposition to the Labour government will tend to favour the adoption of a radical right populist programme on Europe, on immigration, on tax, on welfare and on crime.

The pro-Europeans in the party hope that John Major will win the next election in order to keep the anti-European wing at bay. They also believe, however, that even if the party is defeated and initially lurches to the right, it will recover its balance and in time move back towards the centre. This after all is what happened to Labour after 1979. After first moving sharply to the left the party then shifted strongly back to the centre under Neil Kinnock's leadership. It did require a further election defeat however, and the party has now been out of office for sixteen years.

The anti-Europeans would dispute this scenario. But they themselves are split. Many of them clearly decided to continue to support John Major in 1995 because they were not sure they could take over the leadership at that moment. The game in the Conservative Party is being played for very high stakes. Many Conservatives have concluded that the gap between the two factions is now so polarised that one or other will be forced out of the party in the years ahead. The battle over the leadership is therefore also a battle over what kind of party the Conservative Party is to be in the future. Whose party is it to be? Positions have become so entrenched that on key issues of European policy no compromise between the anti-European and pro-European factions appears possible. Both try to claim that John Major is closest to their own view and moving in their direction.

The two sides of the argument in the Conservative Party are making assumptions about what the electorate wants and will vote for. The anti-Europeans are urging that the party should come out forcefully against the single currency and adopt the slogan 'Labour wants to abolish the pound'.[23] They believe that a fiercely anti-European stance emphasising notions of 'Englishness' can become the populist basis for a successful fight-back against Labour.

The pro-Europeans point to the increasing unease in industry and the City that the logic of the anti-European argument is withdrawal from the European Union. They believe that the adoption of the anti-European programme will complete the demise of Tory England by isolating the party from the support of its core interests and allowing the role traditionally occupied by the Conservatives to be filled by new Labour. The anti-Europeans dispute this. They believe they will be vindicated. The party has moved towards them, and once it has been reunited on a clear programme of national independence, free market economics and social discipline the Conservatives will once again sweep the country. The urge for ideological purity and clarity on the right of the party is extremely strong. They want an end to fudge and compromise. They calculate that in the long run their policy is the one which will command most support from the British people.

NEW LABOUR: A SETTLING OF ACCOUNTS

The legacy of Thatcherism has been an uncomfortable one for the Conservatives. They are divided over the direction in which they should now go. Labour by contrast seems extremely united, buoyed by opinion poll ratings which break all records. The party is confident that its long exclusion from office is about to end.

Thatcherism has had a big impact on the Labour Party. Indeed the transformation of the Labour Party is sometimes regarded as Thatcherism's greatest achievement. It was not the only factor. New Labour thinking has much in common too with the revisionist thinking of the 1950s and the 1960s and with those who split from the party to form the SDP in 1981. But certainly the thoroughness with which the party has reformed both its thinking and its organisation is a tribute to the impact Thatcherism has had on it.

This impact was most immediately felt in electoral terms. The collapse of the Labour share of the vote in 1983 and the close margin between Labour and the SDP/Liberal Alliance meant that Labour either had to change drastically or risk being marginalised in British politics, ceding its role as an alternative government to the Alliance. The need to restore the electoral credibility of the party dominated the leadership's thinking following Neil Kinnock's election as Leader in 1983. Despite encouraging mid-term polls, by-election and local election successes, however, the party made only slow progress towards its goal in 1987 and 1992. Although the party adjusted its policies – particularly on defence, Europe, public ownership, and industrial relations – it failed to convince enough voters that it was economically competent, and on this measure it continued to trail the Conservatives. What Labour would do on tax was the greatest problem in winning voters beyond its core vote, a fact which the Conservatives played on with great skill in the 1992 election.[24]

The strategy behind the concept that is new Labour is that Labour is required not only to readjust its policies, but to undergo a cultural shift, to embrace new assumptions and perspectives, many of them quite different from those of the Labour Party of the past. It is in this area that the party is showing most clearly the impact of Thatcherism. The themes of choice, individualism, and anti-statism are all prominent in a way which would have been unthinkable at one time. Tony Blair has recently praised Margaret Thatcher for her radicalism, and her drive against the privileges of the British establishment. In endorsing this radical, anti-statist line of Thatcherism, Blair implies that this is the ground Labour must take as well. It is a particular kind of moral discourse which gives highest priority to the values and preferences of individuals as the touchstone for evaluating policy agendas and policy outcomes. What individuals want for themselves and their families is regarded as possessing higher moral authority for the conduct of government than the agendas of organised interests. It is because of Tony Blair's particular moral stance that Thatcher has given him her own cautious endorsement, while still claiming that he is completely unrepresentative of his party.

The significance of new Labour is not so much an endorsement of explicit items of Thatcherite policy, although this is extensive enough,[25] but the acceptance that if socialism is to regain its appeal then it has to reconnect with the radical egalitarian individualism of the Enlightenment from which it was born. This tradition has tended to be overlaid by a commitment to collective organisation and statist policies in the twentieth century, whose hallmarks were an increasing public sector through nationalisation, universal welfare benefits, particularly social security and pensions, and policies to promote full employment and economic growth. In so far as it is seeking to rethink the fundamental purpose of the party new Labour is about much more than simply the policies and tactics which are most likely to maximise its vote. This is a lesson that has been learnt from Thatcherism. One of Thatcher's great strengths was her moral conviction and her readiness to reason from principles, rather than from expediency. The success of the argument she was able to develop against the bureaucratic welfare state was in important respects not a Conservative but a radical liberal critique, which was harnessed to a Conservative policy agenda. In seeking to move onto this ground new Labour is seeking to repossess the classic ground of the Left.

This classic ground is that of democratic egalitarianism which employs the principle that everyone should enjoy equal liberty to criticise all those institutional and organisational obstacles to its realisation. These weapons have been particularly strong in the hands of the New Right against state bureaucracies, both their inefficiencies and unresponsiveness. The way of improving their performance may often be to give individuals the right to 'exit', by introducing competition, rather than seeking to improve 'voice' by improving accountability and representation. The tradition of co-operative enterprise was an anti-statist, communitarian but also market solution to the problems facing working-class communities in the nineteenth century. This tradition was lost when all effort became focused on using the powers of the central state to manage and control the economy and the society. The need for local initiative and local knowledge outside the central state was neglected. What new Labour is now emphasising is the need for government to play a strategic role rather than a detailed planning role. It has to promote new forms of local and regional institutions which will be self-reliant and self-sustaining, and which will assist in the overall goal of dispersing economic and political power, and increasing the autonomy of individuals.

The apparent direction of British politics over the last ten years has been towards the creation of a new neo-liberal consensus replacing the old social-democratic consensus of the post-war period. Superficially this appears to be so, and the parties have certainly moved very close together on some of the key questions of domestic and external economic management. But underlying this are deeper questions of the cultural and intellectual forces which will shape the future of politics in Britain and other European countries. Egalitarian individualism can renew the radical purpose of parties of the left, but in communitarian rather than neo-liberal directions, while on the right, the politics of national identity seems certain to figure prominently. Both developments can be seen as rooted in Thatcherism, and are part of its contradictory legacy for British politics.

Thatcherism was so potent precisely because it combined these two different politics of identity, a discourse about freedom and a discourse about order. Thatcher's successors have proved increasingly unable to perform the same feat. But these two discourses still mark out the terrain for contemporary political debate, both within the parties and between them. National populism is moving in increasingly illiberal directions, and is fundamentally opposed to European integration and an open society and economy, but it has solid roots. Neo-liberalism has become unpopular because the policies associated with it are held responsible for undermining so many established institutions and communities. If Labour is to find a new role in British politics it has to find ways of using the state not to plan society but to preserve and enlarge individual autonomy by making use of both democracy and markets as institutional mechanisms for sustaining those forms of association and community that citizens value and desire, without sacrificing the benefits of an open society and an open economy. It has to start to take the shaping of institutions at the local and regional level seriously again.

REFERENCES

1 See for example Stuart Hall, *The Hard Road to Renewal*, Verso, London 1988; Bob Jessop, Kevin Bonnett, Simon Bromley and Tom Ling, *Thatcherism: A Tale of Two Nations*, Polity, Cambridge 1988; Martin Holmes, *The First Thatcher Government*, Wheatsheaf, London 1985; and *Thatcherism: Scope and Limits*, Macmillan, London 1989.

2 See for example Peter Riddell, *The Thatcher Era*, Blackwell, Oxford 1985.

3 For 'Thatcherism' its meaning and use see Stuart Hall and Martin Jacques (eds), *The Politics of Thatcherism*, Lawrence & Wishart, London 1983; Andrew Gamble, *The Free Economy and the Strong State: The Politics of Thatcherism*, Macmillan, London 1994, ch. 1; Bob Jessop *et al*, *Thatchersim*, and Dennis Kavanagh, *Thatcherism and British Politics*, OUP, Oxford 1990.

4 See Hugo Young, *One of Us*, Macmillan, London 1989, and Dennis Kavanagh, *Thatcherism and British Politics*.

5 For a discussion of these trends see Andrew Gamble and Anthony Payne (eds), *Regionalism and World Order*, Macmillan, London 1996.

6 See Stephen George, *An Awkward Partner*, OUP, Oxford 1992.

7 See Helen Margetts and Gareth Smyth (eds), *Turning Japanese? Britain with a Permanent Party of Government*, Lawrence & Wishart, London 1994; and Andrew Gamble, 'Loves Labour Lost', in Mark Perryman (ed), *Altered States*, Lawrence & Wishart, London 1994, pp23-45.

8 Particularly Charter 88.

9 See Geoffrey Maynard, *The Economy under Mrs. Thatcher*, Blackwell, Oxford 1988; and William Keegan, *Mrs. Thatcher's Economic Experiment*, Allen Lane, London 1984.

10 See Kavanagh, *Thatcherism and British Politics*.

11 See especially Maynard, *The Economy under Mrs. Thatcher*, and Alan

Walters, *Britain's Economic Renaissance*, OUP, Oxford 1986.

12 See especially Jonathan Michie (ed), *The Economic Legacy 1979–92*, Academic Press, London 1992; Nigel Healey (ed), *Britain's Economic Miracle: Myth or Reality*, Routledge, London 1993; and Stephen Wilks, 'Economic Policy', in Patrick Dunleavy *et al* (eds), *Developments in British Politics 4*, Macmillan, London 1993.

13 See Will Hutton, *The State We're In*, Cape, London 1994; and David Marquand, *The Unprincipled Society*, Cape, London 1987.

14 The identity of the three was the cause of some speculation, but the general view was that John Major was referring to John Redwood, Michael Portillo, and Peter Lilley.

15 These became the subject of the Scott Enquiry.

16 See George, *An Awkward Partner*.

17 A survey of Conservative MPs at the time of the 1994 European Elections found substantial majorities opposed to current proposals for deepening integration , and in favour of reversing the progress to greater integration in several key areas. See David Baker, Imogen Fountain, Andrew Gamble, and Steve Ludlam, 'The Blue Map of Europe: Conservative Parliamentarians and European Integration Survey Results' in *British Elections and Parties Yearbook 1995*, Frank Cass, London 1996; and David Baker, Andrew Gamble, and Steve Ludlam, 'Backbench Conservative Attitudes to European Integration', *Political Quarterly*, 66:2, (1995), pp221–33.

18 See David Baker, Andrew Gamble, and Steve Ludlam, 'Whips or Scorpions? Conservative MPs and the Maastricht Paving Motion Vote', *Parliamentary Affairs*, 46:2, (1993) pp151-66; and 'The Parliamentary Siege of Maastricht 1993: Conservative Divisions and British Ratification', *Parliamentary Affairs*, 47:1, (1994) pp37-60.

19 See Enoch Powell, *Still to Decide*, Batsford, London 1972.

20 See Alan Duncan and Dominic Hobson, *Saturn's Children*, Sinclair Stevenson, London 1995.

21 See Ian Gilmour, *Dancing With Dogma*, Simon & Schuster, London 1992.

22 Whether this proves correct may depend on how big a swing takes place to Labour in the general election, and how many Conservatives lose their seats, and who they are. Conservative MPs alone comprise the electorate for any leadership election. The chances of rival candidates may depend crucially on which MPs succeed in holding their seats in the event of a Labour victory.

23 This slogan has been strongly advocated in *Sunday Telegraph* editorials.

24 See Ivor Crewe, 'Voting and the Electorate', in Patrick Dunleavy *et al* (eds), *Developments in British Politics 4*, Macmillan, London 1993, pp92-122.

25 It includes the acceptance of most of the privatisation measures introduced by the Thatcher government; many of the education and health reforms; most of the trade union reforms; the restructuring of the civil service; the sale of council houses; the abolition of exchange controls; and the acceptance of much lower levels of direct taxation.

Section Two: Leadership, Loyalty and Loss on the Road to New Labour

MODERNISATION, MODERATION AND THE LABOUR TRADITION
Nina Fishman

British politics are in an unusual state of flux. Their unpredictability is both exhilarating and profoundly disturbing. A typical reaction around Westminster is that the virtual reality of a decrepit political culture has to change in order to reflect the actual reality of the present day. But the shape of a new constitutional settlement is far from clear. There have been a number of powerful critiques of the status quo from various points on the political spectrum, beginning with David Marquand's *The Unprincipled Society* in 1988, and including those of Ferdinand Mount, Tony Wright MP, Andrew Marr, and of course Will Hutton.[1] The runaway popularity of Hutton's *The State We're In* reflected the disquiet of people deep in middle England who were not natural *Guardian* readers. They have been strongly attracted to its arguments not merely because of his searing observations of our economic weaknesses but also his strong belief that these weaknesses can only be resolved if the political establishment cleanses and renews its ties with society on a sound democratic basis.

Tony Blair's determination to modernise the Labour Party by marginalising trade union influence and replacing Clause Four have coincided with the popular perception that the old political ways have failed Britain. The reaction in the media has been strongly favourable. Trade unions and socialism are as inextricably part of the past as Alec Douglas Home and grouse moors. Blair and his associates have worked hard and richly deserve the political capital they have earned from exploiting opportunities shrewdly, whilst standing up for the social-ist principles of the new party they are moulding.

During 1995, there was a fascinating juxtaposition of the growing momentum for a new political settlement and the fiftieth anniversary celebrations of Britain's victory over Germany. The political establishment was properly respectful of the Allied defeat of fascism. But a number of articulate dissident voices were also insistent that the victory had produced a dangerous complacency. The post-war generation imbibed the lessons of the war as enunciated by the generation who had fought it. They absorbed a moral imperative to preserve the British political system, which had successfully defended liberty and freedom against fascism, inviolate in every detail. Hence its current senility.

As the year of anniversary closed, the outlines of a new domestic political battleground could be discerned on the horizon. The most vociferous and active opponents of new Labour were not the old centre of the Conservative Party, but Michael Portillo and John Redwood, the determined harbingers of the new Conservatism. Their message has a shrill, *poujadiste* tone. Confronted with their prescriptions for re-gluing British society, liberal-minded observers understandably blanche and start searching for bolt holes. Nevertheless, the Portillo/Redwoodites are entitled to view their mission as the equivalent to Tony Blair's. They are trying to free the Tories from traditional habits which they view as the outmoded shackles of the past.

The terrain upon which the general election will be fought is evident. John Major and Kenneth Clarke have been trying to hold on to a centrist, old conservatism. Yet, in spite of their determination to maintain continuity and preserve the fundamentals of the post-war consensus, they have been forced to concede crucial ground to their radical right wing. Because the political establishment has lost the will to maintain the political culture and dispositions of the state which it inherited, the essential issue in the general election will be the shape of Britain's new constitutional settlement.

At this important juncture a Burkean note of caution is required. Before proceeding to construct a new compact between politicians and the people, we need to understand just why the old order has broken down. The newly fashioned explanation is that our victory in the anti-fascist war produced overweening hubris and unthinking resistance to necessary political change. Its element of *mea culpa* contains the stuff of a new myth, and might furnish some of the ideological emollient needed to cure the present dysfunction in British politics. However, it is also a serious distortion of what actually happened in the post-war period. Sustained efforts at reform were made by Harold Wilson's governments in 1964–9 and Ted Heath's government of 1969–74. In domestic and international politics, the two Prime Ministers were both committed to adapting the political settlement they had inherited to take account of Britain's changed circumstances.

Though they were very different in their styles and approaches, the Wilson and Heath cabinets shared a common socialisation. Their members' initiation into adult life was the collective effort of the anti-fascist war. They participated in its pervasive reforming zeal, and drew strength from the faith that the post-war world would be a different and better place. Belief in the people's war enabled those who fought it to cohere, endure and co-operate in a total war for the second time within a generation. The effect of their accumulated experience was not surprisingly enduring.

This cohort hardly emerged in 1945 as complacent triumphalists. Their attachment to British society and political culture was strong but unsentimental and realistic. They knew just how contingent and close-run the Allied victory had been. They evaluated Britain's contribution in the light of their own experience on the one hand and the pervasive propaganda of the inherent superiority of democratic representative institutions on the other.[2] Because they could not ignore the shortcomings of British society which they had witnessed at first hand, they dedicated their political lives to achieving the aspirations of the people's war. They were determined to build a *new world*, built upon the strengths of the old to be sure, but which also addressed the problems which had marred inter-war society.

WINNING THE PEACE

The reforming zeal which had gathered momentum during the war had been translated into legislation and policy by the Attlee government in many ways. The nationalisation of coal, electricity, gas, the railways and road transport was seen not only as a vindication of socialist planning but also as a fulfilment of Labour's commitment to democratise British society. The construction of the welfare state also proceeded along democratic, egalitarian lines. Nevertheless, when the Conservative government took office in 1951, there was also a sense that the Labour administration had fulfilled neither the promise of being the first majority socialist government nor the popular expectations accumulated during the war of great social changes to come.

We can see with hindsight that the Attlee administration were consolidators not innovators.[3] But this judgement should not be interpreted as damning them with faint praise. It is rather a recognition that the mantle which the 1945 Labour government inherited from its predecessors was already in essence a corporate social democratic settlement. A critical mass of the changes which the radical democratic and socialist forces in British society had campaigned for had actually been achieved by 1945. Moreover, that was very much how it felt at the time to most of the British people.

Attlee's cabinet was notably reluctant to embark upon legislation to codify and legitimate the *de facto* social democratic settlement.[4] Their horizons remained firmly fixed within the terrain which had already been explored and marked out by Lloyd George and then developed by Ernest Bevin. In the fifty years from 1880 to 1930, British politics had been marked by mounting uncertainty. The pace of class struggle and political conflict had quickened, at times it even approached turmoil. Most of the political establishment resisted the rising democratic forces which they found distasteful and disorientating. They went down the bumpy road to a more egalitarian society resentfully, with great pique and often in bad faith.

According to the perceptions of that establishment, the rise of the democracy – as the masses were denominated in Edwardian political culture – presented an endless succession of distasteful and apparently insoluble dilemmas. Democracy was synonymous with anarchy. It feared that the pressure being placed on the body politic by the increasingly self-confident demands being made by the democracy would prove fatal. The requirement to preserve stability and order was under threat from ordinary people's strident insistence on disturbing the social and economic equilibrium with demands for more wages, better housing, and a voice in government.

Parliament consistently refused to grant the vote to the property-less proletariat. There was also a successful rearguard resistance mounted to prevent women getting the vote. Principled reactionaries in the establishment utilised the forces of inertia and deployed their own determination and immaculate tactical sense to keep democracy repeatedly at bay. If total war had not intervened, it is likely that the forces pressurising civil society towards democratic change would have been stymied. The likely result of continued stalemate between the establishment and the democracy is unknowable. However, some form of extreme rupture in British society with Lloyd George and Keir Hardie at the head of a radical democratic alliance would certainly have been possible.

LAND OF OUR FATHERS, AND MOTHERS

It was the coming of war in 1914 which finally undermined the domestic impasse. Lloyd George, that pre-eminent man of the people, became Minister of Munitions and then Prime Minister. He presided over the construction of a highly efficient total war machine designed to mobilise civil society fully for the war effort. He combined the powerful moral pressure of patriotism with the economic incentives of wage increases and assured profits to persuade employers and unions to co-operate together with the state.[5] The impressive increases in production and productivity which resulted excited the keen envy of the German general staff. They supported the German trade unions and progressive industrialists in their arguments for emulating British tripartism.[6] German industrialists, trade union leaders and liberal civil servants laid the foundations of their social partnership and the corporate state in this period, using the British achievements as a blueprint.

The makeshift, but workable arrangements Lloyd George had fashioned survived the political upheavals and class conflicts of the 1920s. With notable exceptions, British industrialists appreciated the advantages which the wartime *modus vivendi* had achieved. They acquiesced in the democratic currents of the time and were content to grant their organised workforce the same position at work that they had won in the political sphere. They found the new social partnership made their human resources problems both predictable and soluble.

In the political sphere, the establishment was compelled to come to terms with the democracy. Having required every citizen to make supreme sacrifices for their country, they could hardly deny them political equality. Universal manhood suffrage at the age of 21 and votes for women over the age of 30 were conceded by the House of Commons only under extreme duress in 1918. And despite sanguine optimism from young socialist revolutionaries, including foundation members of the British Communist Party, the British state did not collapse under democratic pressure. The establishment adjusted to the concessions which they had been forced to make during the war and in the process they discovered that their worst fears about the democracy were misplaced and unfounded.

The working class gained a greater share of the domestic product. It also grasped the opportunities for greater social mobility and appreciated the degree of social levelling of the wartime emergency. By the late 1920s it was clear that the British masses had no desire to tear down the social and economic edifice within which they co-habited with 'their betters'.[7] The political establishment was still in possession of a position at the top of the social order which had been eroded, even though they now shared it with those genuine representatives of the democracy, the Labour Party and the trade union movement. Those unregenerates who were convinced that the new equilibrium was dangerously egalitarian and ultimately disastrous were proved wrong.

By the mid-1930s, the spectre of the intensifying class conflict which had loomed before 1914 and reappeared in the early 1920s had been banished. There was no political crisis in Britain nor was fascism ever a serious threat. Stanley Baldwin and Neville Chamberlain presided over a stable, comparatively democratised social order. Neither attempted to roll back the forces which had promoted these changes. Their governments did business with the trade union movement and fulsomely espoused what is currently described as stakeholder capitalism. Unlike the tripartism of 1914–8, the unions' place was not co-equal with employ- ers and the Tories, but they were nevertheless acknowledged to have a rightful place in the social, political and economic order. And the prospect of the Labour Party governing the country and unions winning greater equality at the workplace at some point in the future was hardly viewed with alarm by the Conservative cabinet or leading industrialists.

REFORM NOT REVOLUTION

During the 1939–45 war, the balance of forces moved decisively away from employers and back towards the centre where it had last been found in 1914–8. There were changes of degree which began in 1939 and continued their unbroken course into the 1950s and 1960s. Over time these gradual movements resulted in greater social and economic equality. There was undoubtedly a substantial cumulative social levelling and greater equality of opportunity. However, the essential structure of the inter-war settlement remained intact up to the 1960s and appeared to be in an eminently serviceable condition.[8]

The reforming zeal which the wartime cohort still carried strongly within them became newly relevant in the 1960s. By then it was clear that British social partnership was in need of urgent judicious reform. The impact of the Cold War upon the British trade union movement had been serious, complicated and woefully misinterpreted by the political establishment, including the parliamentary Labour Party. The result was that the social partnership was under serious strain. The feel-good factor in terms of material prosperity remained high, but the stakeholders had become fractious and disputatious. The British capitalists who had been certain of winning the post-war economic battle against European competitors were discovering that they could not hold their own on the world market. They viewed the increasingly self-confident mood of British trade unions as a gratuitous and dangerous threat to their already parlous position.

It was a determination to keep the domestic situation in equilibrium, with both sides of industry working together, which motivated the Wilson and Heath governments' attempts to reform trade unions. Both administrations reacted to a general perception that the balance of industrial power had moved too far in one direction, towards trade unions. Their actions in formulating a new legal settlement for industrial relations were firmly anchored within the parameters laid down by their predecessors. They were not concerned to move the balance back towards the employers, but to ensure by means of political pressure backed by statutory guarantee that it remained firmly in the centre.[9]

It was not only political tactical sense, but also opportunism for the socialist left, radical democrats and the trade union leadership to welcome this fresh affirmation of the social democratic corporate system and to press for its widening and deepening in a more egalitarian manner. There was by this time an abundance of evidence that workplace relations between employers and employees could benefit from judicious state regulation. If the enactment were based upon the same corporate principles which had guided the Lloyd George/Bevin model, its effect could be not only in the interest of the capitalist economy, but also to the advantage of working people. The purpose of state regulation would not be to suppress workplace conflict, but rather to provide a framework for its settlement. The conflict would actually be legitimised within the framework, but so would its settlement – taking due account of the needs and aspirations of both sides of the industrial dispute.

THE UNCOMMON MARKET

There was another contentious and problematic situation which required the attention of a serious reform-minded government. This was the urgent need to address Britain's growing isolation in the international political configuration and her lack of any anchor in Europe. If the political establishment still aspired to be a nation state with a voice in what happened in the disposition of the world order, this question could not be ignored. Nevertheless, unlike the corporate social democratic order, there was no consensus amongst the political establishment about where Britain's place in the world lay.

The question of Britain's place in the world stirred the cockles of the political establishment's heart. The dilemma of pooling sovereignty inside the Common Market excited the prejudice and reflex of MPs throughout the House of Commons. It also inflamed the passions of those citizen activists who in the 1960s still abounded in civil society in all parts of the political firmament. There was not only the question which Hugh Gaitskell famously posed at Labour Party conference in 1962 of whether Britons were to cease being citizens of the world and descend into a parochial cabbage patch existence within the continent of Europe. There was also the question of entering into a closer relationship with Germany. Most of the socialist left held attitudes to Germany which were neither realistic, practical nor objective. Finally, there was the view of the Common Market as a capitalist club which pre-empted any opportunities for achieving real socialism. Despite the fact that the social democratic corporate model prevailed throughout the EEC (albeit in many countries with a joint christian democratic/social democratic gloss), the provisions of the Rome Treaty for promoting competition were seen by British left socialists as anathema.

There was also the question of how the state should build upon and legislate to take account of the accumulated changes which had taken place within civil society since 1945. As we have seen, the democratic, levelling content of the people's war propaganda had neither been dissipated nor forgotten. It had merely, and not surprisingly, taken a generation for its impact to be visible upon the face of civil society. Profound social change cannot be produced by legislation or social engineering. It is an organic, complicated and uncertain process, whose results are only apparent some few generations after the first impulse which precipitated it.

Despite the impatience of the angry young generation and their scorn with the formal trappings of hierarchic British society which remained, it is evident that this sea change had indeed occurred by the 1960s. Legislation was called for which reflected the greater popular expectations of egalitarianism, equal opportunity, and the democratisation of civil institutions, including those pillars of the welfare state, the education system and the NHS, as well as nationalised industries and parliament.

The question of the content of state regulation of industrial relations was also affected by these profound social changes. Both companies and trade unions were quintessential institutions in British civil society. They too required reform to reflect the levelling which had occurred and to embody the greater democratic expectations. It is not surprising that those trade union leaders most in touch with the shopfloor embraced the cause of industrial democracy. Nor is it remarkable that industrialists who were observers of social change looked to the German system of *mitbestimmung* (co-determination) and believed Britain should emulate it.[10]

TED AND HAROLD'S BIG ADVENTURE

Had either Heath or Wilson succeeded in their modernising aims, the venerable well-worn shell of British political culture would have been modified in crucial aspects of substance, whilst continuing to be apparently whole and formally more or less the same. Twenty years on, any assessment of Wilson's and Heath's reforming efforts reveals solid achievements: membership of the Common Market, legislation for greater social equality, and certainly earnest good intentions to grapple with problems of the economy and industrial relations. Nevertheless, history will probably judge their contributions to have been noble, but notable failures.

Both prime ministers were committed to enacting important structural reforms, and on the whole they embarked on their attempts with support from their cabinets. But they encountered dense, interlocking webs of relationships and connections which were conservative, intensely protective of vested interests, and inward looking. Successive attempts to reform industrial relations made no impact on the actual conduct of collective bargaining and failed to moderate the intensifying class struggle at the workplace. Though Britain became a member of the European Economic Community, there was no consequent shift in the orientation of the political establishment towards the continent. There was no serious effort to adapt to the changed circumstances of adhering to the Rome Treaty and being part of a new international political order.

It is notable that the socialist left held fire and declined to take the offensive in support of government initiatives to reform and modernise British society. The dynamics and mechanics of British political culture assume that the radical part of the political spectrum will provide a crucial lever in any reform process. To move a society, to ensure that legislation actually changes civil society, there is much agitation, argument, and also initiative required by those committed to the change. There is no way in which the classic Gladstonian reforms, Joseph Chamberlain's gas and water socialism, or Lloyd George's embryonic welfare state would have succeeded without the substantial campaigning activity undertaken by the radical wing of the Liberal Party, the Fabian Society, the ILP and the trade union movement.

Bizarrely in the 1960s and 1970s, the innumerable sects and groupuscules comprising the socialist left stood to one side. They rubbished the partial reform measures because they were not 'real socialism'. Instead of mobilising popular pressure in support of change, and applying pressure on governments for more radical initiatives, the socialist left coalesced around the ideal of the model socialist world and spent their political energies quarrelling about its shape and plotting to achieve it by ruse or fiat. The tragic irony of the socialist left's pre-occupation with the pursuit of purity and real socialism is that the status quo contained the essential elements of a revisionist socialist order. The interesting point is how widely and deeply the socialist left extended down into many crucial institutions of British society, notably the trade unions, education, and journalism. The cumulative effect of the left, however, was to reinforce the conservatism so powerfully present in every part of British society.[11]

It was still possible in the late 1960s to deploy political argument to devastating effect. By disabling an important part of Labour culture, a space might have been created for something pragmatically radical, of practical substance. But there was no ideological assault upon the bunker of purity and dogma into which the socialist left had retreated.

REVISION TIME

There were certainly erstwhile revisionists on the centre/right of the

Labour Party and inside the trade unions. They might have undermined the circular arguments routinely put by the left to justify their do-nothing position. But when it came to the point of joining serious conflict, the centrist socialist revisionists declined to take the risk of destabilising the Labour Party and possibly disabling it for a period whilst it regrouped ideologically.

The painful, but requisite re-orientation of Labourism might have been precipitated in the 1960s or even the early 1970s if the centrist revisionists in Britain – Crosland, Healey, Owen, Williams, Jenkins – had embarked upon a determined intellectual and political offensive. Instead, they kept their own counsel and consciences inside the gladiatorial rings of party conferences and parliament. If they had been serious about their revisionism, they would have had to do battle not only against the left, but also against the culture and habits of the trade union leadership. However, they declined to offend or challenge these close allies.

In effect, it was not only the left, but also the centre and right who held onto catastrophism and had a millenarian outlook within which there was a cataclysmic difference between the socialism of their dreams and the capitalism within which they had to work and struggle. The powerful defences of militant trade unionism and pure socialism which the left were providing burgeoned and prospered alongside Crosland's *The Future of Socialism*.

Thatcher's governments have been generally credited with enacting radical agendas and sweeping away sclerotic institutions which had provided the foundations for the post-war consensual settlement. It was rather due to the refusal of both left and right in the Labour Party to take a seriously revisionist reforming initiative that these institutions became worn out, discredited and vulnerable. Thatcher merely provided the last push. Moreover, as Heath's most recent biographer pointed out, she did so along the political and intellectual lines which Heath had already pioneered in the early 1970s.[12] The difference between the two Tory leaders was that Heath was (and is) a politician with a sincere commitment to the values of the 1945 generation. He was determined to reform the post-war settlement, not replace it with a radical new model capitalism.

It is hardly surprising that in the wake of Wilson's opportunism during the February 1974 general election, the revisionists lost all hope of retrieving Labour's credentials as a vehicle of positive reform. That election was held in the aftermath of the second national miners' strike in two years and the Conservative government's declaration of a national emergency and a three-day week for business and industry. The strike could easily have been settled had there been pressure exerted by Labour politicians and the TUC on the NUM. The ideological price was the unions' acceptance of the need for a national wages policy. Both the TUC and the Labour Party abstained from bringing the NUM into line with a reasonable incomes policy, essentially for party political reasons.

Wilson dragged the Labour Party into fighting the election on this dubious terrain. He portrayed Labour as the safe bastion of conservatism, the only safe pair of hands. Heath's insistence on the need to evolve a comprehensive incomes policy became an irresponsible, tearaway caprice. His determination to place the resolution of industrial conflict within a new, more organised and publicly accountable framework was labelled as dangerously radical. It was hinted that his unwritten agenda was to destabilise society and deny the British people the rising living standards which they had come to expect as a basic right in the post-war settlement.[13]

Wilson's unabashedly opportunist manipulation of politics for electoral advantage during the 1974 miners' strike was not the first time he had abandoned political principle. Whilst in opposition, Wilson had also reneged on his European orientation. At the time this unaccountable reversal of his earlier position when in government was not resisted root and branch by the centre/right revisionists. They declined to enter into inner party struggle and rather salved their consciences by voting with the government in crucial parliamentary divisions.

After the 1979 general election, the leading centrist revisionists abandoned the entire ideological terrain of the Labour Party to the socialist left without a fight. By forming the Social Democratic Party (SDP), they made a belated but valiant attempt to move British society out of the *cul-de-sac* into which the Labour Party and trade unions had driven it. But even had the secessionists remained and continued to fight the good fight within, it is unlikely that Labour would have won either the 1983 and 1987 general elections. History very rarely metes out second chances. The events of 1974 were a crucial watershed. The moment had passed when the post-war corporate structure of British society with its *de facto* social democratic settlement could have been modernised and reformed (by either a Conservative or Labour government).

CRITICAL CROSSROADS

British society now stands at a new and critical juncture. As a result of the failure to reform, the British political establishment is now operating in a veritable vacuum. The dense and habitual links which bound ordinary people to their political representatives have been ruptured – along with many other previously strong, organic bonds at the workplace and home. Civil society has become disorientated and problematic as a result. The political establishment has yet to provide a coherent, persuasive explanation of what is happening and why. The new ideological fads on offer have simply put a gloss over the great gap opened up in the atrophied political tradition. There is only negative derision for the past on offer, no signposts as to possible directions which civil society could take towards new self-definition and goals.[14]

The vacuum can be filled only by the political establishment offering a frank admission of past mistakes in the post-war period. A serious revisionist programme could enable either the Conservative Party or the Labour Party not just to take and hold the moral high ground but also to seize the political initiative for at least a generation. History has presented Tony Blair not with another opportunity to reform, but with an unprecedented challenge to create. Blair has so far relied on the weakness of the trade unions and the calculated self-interest of Labour activists to carry his point. The force of such circumstances always plays a vital part in determining the outcome of any political conflict. Nevertheless, circumstance and *realpolitik* are insufficient in the present political situation.

As John Major has discovered to his cost, without a new underlying perspective and an accessible body of thought which is clearly relevant to the present situation, a political party is liable to lose its way and fall prey to the ever-stronger centrifugal forces fragmenting and fracturing British politics. For the past five years, the conflict in the Conservative Party over the loss of parliamentary sovereignty to the European Union has never been far from the surface. If the conflict becomes an irreparable breach, it would permanently disable the party as an institution of government. The Euro-sceptics' perspective is narrow and eccentric to the point of being aptly characterised as quaint. No substantial section of British society has been moved by its appeal. Had Teddy Taylor and Teresa Gorman raised their banner high in 1969 or 1975, they might have found themselves leading a crusade against our taking our place in Europe alongside the Germans. In the late 1990s their potential for mobilising popular discontent is nil.

Civil society in Britain has quietly assimilated the dramatic changes in the international scene. The end of the Cold War is the most obvious and visible feature of the transformed international scene. The increasing economic and ideological importance of the Pacific rim, the satisfactory dismantling of apartheid in South Africa and the marked loss of direction and coherence in American society are other important developments. During this period of momentous change, the protests and rebellions of the Euro-sceptics might have provided the occasion for a collective and constructive reckoning up of where Britain now stands in the world. Instead, the arguments in the Conservative Party have degenerated to the level of obfuscation, bad temper, and whingeing self-pity.

MAKING THE CASE FOR SOCIALIST REVISIONISM

New Labour has the opportunity and arguably also the duty to make Blair's social-ism into something more than an ingenious vote-getting device. The party needs to embark on the ambitious job of rebuilding a popular collectivist outlook and reconstructing popular collective democratic institutions. But Tony Blair is a politician of his age, a *fin de siècle* British leader who has neither the ambition nor the will to lead anything remotely collective. He has designed new Labour to make the party more electable. He has yet to sign up the Labour Party for a thorough-going socialist revisionist project which would have more long-run consequences than winning the next election.

The starting point of socialist revisionism, the belief that socialism can only be constructed gradually by modifying elements of capitalism, has never been more relevant. Throughout Europe, but in Britain particularly, there is a clear need for collective opposition to resurgent aspects of capitalism which are threatening living standards, the social fabric and humane values. The advantage of facing up to the intellectual and moral challenge of producing a comprehensive and comprehensible revisionism is that it will provide a guide to action. Its tenets will give the electorate something which they can understand and believe in when voting. A long-term relationship between the electorate and the party could develop – within which there are realistic popular expectations about the limits of a government's ability to effect social change, whilst encouraging people to undertake the important reconstruction needed in civil society for themselves, aided by the political framework which it is a reforming government's job to provide.

For socialist revisionism, the theoretical underpinnings start with the German politician/intellectual Eduard Bernstein, who was actively involved in the formation of the Social Democratic Party (SPD) in the 1870s. Later, Bernstein found England a sympathetic and profoundly congenial place in which to spend his long political exile from Germany. He moved amongst not only the dense communities of political refugees here, but also came to know British workers and socialists intimately. He was a good friend of Ramsay MacDonald, and recounted how he first came to realise that he was a revisionist when giving a Fabian lecture about the fundamentals of Marxism.

During his enforced absence from Germany, Bernstein was not insulated from political and economic developments there. He followed them closely from abroad, and also had the benefit of his political initiation, spent in the intense and formative period of struggle between the Lasalleans and the Marxists for the soul of the infant socialist party. The conventional mythology of the Second International insists that the Marxists inflicted a decisive ideological defeat on the more liberal and collaborationist Lasalle. In fact, Lasalle's influence continued to be important in the SPD's evolution, if only because his pragmatic inclinations and strong will to imprint the young and malleable German Reich with the working-class point of view were shared by so many rank-and-file SPD members and trade unionists. It is no accident that Bernstein took Lasalle's legacy seriously and took no part in the systematic rubbishing of his name.

But Bernstein was also proud to call himself a Marxist. He had been singled out as a young man in exile by Marx and Engels in England, as being a worthy epigone and was accorded the honour of being Engels's literary co-executor with the SPD leader August Bebel. His total immersion in Marxism made his decision to speak and write about his doubts and the need to revise Marxism extremely impressive. No *enfant terrible*, his concern was not to discredit Marxism, but to adapt it before it became misleading and downright harmful as a guide to action for socialists.[15]

Bernstein pointed to three inaccurate and complementary tenets of the socialism then being propagated and espoused by the SPD: firstly, the assertion that when the working class gained political power, socialism as an economic system would automatically follow (the primacy of politics); secondly, the 'scientific prediction' that capitalism as an economic system was bound to end in a big bang, a slump to end all slumps after which socialism would be inevitable (catastrophism); thirdly, the inexorable tendency of capitalism to emiserate the proletariat which would lead to the equally inexorable final rebellion of the proletariat against the intolerable conditions under which they were toiling (emiseration).

Bernstein did not shirk from showing that these propositions were central to Marxist doctrine. He was well aware that an important reason for their strong appeal to many SPD activists was that they coincided with already existing intellectual, political and cultural patterns inherited from previous revolutionary, millenarian, protestant and democratic thought. It is important to note that the British labour movement was equally dependent on these three propositions for its inspiration, without being tied to Marxism for its justification.

In place of these inappropriate conceptions, Bernstein offered the following revisions. Firstly, as socialist/working-class parties won greater representation in parliaments, their strength would be reflected in a greater democratisation of the existing state; this greater political weight would facilitate timely reforms but would not produce any dramatic transformation. Secondly, the many other countervailing tendencies within capitalism (which Marx himself had noted in Vol.3 of *Capital*) were proving more than sufficient to counter-balance the tendency for the rate of profit to fall in large-scale capital intensive corporations; capitalism had an indefinite and evolving future ahead. Thirdly, the industrial working class was proving well able to organise both inside trade unions and politically; as a result the working-class's position was improving both economically and socially (a fact which Marx had noted in Vol.1 of *Capital* in particular with reference to the British proletariat's success in achieving the legal enactment of the ten hour working day).

Bernstein drew detailed practical conclusions from his intellectual insights. He had an acute understanding of the substantial gap which would be left in current SPD activities and assumptions if the three inaccurate central propositions were replaced by his revisions. Reading his practical suggestions, it is striking how applicable they still are to our current perspectives. Revisionist socialism is, above all, a collective project which assumes a functional, organic society in which the people respond to leads provided by an elite (amongst whom socialists are prominent and influential). Whilst there is ample room for individualism and self-fulfilment, as Bernstein observed, a collectively agreed and pursued goal is also essential. His principal conclusions from this analysis were as follows.

- First, there would be no point at which capitalism would cease and socialism begin. Because there would be no dramatic collapse of capitalism nor any dramatic political transition from capitalism to socialism, the aim of socialists must be to increase and intensify the growing strength of collective, socialist tendencies already discernible and gaining ground within capitalism.
- Second, the continuing existence, and in some sectors the increase, of small-scale capitalists was evidence of the health of capitalism. It did not, however, automatically mean that the socialist aims of the working class were thereby diminished. The successful growth of agricultural co-operatives, manufacturing producer co-operatives and consumer co-operatives showed that there was no *a priori* conflict between the aims of the working class and those of small farmers and small entrepreneurs.
- Third, the state was vitally important as a collective expression of the whole people, not merely the industrial working class. The government of a state had to take into account the needs of the collective whole, not merely the special pleadings of employers, trade unions or other interest groups. A socialist party had to be separate from its trade union support as well as to be able to act within parliament and government to safeguard the interests of the whole people.
- Fourth, socialism was an integral part of the collective project embodied in the French Revolution. Integral to the working out of that project was the increasing importance placed on individualism and individual rights. This was a sign of social development and to be welcomed by socialists.[16]

It is worth recalling that Bernstein's body of revisionist thought was rejected by the SPD before 1914, not mainly because of pressure from the revolutionary left wing of the party but because of the hostility of the conventional centre headed by August Bebel, the longstanding SPD leader. Bebel recognised that whilst the SPD's practice increasingly conformed to a Bernsteinian perspective, its culture and orientation were underpinned by an allegiance to the three eternal verities of Marxism/millenarianism which Bernstein was trying to undermine.[17]

After World War II, the German trade unions and Social Democrats finally took the giant step of abandoning the three pillars of their old outlook which Bernstein had sought to replace in the 1890s. They had the undoubted advantage of being forced to start afresh organisationally. There were no active vested interests involved in jettisoning notions once central to the daily practice of activists. Nevertheless, it required great moral and intellectual courage to admit that Bernstein had been right and that their refusal to become revisionists earlier had been a contributory factor in the failure of the Weimar Republic and the SPD's impotence in the face of fascism.

Historians have been inclined to stress the differences between German and British working class movements: the British were untheoretical, oblivious to Marxism and dominated by their trade unions; the Germans were disciplined Marxists, the SPD dominated the trade unions and the proletariat were keen SPD supporters in the 1890s. This historicist mythology has been persistent, and clearly had its political uses for the left-wing academics and practitioners of both countries. The accumulated evidence to the contrary has been published and circulated but consistently ignored.[18]

There were (and are) important differences between British and German society and their respective socialist parties. But the similarities are striking, and arguably more significant. They are easy enough to see once the pre-conception of fundamental difference has been shed.[19] In the Britain of the 1950s and 1960s, the right wing of the Labour Party and the trade unions were like August Bebel and his SPD centrists. They still held fast to an either/or ideological view of capitalism and socialism. They expected and were accustomed to compromise and doing deals with Tory ministers and industrialists, but without abandoning one iota of their strong non-conformist spiritual world-view in which capitalism and its state were enemies of the working class and a threat to the survival of all the things won and held dear by trade unions. This was a culture which was shared and cherished across the whole spectrum inside the labour movement.

REVISIONISM TODAY

It is self evident that a socialist revisionist project today could be no simple repeat of Bernstein's 1890s offensive, the German SPD's painful reckoning and re-orientation of the 1950s and 1960s, or the experience of British Social Democrats of the mid 1980s. However, the different circumstances of the later 1990s do not affect the case for the basic integrity of a revised socialism as an approach to politics. Nevertheless, European society, including Britain, has undergone fundamental change over the past century, and the new ground upon which Blair must sow the seeds of revisionism needs to be carefully examined.

Significant shifts were barely detectable in the 1950s and '60s. Any predictions about their consequences then were highly speculative. It is now possible to observe their effects over a longer time-span and consequently analyse them in greater depth. Eric Hobsbawm's *Age of Extremes*[20] provided the first systematic account and scholarly reflection upon the dramatic changes of the latter half of the twentieth century. Few other academics and political analysts have cared to venture such a comprehensive assessment. There have been many partial observations. But these are inadequate. Our assessment of the political prospects for a revisionist socialism must begin with a recognition that the ideals of the French Revolution (fraternity, equality, liberty) and their cognate social/political developments (democracy, liberalism, socialism, nationalism) have ceased to provide fundamental inspiration and motivation for action. This crucial development has three, complicated origins: first, the grave risks to the social fabric perceived by the political elite in continuing to embark upon open-ended collective national projects; second, the comparative lack of personal rewards, economic security, accumulating capital and social status, compared to the burdens and sacrifices involved in being part of the elite in the post-war world of levelled and 'demotic' culture; third, the profound shock, disillusion and demoralisation consequent upon presiding over the waging of two destructive, total wars.

The European elite no longer have the stomach for leading collective projects: they believe they have learned from the experience of 1914–45 that these require too much material and social sacrifice on their part for unknown, incalculably negative and morally reprehensible consequences. Predictably, there has been no new innovative spontaneous response from 'the people'. It has always been the case that any popular political movement has gestated first inside a small, committed group of liberals, nationalists, socialists, non-conformists, etc. The operation of a lively, unpredictable and energetic democracy is dependent upon inspired thinkers, leaders, a putative elite who are committed to 'serving the people'.

The period since 1945 has provided an unbroken period of unprecedented material prosperity, economic security and social stability. The golden age, as Hobsbawm describes it, brought undreamt-of increases in material and physical well-being with consequent widening and deepening of cultural and social horizons. But there have been significant and decisive changes. Today, compared to 1945, European people as collective social entities, national, class or religious, are more passive and pacific. They are showing no inclination to respond to the threats of falling living standards and deteriorating social fabric by adopting millenarian or reductivist solutions: class war, national conquests, or xenophobic crusading.

Hobsbawm's point is that in the late 1960s to early 1970s, a decisive break occurred and capitalism in Europe ceased to expand and provide rising real wages and full employment. It is important to note that countervailing forces operated with substantial success in the following decade: union strength in preserving wage and employment levels; the safety net of the welfare state; the protectionism of the EEC to maintain Europe's manufacturing base. This has meant that the material and social psychological effects of this decisive break are only now beginning to be felt throughout Europe. Thatcher's defence of the value of the pound pushed a comparatively weak British industrial capitalism into an earlier crisis from which it had neither the will nor the means to recover. On the continent, though the ultimate fate of industrial capitalism is less clear, its importance in shaping society will certainly diminish.

Though the European elite are busily engaged in insulating themselves from ordinary people in terms of political ties, responsibilities and mission, they are by no means separate in terms of world-view, underlying sources of inspirations, and directions. Though democracy has lost its positive dynamism in Europe, European society remains substantially and radically levelled compared with 1945; the contrast with 1895 is even more dramatic.

The delayed but inexorable impact of fighting two total wars for the ideals of the French Revolution combined with the economic, social and cultural dominance of the United States in the post-war world has produced a levelled society in Europe where individuals pursue not only self-interest but also seek immediate, and not deferred satisfaction. European society now values self-development, self-fulfilment above collective development and collective fulfilment. The serious and imponderable problems which exercise both elites and ordinary people are now individual, not collective. Though European people have displayed considerable conservatism in responding to this shift in dominant ideology, the shift has nevertheless had profound consequences on social life, both positive and negative.

Whilst the older value systems, the collective ideological glue of class, nation, religion, are certainly not dead, their current pull and impact as guides to action are much diminished. They are increasingly vestigial in their effect upon people's plans, dreams, ambitions and behaviour.

Before this situation changes, there has to be a fundamental shift in the attitudes of the elite towards society and towards collective projects. The whole ethos of Europe at the end of the twentieth century seems to militate against such a possibility being feasible or even being seen as desirable by a modern politician. There has to be a renaissance in the belief in the efficacy and practical importance of democracy, of levelling, and of the periodic radicalisation of the society through daring to put vested interests at risk by pursuing audacious collective goals.

It is hard to know what event or body of thought might set this fundamental shift off. Certainly once it has started, if the substance of the collective project and the mettle of those championing it are of sufficient quality, there will be a sea change in European society and a new era will begin. In the meantime, we bask in the mellow afterglow of the golden age. Sunsets can be prolonged and very beautiful. What will follow remains an unanswered question.

The historian can find reassurance by drawing attention to the attested openness and flexibility of European society. The sanguine will assert that we can still rely on our much-vaunted ability to rise to the occasion when needed. If we start running out of water, or find our coastal settlements disappearing when the polar ice-caps melt, the elite will respond to the emergency, will provide the lead to which the people will respond collectively.

It is possible still to argue the case for this scenario occurring relatively easily in continental Europe. The changes which took place during the golden age were profound, but not irreversible. The countervailing forces are still sufficiently intact to re-appear when needed. This argument is not tenable at present in Britain. The disintegration of the elite has been going on longer, bitten deeper and been more damaging than on the continent. There is scarcely any form of collective expression left in British society.

Consequently, we need to participate in a collective effort to rebuild our society, including the admission of past mistakes, comparable to the reconstruction on the continent in the decade after the second world war. The destruction of our social fabric has been self-induced. It has been taking place in true British fashion, slowly, gradually but inexorably, from the 1960s. Having funked the modernising attempts of Heath and Wilson between 1964–79, we are reaping the whirlwind of our complacency.

REFERENCES

1 David Marquand, *The Unprincipled Society: New Demands and Old Politics*, Fontana, London 1988; Ferdinand Mount, *The British Constitution Now*, Mandarin, London 1993; Tony Wright, *Citizens and Subjects*, Routledge, London 1993; Andrew Marr, *Ruling Britannia: The Failure and Future of British Democracy*, Michael Joseph, London 1995; Will Hutton, *The State We're In*, Jonathan Cape, London 1994.

2 The classic history of Britain's war is Angus Calder, *The People's War: Britain 1939–45*, Cape, London 1971. For an exemplary comparative analysis of the total war economies see Alan S. Millward, *War Economy and Society 1939–1945*, Pelican, London 1987.

3 There is an ever larger volume of historical analysis of the Attlee administration. Examples of positive appraisals are Paul Addison, *The Road to 1945. British Politics and the Second World War*, Quartet, London 1982; Kenneth O. Morgan, *Labour in Power, 1945–1951*, Clarendon, Oxford 1984; Nick Tiratsoo (ed), *The Attlee Years*, Pinter, London 1991, Nick Tiratsoo and Jim Tomlinson, *Industrial efficiency and state intervention: Labour 1939–51*, Routledge, London 1993.

4 See James Hinton, *Shopfloor Citizens. Engineering Democracy in 1940s Britain*, Edward Elgar, London 1994.

5 See Hugh Armstrong Clegg, *A History of British Trade Unions since 1889, Volume II 1911–1933*, Clarendon, Oxford 1985, chapter 5, and G.D.H. Cole, *Trade Unionism and Munitions*, Clarendon, Oxford 1923.

6 See Gerald D. Feldman, *Army, Industry and Labor in Germany 1914–1918*, Berg Publishers, London 1992.

7 See Ross McKibbin, *The Ideologies of Class: Social Relations in Britain 1880–1950*, Oxford University Press, Oxford 1991. For the connection between total war and democratisation see Nina Fishman 'Extending the Scope of Representative Democracy', *Political Quarterly*, October–December 1989, pp442-55 and Michael Howard, *The Lessons of History*, Oxford University Press, Oxford 1993. Within literary culture, the shift in the balance of class forces was perhaps best represented by the popular novels of Neville Shute and A.J. Cronin. Both these men are interested in people 'in general' and their heroes and heroines come from any and all

walks of life. Of course, the novels of H.G. Wells and Arnold Bennett reveal the strong influence of the levelling forces from the turn of the century.

8 See P. Inman, *Labour in the Munitions Industries*, HMSO, London 1957, and Hugh Armstrong Clegg, *A History of British Trade Unions since 1889, Volume III 1934-1951*, Clarendon, Oxford 1994, chapter 3. The levelling impact of World War II is described particularly well in Robert Blake, *The Decline of Power 1915-1964*, Paladin, London 1986, chapters 15 and 16.

9 See Peter Jenkins, *The Battle of Downing Street*, Charles Knight, London 1970 and John Campbell, *Edward Heath*, Weidenfeld & Nicholson, London 1994.

10 See John Elliott, *Conflict or Cooperation? The Growth of Industrial Democracy*, Kogan Page, London 1978, pp228-30. The head of GKN, Barrie Heath, was particularly impressed by *mitbestimmung* when he visited Germany in 1976 as a member of the Bullock Commission on Industrial Democracy.

11 In the 1960s and 1970s, the left was an amorphous admixture including the vestiges of the Bevanite wing of the Labour Party; traditional left-wing Labour socialists; the Communist Party, clearly delineated into intellectuals, local citizen activists and trade union militants; assorted Trotskyists, Maoists, and their intellectuals and union militants; and a small but tangible sprinkling of anarchists, anarcho-syndicalists, and libertarians. These categories were hardly hermetically sealed. People moved from one to the other with ease and often were part of social or work groups which were highly catholic in content. The shop stewards' committee of Austin's Longbridge, a not unimportant institution in this period, is a good example. It was led by a gifted Communist, Dick Etheridge. Its prominent members included Trotskyists, Labour loyalists, ex-Communists who had become Labour Party members, Trotskyists who had become Communists, and Trotskyists who were practising entryism into the Labour Party. For the more exotic and esoteric groupuscules (but also including the Communist Party) see John Callaghan, *The Far Left in British Politics*, Blackwell, Oxford, 1987.

12 See John Campbell, *op.cit.*

13 John Campbell's biography draws heavily on Hugo Young and Stephen Fay, *The Fall of Heath*, London, a pamphlet written in 1974, a lapidary example of investigative journalism at its height. In an interview with the author (2 November 1995), Len Murray stressed that the TUC General Council, and notably Jack Jones and Hugh Scanlon, had done their best to present the Heath government with a face-saving way out of the situation. Murray, Jones and Scanlon had offered to view the miners' wage claim as a special case which did not affect the overall integrity and coherence of the government's income policy. Campbell's account makes a similar point. The definitive history of this crucial episode clearly remains to be written. Nevertheless, the Labour Party and the shadow cabinet in particular remain highly culpable. What Murray and Campbell both perceive as Heath's bad judgement and unaccountable refusal to accept the General Council's offer was used by Wilson for short-term political ends. The long-term

consequences of this opportunism for the Labour Party, the trade unions and British society have been profound.

14 The abrupt change of tone towards politicians on the *Today* Programme on Radio 4 is symptomatic of civil society's disorientation. The discreet respectfulness which bordered on unctuousness, though never obsequiousness, has been replaced by barely repressed hostility. In the place of the previous couth and correct relations, *Today* presenters now stand up for England by brazenly insulting politicians and routinely disbelieving their statements. They have become self-appointed tribunes. Because there are no longer any ties binding us (ordinary people) to them (the political establishment), the presenters feel evidently bound to behave without manners or normal politeness. Perhaps the presenters believe they are reflecting our feelings as well as their own towards these politicians who have been revealed as men and women with feet of clay.

15 For Bernstein, see J. M. and H. Tudor, *Marxism and Social Democracy: The Revisionist Debate 1896–1898*, Cambridge University Press, Cambridge 1988. This is a collection of the original revisionist articles by Bernstein and the opposing replies including articles by Belfort Bax, Rosa Luxembourg, and Karl Kautsky, edited and translated by H. and J.M. Tudor with an introduction by H. Tudor. See also N. Fishman, 'Eduard Bernstein from a post-revisionist perspective', unpublished paper 1991.

16 The revisionist case was stated most fully by Bernstein in *Die Voraussetzungen des Sozialismus*, first published in 1899. It was translated in 1909 as *Evolutionary Socialism* in a highly attenuated form. It has been newly translated by Henry Tudor and published as *The Preconditions of Socialism*, Cambridge University Press, Cambridge 1993. The essentials of Bernstein's position are, however, easily accessible in his original polemical articles, many of which are translated in J.M. and H. Tudor, *Marxism and Social Democracy, op.cit.*

17 Bebel relied upon Karl Kautsky to do his bidding and rid the SPD of the troublesome revisionist contagion. Even though he actually agreed with Bernstein, Kautsky complied. Insufficient reflection and attention has been paid by academics to this episode. For an appraisal of the impact of Kautsky's apostasy and Kautsky's responsibility for the character assassination of Bernstein, see Fishman, unpublished paper, 1991.

18 The similarities are explored in Stefan Berger, *The Labour Party and the German Social Democrats 1900–31*, Oxford University Press, Oxford 1994.

19 The classic academic work is Paul Kennedy, *The Rise of the Anglo–German Antagonism 1860–1914*, Allen & Unwin, London 1981. Notable British Germanophiles have included George Eliot and R.B. Haldane.

20 Eric Hobsbawm, *Age of Extremes, the Short Twentieth Century*, Michael Joseph, 1994.

'The Centre of My Political Life': Tony Blair's Sedgefield

Gareth Smyth

'It's the centre of my political life,' he said, matter-of-factly. Tony Blair was talking not about Westminster, nor even Islington, but about Sedgefield, the undulating slice of Counties Durham and Cleveland he has represented in the House of Commons since 1983. 'I see the Labour Party here as the model of what the Labour Party (nationally) should be. It's a big party, with roots in every part of the community. It's one of the things I'm proudest of in my political career.'[1]

This was late February 1995. Blair had been leader of the Labour Party for just six months. He sat in the passenger seat as I drove the 15 miles from his local advice surgery in Trimdon village to Darlington, where he was to present prizes for swimming to disabled children. I had expected an interview in an office. This was his idea. He and I followed the large Ford Orion with his driver and minders.

Despite the unusual setting, Blair relaxed very quickly. 'Sedgefield has had a big impact on my political development and thinking,' he said, above the burr of the engine.

> When I came here I was pretty convinced that Labour had to modernise. What this area did was to teach me that this was what so-called traditional Labour supporters wanted. The people here have not been reluctantly accepting change but, on the contrary, agitating for it and moving it. People here are in many ways responsible for encouraging me to be fairly bold and radical.

That a leading politician could learn from 'ordinary folk' seems unimaginable to so many of the political class. It has been far easier for commentators, who generally inhabit the same London milieu, to portray Blair as 'Islington man' (to be understood in terms of the bistros at one end of a very mixed borough) and to explain his belief in individual responsibility as something stemming from – or designed to appeal to – 'Middle England'.

Islington Man Appealing to Middle England is a theme the political class uses to explain the transformation Blair has brought in the Labour Party. And even within Labour, Blair's critics argue he has simply moved the party along a political continuum defined by the bipolar terms 'left' and 'right', away from the aspirations of the poor and 'working-class' to the better-off and the 'middle class'. But those critics' belief that aspirations like, for example, patriotism or discipline are 'right-wing' or 'middle-class' reflects, in Blair's view, how out of touch some within Labour's ranks have become.

Blair unsettles. The left has spent too much time talking to itself, he told me, on our car journey. But the Sedgefield party is different.

Tony Blair's detractors love to argue, with less and less conviction or credence, that he is all smile without substance. But the people of Sedgefield, a mainly 'traditional' working-class ex-mining constituency, are the last people in England to be impressed by glitz. Loyalty here is not easily earned. When Blair was reported – erroneously, he says – to have paid £60 for a haircut, reporters arrived from London to scour the pubs. But, in an area with high unemployment and low wages, the reporters' wallets stuffed with ten-pound notes failed to produce the critical voices their editors demanded.

There was no constituency called Sedgefield between 1974 and 1983. The Boundary Commission first abolished the seat – ending the parliamentary career of David Reed – and then revived it at a fortunate time for a young lawyer seeking a more promising parliamentary nomination after an eye-catching performance in a 1982 by-election in the safe Conservative seat of Beaconsfield in Buckinghamshire.

Sedgefield village is genteel. It has been an active market town since the fourteenth century. Its rowdy Shrove Tuesday football match whose object is to 'alley' the ball by forcing it into the end of the village defended by the other side, has been played on the village green for 800 years. Today Sedgefield village is very lively on a Saturday night but quiet during the week.

The centre of gravity of Sedgefield Constituency Labour Party lies in the villages whose pits closed in the 1960s and 1970s – the Trimdons (Trimdon village, Trimdon Grange and Trimdon Colliery), West Cornforth and Ferryhill. These are tightly-packed pockets of terraced houses separated by green, gentle hills. One larger industrial town, Newton Aycliffe, replaced another, Spennymore, in the 1995 boundary revision of the Sedgefield constituency.

At the hub is the Labour Club in Trimdon village. 'I'm just a working-class lad,' says its manager – the large, bearded Paul Trippett who was born in the village 39 years ago. Once a member of Militant, Trippett runs the Labour Club at a healthy profit, selling around 3,500 pints of beer every week and attracting a different, daytime clientele with tea, coffee and biscuits.

The club avoids the two extremes of Labour Club culture elsewhere – the politically-correct meetings-based 'centre', and the more widespread, if waning, traditional (overwhelmingly male) working men's club which is basically a glorified pub-cum-snooker-hall. The broad appeal of Sedgefield Labour Club makes it a going concern: over £50,000 has been spent on refurbishment, and the Federation Brewery has lent £32,000 interest-free for new toilets.

Trippett often pulls a pint for Tony Blair: 'When he's in the constituency, he likes a night in the club. People know him as a friend, and tell him what their problems and hopes are. Tony knows what the people around here expect of him. We do want fairness and justice, and jobs and security. Tony's listened. That's what drives him.'

A PRACTICAL GAME

The North East is football-mad, and Sedgefield is no exception. Owen Willoughby, his house next to a bookies in Trimdon colliery, still scouts for Tottenham at the age of 76 – reporting to White Hart Lane on promising players or on teams due to play Spurs. Terry Fenwick, now managing Portsmouth, and Nottingham Forest defender Colin Cooper are among the local lads he brought into professional football.

Willoughby is a gentle, thoughtful man who hates swearing. His passion for football coexists with strong support for Labour and a deep admiration for the honorary president of Trimdon Juniors FC, Tony Blair. 'Football is a practical game,' says Willoughby. 'You have to win matches. You have to win the tackle, make the pass. It's the same in politics.'

When Tony Blair came to Sedgefield seeking selection for the newly-created constituency in 1983, just three weeks before the general election, the party had around 400 members, the kind of figure still typical in the Labour-dominated North-East. 'Even then he was saying that if we wanted to reflect the views of the ordinary men and women, we had to broaden the party,' says John Burton, the 55-year-old chairman of the local party and Blair's full-time agent since retiring early in 1994 as a PE teacher.

Blair has said of Burton that: 'I trust his political judgement almost more than anyone else.' Certainly Burton is pivotal in the Sedgefield party. 'The Sedgefield experience wouldn't have happened without the strength and vitality he brought to us.' says Blair. 'He's a remarkable person. Had things worked out differently he would have been a big political player in any field he chose to go into.'

Burton is a bustling, large-set, furry man with a big moustache, bushy eyebrows and a deep, growling voice. His pronounced limp is the result of spending much of his youth on the football field, where he once scored 70 goals for Stockton in one season. The twinkle in his eye and his affable manner complement a political astuteness and a warm worldliness.

He remembers his boyhood in Trimdon village with a mixture of emotions.

> There was poverty. I can remember people running around with no shoes on their feet. But there was tremendous community spirit. The roads were ash, the pit heap rose from the middle of the village. That was the life of the place. You left school and you got a job in the mine. If you were fortunate you got an apprenticeship (for skilled work) down the mine.

The centrality of coal mining shaped the politics of the era. 'The NUM (National Union of Mineworkers) picked the MP. It was as simple as that. They decided at a closed meeting who would be the MP, and that used to happen throughout County Durham.'

The role of the NUM had already declined when in 1983 a 30-year-old aspirant MP went to Burton's house seeking the Labour nomination for the Sedgefield constituency. Tony Blair had grown up in nearby Durham, where his father Leo Blair (then a leading Conservative in the region, but who joined Labour in 1995) was a law lecturer at the University. When Ossie O'Brien, a county councillor and briefly MP in 1983 for Darlington, was a mature student at Durham in the early 1960s, Blair senior was his tutor for constitutional law:

> Leo Blair was a very curious combination of a man, with very right-wing political views combined with being an extremely nice person. I remember visiting the Blair house sometimes with other students for sherry

and Tony coming in from the Choristers School in his school uniform.
He must have been about eight years of age at that time.[2]

Blair moved on to public school at Fettes in Edinburgh, to university
at Oxford where he became a practising Christian and where his
political views shifted leftwards, and then to London to work as a
lawyer. There was nothing inevitable, then, about Blair returning to the
North East to find a seat – even if John Burton tells the story in such a
practised way that Fate, you feel, must have played her part.

Burton recalls the night Blair arrived at his house: 'There were five
of us meeting to discuss the district council results. We'd done very
well and were going to send out thank you letters.' But there was a
football match – the European Cup Winners' Cup final no less –
between Aberdeen and Real Madrid to watch on television and Blair
had to wait while the match went into extra time.

When the game finally ended, the group asked Blair some questions.
Burton was impressed by 'his youth, his vitality, his ideas', he says.
'He was charismatic and was saying things even then that weren't party
policy, and he knew where he wanted the party to go. Whilst we
would never have thought, I suppose, that he would have been leader
of the party in eleven years, we certainly knew he was something
special, even at that first meeting.'

Burton and the three others present – Paul Trippett, Peter Brookes
and Terry Ward – agreed they would work to secure the nomination for
Blair. It was a strong field, including Les Huckfield, whose Nuneaton
seat had been tilted towards the Conservatives by the Boundary Commission, Reg Race, political advisor at the Greater London Council, and
the then leader of Sedgefield district council, Warren McCourt. At the
eleventh hour Burton persuaded the constituency's general committee
to include Blair's name on a shortlist of six, largely on the strength of a
letter from Michael Foot praising Blair's efforts as the candidate in
Beaconsfield. At the selection meeting in Spennymore Town Hall, it
took five rounds of voting to overcome Huckfield.

Ironically, Blair might have faced a sterner challenge. Arthur
Scargill revealed to me in 1995 that, unbeknown to John Burton, he
had tried to persuade Tony Benn to seek the Sedgefield nomination.
Benn decided to stay and fight his ground in Bristol, where his
majority was threatened by boundary revision. Benn lost, and then
became MP for Chesterfield in a 1984 by-election. The possibilities of
Benn sitting in parliament when Michael Foot resigned in June 1983

and so being eligible to stand against Neil Kinnock for the leadership, and Tony Blair perhaps having to wait until 1987 to become an MP, make interesting material for students of the 'what-if' in politics.

The Blair bandwagon gathered speed. 'Everything happened so quickly,' John Burton continues. 'Cherie says he left home with his suitcase and never went back. He left his job as well, and never practised as a lawyer from that point. He stayed with my wife and family at our house in Trimdon village for a year and a half. Cherie used to come up at weekends.'

So began a political journey watched locally with growing interest outside the party. Father John Caden has spent 29 of his 72 years as a priest in Sedgefield, first as a minister within the local psychiatric hospital and then as parish priest at St John the Fisher, the church in a terrace at the top of Sedgefield village green. Sitting in the presbytery, Caden recalls the inspiration of Pope John XXIII, who was installed as an elderly, caretaker pontiff in 1958 but proceeded to transform the Catholic Church by reviving the long-dormant Vatican Council.

Pope John XXIII's emphasis on the social dimension to the Church's ministry was an important fillip to 'liberation theology' in the 1960s. John Caden took up the challenge. He was directly involved in politics as an independent county councillor for 16 years, retiring in 1989 at the age of 66. Caden has been both an observer of Tony Blair and an influence upon him.

> It was John Burton and the late Mick Terrens (leader of Durham County Council and chair of the Sedgefield party) who took Tony Blair to heart. When they listened to him they thought: this fellow has a vision for the future. Every pit here had been closed down, the coke works were closing. Anything where the unions had said 'you can't do this, you can't do that' had failed. Burton and Terrens realised the way forward was to try and have a different vision of things. Other members of the Sedgefield party gathered round and began to spread the Blair gospel. His ideas for community politics and Christian socialism came to fruition in Sedgefield.

Father Caden baptised Blair's three children, and introduced the future Labour leader to his tennis circle. 'The first time he came to my house he saw my racket. He would have a game when he came up. The people in my little tennis group – doctors, housewives – have all met Tony at different times. Quite a number would be anything but socialists but he always managed to get a good rapport.'

A POUND A YEAR

Increasing the size of the local party has been crucial to the Sedgefield project, and a scheme which allows people to pay as little as a pound a year has helped swell membership to nearly 2,000 since it was introduced in 1993. 'Increasing the membership keeps you in touch with those communities you say you represent,' says Phil Wilson, who helped as a local activist to frame the scheme in Sedgefield and now works for Labour's national headquarters on recruiting trade unionists to the party at reduced rates. 'My definition of a mass party is where everybody knows someone who's in the Labour Party. If you have a mass party you start discussing real issues – whether your kid should wear a school uniform, the minimum wage, the NHS, crime – and the party ends up being in tune with the local community.'

Critics of the Sedgefield scheme have alleged that the influx of members has diluted the party, taking it away from policies they judge socialist and diverting it into activities they feel are lightweight. 'There is certainly a mass membership,' says Derek Cattell, party member and full-time official of the GMB trade union. 'But that doesn't necessarily mean there is mass participation. We can't say that because it's possible to join for as little as a pound that suddenly lots of people are entering into the political process and debate.'

The constituency party still must pay two-thirds of the full membership per member of £15 to Labour's national headquarters, and this necessity sets its own priority. 'Sedgefield is constantly fundraising – in fact that's its sole activity,' alleges Derek Cattell. 'I warn anyone who follows the Sedgefield model, they'd better start printing their raffle tickets now.'

Rita Taylor, the Sedgefield party secretary, disagrees. 'We ask people to pay what they think they can afford, and they do. Some people do give us a pound, but some people make a standing order out and perhaps pay £100 in a year. About half the membership fees we have to pay to Walworth Road come in through membership.'

This does leave the other half to be raised through fundraising. But, Taylor argues, fundraising is part and parcel of the flow of views and the pooling of experience: 'It means we're constantly in touch with our members. All the time we are engaging in political discussion and campaigning. It's all tied up together.' When she joined the party in 1984 in Sedgefield village (having left the SDP, disillusioned, after only six months on board), it had fewer than 20 members in the village. 'The party was quite moribund,' she recalls. There are now 160 people in the party in Sedgefield village, meaning that one in four Labour supporters has joined the party.

The Labour Club manager Paul Trippett, too, has a relaxed view of politics.

> I've got two guys who joined the Labour Party through the club, and they're both school governors now. They don't come to Labour Party meetings very much. They come to governors' meetings because they are contributing to the community by doing that. So you get people who don't think they are political, but they do a political act by becoming a school governor. Then, hopefully, the same two guys will put their names forward when it comes to the election of the new parish council.

The Sedgefield stalwarts are keen to avoid politics with a hairshirt. 'We have meetings where people laugh,' says John Burton. 'In the past I've often said there were members of EXIT trying to get in.'

But Burton is realistic about the attractions of formal meetings:

> We had a discussion a few weeks ago about the number of young people in the party. They were saying – 'why isn't the room full of teenagers?'. And I said: 'The last thing I wanted to do when I was a teenager was to sit in a room and discuss politics. I was playing football, I was courting, I was going out.'

Tony Blair's notion of Sedgefield as a 'model' for the party nationally gained ground with the upsurge in Labour's national membership to 350,000 at the end of 1995, the highest for ten years. This increase came at a time when Conservative membership fell and when many commentators extolled the rise of single-issue pressure groups and consigned political parties to the dustbin of history.

Only three other constituency parties – including Gordon Brown's Dunfermline East – have chosen to operate the scheme adopted in Sedgefield, although all can sign up trade union levy members at a reduced rate. But, Labour says, it has become a party with a genuinely new flavour reflecting the kind of openness Blair has championed. 'We are more welcoming,' says Nick Smith, the official at Walworth Road with overall responsibility for membership development. 'The Ispwich party, for example, has adapted its general committee and introduced all-members meetings. Many local parties have a new emphasis on political discussion through smaller group work rather than the old, adversarial approach of submitting resolutions and then fighting your corner to the death.'[3]

While Labour has employed modern marketing techniques to recruit new members, the most successful single method has been 'member-get- member' initiatives through which existing members are encouraged to enrol their friends and associates – essentially the model followed in Sedgefield. 'Member-get-member' is encouraged by the party's internal communications including *Mew Labour, New Britain*, the magazine which is mailed direct to all members.

Labour's success in recruiting members is recent, dating from just before Blair's election as leader. The extent of decline in membership had become apparent after 1981, when the real membership figures were recorded for the first time: previously it had simply been assumed that each constituency party had 1,000 members. By 1988 the party had only 250,000 members. A succession of targets for growth floundered throughout the 1980s: famously, Neil Kinnock proclaimed in 1983 that 'A quarter of a million new members in the next 18 months is not a pious hope.'

The extent to which Labour's culture alienated potential members is illustrated by a pamphlet published in 1982 by the Labour Co-ordinating Committee[4] – one of whose authors, Charles Clarke, was later head of Neil Kinnock's office. 'What, then, do we mean by a "campaigning Party"?' the pamphlet asked, before supplying a very reasonable solution. 'In its most obvious sense, this is a question of turning the party outwards – of speaking to others not just to ourselves.' But in turning outwards, the imagination of the pamphleteers was rather limited: they went on to cite 'nuclear-free zones' and 'Sheffield's decision to break all links with apartheid' as 'pioneering examples of what can be done' and bemoaned that 'the party and the LPYS (Labour Party Young Socialists) have no real contact with even the more progressive youth organisations such as the Woodcraft Folk or Young Christian Workers.'

Evidence of more practical thinking appeared with a Tribune pamphlet written by Gordon Brown and published just before the 1987 election. Drawing unfavourable comparisons with European socialist parties, especially the Swedish Social Democrats, Brown advocated recruiting trade union levy payers as individual members at a reduced rate: 'British socialists have an army waiting in the wings, ready to be mobilised for socialist change'. With the backing of the GMB general secretary John Edmonds the 1988 conference laid the basis of a new membership structure: approving a reduced membership fee of £5 for levy payers, and approving the introduction of a computerised, national membership scheme.

These institutional and organisation changes were not enough in themselves to revive the party. Blair and Brown saw them, along with the introduction of One Member One Vote, as part of a wider change in political culture needed if Labour were to become an effective party of power. Shortly after Labour's defeat in the 1992 election, Brown produced a second pamphlet *Making Mass Membership Work* which summarised the modernisers' case:

> The renewal of Labour is not a distraction from winning power. Indeed the modernisation of the Labour Party is the first step to the modernisation of Britain. That is why the task of regenerating Labour must lie at the heart of a political strategy for winning and sustaining power ... The world of politics must not exist in a vacuum separate from the every day concerns that people have ... With more members and direct democracy, our party will be able to speak with greater authority than ever before. Our party will reflect the communities that our members live in ... The 'electorate' isn't a mystical body. They are the people around us, our neighbours, colleagues and friends ...

COMMUNITY FORCE

The 'day to day' concern most associated with Tony Blair's rise to pre-eminence in British politics is crime. In no area of public policy has he been more successful in shifting public perceptions of Labour and in wrongfooting the Conservatives. The kind of approach Blair follows has its echoes in Sedgefield.

Crime in Sedgefield is basically of two sorts, says Detective Chief Inspector Barry Peart. Sedgefield village is prone to the 'better class burglary' by professionals travelling along the nearby A1(M): 'The more socialist and traditional old colliery villages tend to have the more opportunist thief, probably because they know there's not a lot to be had money-wise.'

In the 'close-knit, hardline' ex-mining villages, says Peart, there has been a reluctance to help the police. But that is changing. Crime is on the mind of many who attend Tony Blair's Saturday morning advice surgery in Trimdon Labour Club. Jeanette Brown disturbed someone breaking into her bathroom window in Trimdon Colliery. 'Youths in the street just taunt the police,' she says. 'It's terrible.'

But Detective Inspector Peart – a softly-spoken 44-year-old with a colourful tie – believes that new police tactics are bringing success. There is close co-operation with Labour-controlled Sedgefield District Council, whose uniformed Community Force acts as 'eyes and ears' for the police and whose Housing Department repairs damage from burglaries free and within two hours.

'The Community Force has no powers of arrest, but they do drive around in cars which look very similar to a County Durham police car,' says Sean Edmunds, reporter for the *Northern Echo*. 'An independent survey has shown that a large majority of people welcome the Community Force.'

The police target suspected criminals. 'A lot has to do with observation – surveillance if you wish,' says Peart. In a typical operation, in Ferryhill, a village with a relatively high crime rate, raids on twelve houses found drugs, electrical gear, jewellery and mountain bikes. Police made twelve arrests.

This proactive style of policing has been encouraged nationally throughout the many years of Conservative Home Secretaries, yet in the 1980s many Labour local authorities, especially in London, tended to regard the police with deep suspicion and even eschewed formal links. Tony Blair made his mark as Shadow Home Secretary by reclaiming much of this crucial political ground for Labour.

Back in my car, he freely admits the importance of Sedgefield in shaping his approach:

> Tough on crime, tough on the causes of crime arose from the experience I had here. It brought home very clearly that people understand that there are causes of crime we should tackle, but they also believe very strongly in personal responsibility. They don't believe that you can ever allow the identification of those causes of crime to become an excuse for not having an effective criminal justice system.

Blair readily identifies the causes of crime in Sedgefield: 'Family instability, young people with nothing to do, drug abuse, poor educational opportunity – these things create a context in which young people are less likely to be responsible citizens.' This is more than a question of unemployment. In stressing personal responsibility, Tony Blair seeks to return Labour to deeper values than common ownership of industry. In Sedgefield, the case for reforming Clause Four was very easily won. 'We're not going to nationalise ICI and Black and Decker,' said John Burton. 'We're not going to take the corner shop off the bloke. Why not let's be honest and say what we're going to do?'

When Arthur Scargill came to the constituency during the controversy over revising the clause, he attracted a 180-strong audience. Around two-thirds were Labour left-wingers from across the region and a third were ex-miners keen to see a living, if fading, legend. 'Clause Four is timeless,' tub-thumped Scargill. 'The only thing wrong with Clause Four is that it's never been implemented. This is about the very soul, faith and belief of this party. Without Clause Four our party is indistinguishable from the Liberal Democrats and the Tories.'

Scargill left the rally quickly after a ritualistic dig at the BBC. But he found time, just, to recall that he (Scargill) and Blair had appeared together on a platform earlier that year when, according to Scargill Blair had praised the National Union of Mineworkers' president as an 'outstanding socialist'.

Since then the NUM President and the MP for Sedgefield have moved further and further apart. 'Blair has declared war not just on Clause Four but on socialism itself,' Scargill told his rally. During our trip to Darlington Tony Blair openly acknowledged that Margaret Thatcher attacked 'some abuses that needed to be tackled', a remark which would have constituted heresy in the Labour Party of the early 1980s.

After Scargill's meeting, its organiser John Piggott of the local Trades Council could introduce me to only one member of Sedgefield constituency party present. I later discovered that the Sedgefield party's youth officer, Dawn Wilson, had been in the audience. In some ways hers was the most sceptical voice I encountered in Sedgefield. But she had little time for Arthur Scargill. 'The policies he proposes are way back in the 1930s,' she said. 'Society's changed.'

Dawn Wilson lives in West Cornforth village where many of the friends she grew up with are unemployed. 'There's a problem of lack of facilities, lack of things for young people to do. Not many people go on to further education. The year I was in, there were only four of us out of a class of 30 who went on to take A-levels or resit GCSEs. A lot of people leave at 16, perhaps get a temporary job in a factory and then find themselves unemployed. The girls get married very young and have children by the time they're about 20.'

She was well aware that the challenges facing her generation go far deeper than reversing the 'wrongs' of Thatcherism. She is no pie-eyed idealist about her village. 'Among the young people there's a general sense of hopelessness. Among older people, they see it as more of a community. The way society's gone over my generation, there isn't much of a sense of community left. People are very individualistic.'

The sense of community, she said, had been eroded by unemployment, lack of education and increased mobility. 'People are a lot more isolated. At one time my parents say they knew everybody in the street. Nowadays, people move about a lot more, they don't pull together as much.'

Interestingly, she argued that the columnists, seers and professional prophets of doom missed the point in expecting a crisis of expectations in the aftermath of Tony Blair entering Number 10. They both underestimated the scale of the problems society faced and misread the popular mood, at least of the young. 'I can't remember a Labour government,' she said. 'Things have got that bad, they can only get better. From Sedgefield's point of view, a Labour government couldn't suddenly turn the economy around, open all the pits and shipyards. People do realise that it is going to take time to change things.'

In the time change takes, and in the pressures of Labour's first government in a generation, will Blair's Sedgefield people remain important to him? John Burton laughed out loud when I suggested he would be a power behind the throne of the next prime minister.

'I was at a ceilidh in the club last night. Tony and I spent about ten minutes – I was on the phone at the bar – talking about things. It's exciting to be involved, and it's nice to have access to someone in that kind of position because that can be used to help other people to get access. But while we might bounce things off one another, Tony's his own man. He knows where he's going.'

That said, John Burton is in no doubt that Blair will continue to draw on the warmth and wisdom of Sedgefield people. 'They'll tell him if they don't agree with him,' he chuckled. 'That keeps his feet on the ground.'

REFERENCES

1 The interviews on which much of this chapter are based were mainly conducted in the Sedgefield constituency in February 1995. I should like to thank Tim Allan, John Burton, Yvonne Harrison, Rita Taylor and Paul Trippett for their help and hospitality.
2 Interview, Durham, February 1995.
3 Interview, London, December 1995.
4 Charles Clarke, David Griffiths et al, 'Labour and Mass Politics: Rethinking our Strategy', Labour Co-ordinating Committee, London, 1982.

THE IMPERMANENCE OF NEW LABOUR

Kevin Davey

Although Tony Blair has done much to transform the culture and ideology of the Labour Party, there are few signs that new Labour is anything but a temporary political formation. There is also good reason to believe that the leadership does not regard it as sustainable in its present form. For some close to the centre of events, this uncertainty is a welcome and desirable state of affairs.

Blair has successfully reassembled and expanded the coalition of support for Labour that flew apart in the wake of the 1979 election defeat, the growth of Bennite activism and the formation of the SDP. Electorally speaking, Labour can no longer be regarded as a loser. But as the example of Thatcherism demonstrated, real and hegemonic political power is the consequence of creating a modernising alliance across class, regional and interest groups, at macrosocial and at microcommunity levels, which is both ethical and economic in its concerns. The popularisation of a wide-ranging and coherent set of principles, expressed in a comprehensive agenda for change, is therefore a precondition of a lasting change in the way in which the country is governed.

There is no doubt that Tony Blair aspires to be a counter-hegemonic politician on this scale. But the ambition is falling short of the reality. For all the talk of a new consensus and vision, of One Nation Labour, of a new morality and stakeholder capitalism, the unity of the heterogeneous and growing coalition of interests that new Labour has amassed remains tactical, temporary and pragmatic. The party's attenuated pluralism is based on a set of compromises imposed by a short term objective: political office. On decisive issues like tax cuts, for example, it is already proving difficult to maintain the marriage between 'the moderate middle income majority' and Labour's poorer but traditional support. Robin Cook has described the political culture of conformity which results only too vividly: 'We are united and disciplined and biting our tongue ... we are giving support to our colleagues and restraining criticisms of our colleagues. We have always believed in solidarity and the collective ideal, but in the past we have never practised what we preached.'[1]

Complementary to the long term repositioning of the party in the media and the political marketplace, which began under Neil Kinnock, there is a more transient internal settlement based on realpolitik. Krieger's under-estimate of the the force of Thatcherism is far more useful as a way of analysing the nature and scope of new Labour: 'Thatcherism is based on arithmetic politics. It relies on the sum of diverse and particularistic appeals; on housing, race, anti-Labour or anti-union sentiments, entrepreneurial ethos – but does not represent a unified coalition such as that which lay beneath the Butskellite programme of the Keynesian Welfare State.'[2]

Despite an energetic attempt to appropriate and popularise a vision of a stakeholder society combining economic efficiency and social justice, it is the base of new Labour's support which increasingly appears to be arithmetical, held together only by the unstable and undisclosed sum of the sectional fruits each partner expects of the party in office. Middle England wants its lifestyle secured, and the welfare state repaired; the Scots want independence; manufacturing industry wants infrastructural development and lower interest rates; the trade unions are desperate to reverse the attrition of their legal rights; the low paid – and many who are better paid – want higher wages and job security; the unemployed want work. Substantial majorities of each of these constituencies now believe their priorities were never, or are no longer, serious objectives of the Conservatives.

The political identity that has been constructed by new Labour is therefore improvised and fluid. Although it aspires to be sovereign, its unity is fragile. Despite the continual striving after a common voice, the cautiously articulated understanding that has been reached by the allies now gathered under the party's umbrella is mostly prompted by electoral discipline. Short of an absolute transformation of Labour's culture – and for that there is precious little time – it is likely that the rewards each partner seeks for its contemporary self restraint will prove incompatible.

Some of the divisions – those between the party leadership and the trade unions, or between the leadership and the left of the PLP – are already public even if much of the detail is private. Some issues – the scope and pace of European integration, the imposed acceptance of Conservative educational reforms and the purchaser-provider split in the NHS, ambivalences over constitutional reform and pluralism, and the tensions between Labour's new touchstones of community and responsibility and its civil libertarian traditions – trouble the party at every level, from the constituencies to the Front Bench. Others – like the disparity between new and Scottish Labour,[3] or the divergent priorities of new Labour in Westminster and new Labour in the Town Halls – are currently visible only as hair line cracks. Yet others deriving from the limits on redistribution assumed in the public concordats between the party and Middle England, the party and the City, the party and the European Union – are likely to burst through with little forewarning.

The origins of new Labour's political identity have been variously defined by the left. Orthodox marxists and leftists argue that Blair is either the offspring of two revisionists – the late nineteenth century marxist Bernstein and Labour's Anthony Crosland – an unashamed exponent of the corporatist politics that failed Labour in the 1970s, or the son of Thatcher herself. They frequently characterise the incoming administration as the most right wing since Ramsay MacDonald's National Government in the 1930s.[4]

Apart from its acceptance of a number of Thatcherite reforms, new Labour's search for a fresh identity has been global rather than indigenous. It has turned to the American Democrats for lessons on how to win power, the Australian Labour governments of Hawkes and Keating on how to retain it, and to the Asia-Pacific for a vision of the future. There have been many long haul flights and much cloning of policy: a Jobs and Enterprise Training (JET) programme for the long-term unemployed was extricated from Australia's otherwise unwanted government-union accords; communitarian themes were imported from the United States. Asian values and the models of industrial development and welfare which have generated the 'Tiger' economies of the Pacific 'Rim' have also been called upon.[5]

It has become a commonplace to point out that today the only political constant is change. The post-war stability of institutions, ideologies and issues has gone. The Blair leadership accepts that every tradition now has to justify itself anew, and every assumption about policy has to be re-examined. But the shifting sands of political life exacerbate the problems of new Labour more than for any previous incoming Labour administration. The status of politics and politicians is on the decline. There is a diminishing expectation, even amongst the political class, of what governments can do. The policy convergence between the main parties that results contributes to the volatility of electorates. A proliferation of cultural and political identities further stimulates the appetite for devolved decision-making and democracy. Seen from within this context, new Labour's transformation still falls short of that which is needed to overcome the crisis of representation in British politics. Far from a finished product, new Labour is merely a staging post and herald of far reaching change.

A PRECARIOUS PARTNERSHIP

Sixteen years of Conservative rule, 'the worst set of defeats of any social democracy in Europe,'[6] has forced an unusually diverse range of interests together. The heterogeneous coalition that is addressed by new Labour consists of the traditional, if now arms length, labour movement alliance – trade unions, approved socialist affiliates, the professional middle class still committed to welfare ideals, the CLPs, and the PLP. It also embraces those who seek their own new parliaments and those who want to defend the Union; people living in regions with distinct interests and needs and an enduring and traditional distinction between left and right; clashing civil libertarian and communitarian voices; pluralists and constitutional reformers as well as party triumphalists; people in and out of work; party members lodged in different tiers of representation in the state and local government; male members with a tradition of over-representation and female members seeking to overcome it; pro-Europeans, tentative Europeans and Euro-sceptics; Keynesians, monetarists and neo-Keynesians. It reaches beyond the party to include the non-Conservative voices in the City and the private sector with whom partnerships are being sought, the voluntary sector and the floating south of England voter.

Because of the structure of the state and the requirements of the electoral process, Blair insists, the first commitment and overriding responsibility must be the installation of new Labour in office. Particularistic identities and interests must become subsidiary to the party and the nation. New Labour prefers not to acknowledge its real identity as an imposed and temporary coalition but unless it does so, and unless it carries out the kind of constitutional reforms that will enable its components to assert and negotiate their interests in public and claim their autonomy, it will neither deepen the forms of political representation nor remain sustainable as a coalition.

Is this alliance cemented by anything more than a shared, short-term interest? The ruthless press and patronage policy of the leadership suggests not. Three controversies in the summer of 1995 revealed a project willing to resort to force under cover of its public commitment to dialogue and consensus. The first involved the removal of the party's General Secretary, followed soon after by the removal of the Chief Whip and the transfer of responsibility for selecting whips from the PLP to the Leader; the second was a leaked memorandum by Philip Gould addressing the need for a 'unitary command structure' in the party;[7] the third was over the selection and then non-recognition of a socialist Islington councillor, Liz Davies, as a parliamentary candidate. Determined to/travel light on policy and give few hostages to fortune, the leadership has also introduced strict procedures for the management of the policy process. To become hegemonic in society Blair has not shrunk from being coercive in the party.

New Labour has not just discarded unpopular policies. It has become disciplinary in its determination to win and retain office. Despite the formal empowerment represented by the system of One Member One Vote (OMOV), the Leader's Office has continued to strengthen itself at the expense of the different tiers of representative democracy embodied in the shadow cabinet, the NEC and the party conference. A series of advisory groups, consultative forums and commissions have displaced former adversarial or back-room forms of decision making – the NEC and party conference. As John Evans wrote in *Tribune*, 'Increasingly the NEC is being bypassed and major policy and other decisions are taken by Shadow Cabinet members or party officials and Leaders Office staff'.[8] The downgrading of Labour's women's conference to a biennial, non decision-making forum is further evidence of the process. Paradoxically the real context of the empowerment of party members is that the purchase of the vote given to each member of the organisation has been reduced.

Members offer three grounds for their acquiescence: first and foremost a desire to see their party in office, secondly the range of immediate benefits that are expected, and thirdly, the absence of any coherent alternative, whether pragmatic or utopian. Although expectations are being lowered, the likely rewards of office will still be tangible for Labour's supporters. The unions will get a statutory right of recognition, the abolition of check-off and compulsory competitive tendering and the benefits enshrined in the Social Chapter; local authorities will benefit from the reintroduction of accountability into the quango state; Scotland may get a long awaited Parliament and Wales an Assembly; constitutional reformers will celebrate reform of the Lords, a Bill of Rights, a Freedom of Information Act and, just possibly, a referendum on electoral reform for the Commons. There will be some repair, albeit on an undisclosed scale, to education and the welfare state. And the low paid may benefit from a minimum wage, depending on the level at which it is set.

Although most eyes are firmly fixed on the prize of office, in the medium term new Labour's political settlement is unstable and precarious. Many elements of the party who defend the official positions also hold a number of potentially subversive particularistic beliefs or sectional interests, expect more than is projected, and will be disappointed with what Labour is likely to deliver.

To date there is no left capable of matching or outflanking the Blair leadership's new hegemony in the party, nor its ability to reposition Labour in the political marketplace. The left inside and outside the party has no alternative strategy capable of delivering new reforms to match the changed dynamics of Britain's political system, economy and cultures. In the main it does not accept that there is any need to renew or extend the coalition of interests identifying with the Labour Party. Like Kinnock before him, Blair is denounced as the leader of an SDP Mark 2, a liberal or a democratic party on the US model. Blair is pressing ahead with what Tony Benn can only see as 'an attempt to dismantle the Labour Party by breaking the links with the unions and disavowing socialism'.[9]

Others on a marginal but stubborn hard left go further and argue that in the mid-1990s new Labour succumbed to Conservative thought. The period between the two Labour conferences in 1995 appears to have been a watershed for the left. 'The biggest irony for the Labour Party,' wrote *Tribune* editor Mark Seddon during the debate on Clause Four of the party constitution, 'is that, just as the majority of the people recoil from the exigencies of the market economy, the party seems prepared to write it into its constitution.'[10] That spring *Tribune*'s parliamentary correspondent, Hugh MacPherson, warned that 'the Labour Party must face the fact that there is now the most determined intention, not only to change it into a Liberal Conservative organisation, but also to destroy the democratic way in which it has made policy in the past'.[11] Five months later it had happened: 'New Labour is nothing short of One Nation Conservatism,' he declared.[12] In the *New Statesman & Society* in the spring John Pilger insisted that new Labour's leaders were 'newly cloned Conservatives'. He went on to argue that 'The defeat of the Tory Party is pointless if the replacement is its literal shadow'.[13] By the autumn he also believed that he had been correct to fear the worst. 'New Labour is an authoritarian party of the new right,' he concluded.[14]

In this displaced left there are critics of Blair aplenty. But apart from a few redoubts in trade unions, *Tribune* newspaper, and in the founding manifesto of Arthur Scargill's Socialist Labour Party, little confidence remains in the Keynesian and statist solutions traditionally associated with the Labour left.[15] Even fewer still hold to the anti-European, public ownership aspirations of the high-points of left influence, Labour's 1973 and 1982 programmes, still sustaining the Campaign Group. Perspectives and policies capable of holding Labour's old coalition together and winning it new friends from contemporary social movements have yet to be established.

The centre of gravity has shifted, irreversibly, away from the unions and CLP activists and the statist left. But to achieve electoral victory, its overriding interest, the shadow ship of state has had to keep these traditional interests on board, albeit sometimes in chains. This may be the last time Labour strikes this particular compromise. The achievement of office, the introduction of state funding and the mediatisation of campaigns could end the party's financial reliance on the unions and its inherited membership for good.

MEMBERS, WHO NEEDS THEM?

During the 1980s, when 60,000 people decamped from the Labour Party in the wake of its double humiliation at the polls, a debate opened on whether this was an understandable display of war weariness or confirmation of a wider trend in which cultural and political differentiation were eroding the very ground on which mass membership parties stood.[16] In the autumn of 1995 the Labour Party silenced the academics who had been speculating about the end of the mass party by disclosing that its membership had surpassed 350,000. One third had joined since Blair's selection as leader.

The expanded party is not simply a larger version of its former self. Its structures have been re-engineered to encourage growth based on a national rather than a neighbourhood identification with its political project. The relationship between members and the party's constitution is no longer mediated by local officers and branch meetings but by a centralised and computer-based register of members, banker's orders, postal ballots, and the increased rights that accrue from the introduction of OMOV in 1993.

New Labour's membership campaign – the Regeneration Project – has certainly produced impressive and unexpected results. But has new Labour simply bucked, for now and for very specific reasons, a trend that will reassert itself? Or has it discovered a participatory form that goes with the grain of an increasingly non-political age? It is still too early to say. No one knows the stress capacities of the new relationships that have been established nor how many of the tensions and the conflicts described in this chapter they can bear, and for how long. It is possible that we may never find out. For some of those involved in its reconfiguration, the party's diverse and hastily gathered membership is instrumental, no more than a temporary necessity imposed by the need for parties to win funds in the social marketplace.

Will the introduction of state funding for political parties really displace the need for a mass membership? Much depends on the system that is adopted.[17] The level of party membership is actually higher in Germany, where state funding was introduced in 1982, than it is in Britain today. In Germany the amount of financial support given is based on the size of the party's vote and the amount of money that it raises for itself. One outcome, the subject of much envy in Walworth Road, is that the main left of centre party – the Sozialdemokratische Partei Deutschlands (SPD) – does not depend on trade union donations. The introduction of a similar system in the United Kingdom might help to free new Labour from a vested interest they find it increasingly difficult to accommodate. But the precondition would be a large card carrying membership or high levels of donation by the party's supporters.

The orthodox left's anxieties about state funding have been most dramatically voiced by Tony Benn: 'MPs will become civil servants and Labour MPs will no longer have any link with the trade unions that set up the party, because their new paymasters will be the Treasury, which will then be free to withdraw funding from any MPs following policies which are unacceptable to the establishment.'[18]

Benn's argument assumes a great deal about methods of payment. There is no reason to believe that the monies would not be distributed using the same centralised structures and priorities that determine the present allocation of Labour's disposable funds to think tanks, experts, agencies and advisers. Both scenarios are dismissed by Peter Hain, who insists that state funding would enable Labour to appoint organisers who could develop its participatory structures and political culture at all levels.[19]

Whether voluntary or subsidised, new Labour's programme of organisational reforms involves a risk. If the modernisers engineer a party that is massive but passive, they may well have thrown away one of Labour's greatest assets. The authors of the most exhaustive published research on Labour's ranks concluded that 'an active party membership is absolutely vital to the electoral performance of the Labour Party'. They even concluded that 'the Labour Party is unlikely to survive as the main alternative party of government, and a major electoral force in British politics, without a thriving grassroots organisation'.[20]

Given that members do serve as local ambassadors, persuaders and mobilisers for the party, this argument should not be dismissed as activist special pleading. However in a leaked document, Andrew Stunnell, political officer of the Association of Liberal Democrat Councillors, observed: 'Even where Labour is not running an active campaign and it is clear that the party are unlikely to win the seat, electors are attracted to vote for them. The Blair effect does not rely on a strong local campaign to be effective.'[21] When Labour's electoral opponents fear a branch with low expectations as much as a well oiled campaign machine it surely suggests that the decisive political encounters no longer take place in the localities.

Of course, the reforms are not yet over. There are calls for Labour's conference to become a US-style convention rally and, for reforms to local party committees and the NEC, regional conferences and the policy process.[22] Roger Liddle and Peter Mandelson are urging the adoption of a constitution – wholly based on OMOV and without any federal arrangement – modelled on the SDP that broke away from Labour in the early 1980s.[23]

New Labour's emphasis on national membership, the centralised management of the party's profile and campaigns, and the prospect of state funding all tend to relocate politics outside local spaces and structures. In doing so, they complement the centralising thrust of recent Conservative politics. If there is no countervailing engagement with the local, these reforms will narrow the forms of representation and participation that will predominate in our political culture.

WHAT'S LOCAL ABOUT LABOUR'S AUTHORITY?

Even before the 1994 landslide victory in the local government elections, which installed 12,000 Labour Party councillors in office, Conservative strategists were hoping that Labour's local authorities would prove to be the reborn party's Achilles' heel.

As Labour has been out of office so long, its performance in local government is one of the few public foretastes of how it might operate in Westminster. The thin seam of municipal sleaze that does exist is voraciously mined by new Labour's opponents. As a result the party now demands high standards, and political discipline, from Labour Groups across the country.

Labour accepts that its record in local government is a potential weakness. In 1995, at the first suggestion of resistance to its decentralisation policies – and Conservative interest – the NEC suspended Walsall District Labour Party. The possibility that the Conservatives will draw further attention to misconduct, past or present, in Lambeth, Birmingham, Hackney, Monklands or Tyneside – familiar and all too easy targets – is the recurring nightmare of the party's strategists. But as Ivor Crewe has pointed out, 'Lambeth-style councils of 1980s vintage – a gift to the Conservatives in the Thatcher years – are not about to sprout in Bracknell Forest, Exeter, Fenland and Hove'.[24]

In reality, a fissure between the Millbank Tower and the Town Halls is likely to open after, not before, a general election. The levels of frustration and pent-up demand in this sector are enormous, from the long-term restrictions on public sector pay, to the compulsory competitive tendering (CCT) of contracts for the delivery of services, to the transfer of many responsibilities from local and accountable bodies to a parallel quango state. Although they are too polite – and tactically astute – to say so in public, the Town Halls want their powers back, and they want increased funding.

As the party's Treasury team fear the outbreak of a local government spending spree soon after the election, a deal has been struck. New Labour plans to keep the ratecapping powers it will inherit from the Conservatives, at least until it has introduced annual elections in every council as a democratic check on excess. Labour's policy statement

Renewing Democracy, Rebuilding Communities made a series of concessions to the local government wing of the party. The procedures for compulsory competitive tendering, a much resented imposition, will be replaced with a system of targets and bonuses. The business rate will also be returned to local control. In return new Labour has insisted that in future mayors will be directly elected and local authorities that are deemed to be failing by the Audit Commission will be replaced by an independent management team.[25]

There will be structural change too. An elected authority for London is a popular commitment that goes some way to appeasing the capital's local government lobby. Labour's controversial retreat from the immediate introduction of regional government – it must now be preceded by a referendum and receive the blessings of the local council and of parliament – was sweetened by the promise that a new tier of regional chambers would be established. Hostilities still haven't been suspended. Northern politicians still want a regional assembly of the north within a year of Labour taking office.

The interface between local and national government, and between the cohorts in the Labour Party attached to each level of the state – school governors, councillors, regionalists, parliamentarians – will continue to be a major source of friction. If the rate of funding or the pace of decentralisation is perceived to be too slow, when Labour's local electoral support falls from its current artificial peak, as it must, this will become a fierce battleground.

PICKETS ON DEATH ROW? THE POLITICAL FUTURE OF TRADE UNIONISM

The inner tensions of new Labour's coalition have been most visible in its relationship with the trade unions. Conflict on issues like the level of the minimum wage, the scope of public ownership, trade union law reform, market mechanisms in the NHS, the firmness of Labour's commitment to full employment and the constitutional weight of the trade unions within the party's decision-making process are barely contained and are likely to escalate after the general election.

There has already been a significant flexing of muscle. One of the most significant was the re-election of Bill Morris as General Secretary of the TGWU despite the public preference of Blair for challenger Jack Dromey. Not only will Morris – an advocate of collective rights, full employment and public spending – now lead the union through the first term of office of any post-Conservative government, he is more accountable to the democratic structures of his organisation (which has an active Executive and biennial delegate conference, and a backlog of grievances) than most trade union leaders. Rodney Bickerstaffe, who favoured the retention of the old Clause Four of the Labour Party constitution, has also become the head of UNISON. The pair will strike a deal with Blair, but the price of peace, particularly in the public sector, will not be cheap. GMB leader John Edmonds and John Monks, General Secretary of the TUC, will attempt to moderate and urge the virtues of social partnership. Nevertheless public sector pay, after the election, will be an explosive issue that may move out of their control. And if pay differentials for skilled workers are to be recalibrated on the basis of a new minimum wage, as has been threatened, major conflicts over pay loom. There will be plenty of political openings for the militant left that remains in the public sector unions.

The unions are right to suspect that a policy of 'fairness not favours' may turn out to be punitive. After all, the party has proved itself far from reliable in internal horsetrading on the terms of its political project. John Smith's reassurance that Labour remained committed to full employment helped to get the OMOV reform passed at Labour Party conference. The objective has been redefined, heavily qualified and frequently overlooked ever since. Blair's promise of a high minimum wage helped secure the redefinition of Clause Four. Soon after he deferred all detailed discussions to a date after the general election.

In return for their affiliation fee, trade unions linked to the Labour Party have undergone a sustained challenge to the legitimacy of their basic mission – the defence of their members' interests and conditions in the workplace – as well as to their past militancy and weight in the party.

In both the public and the private sector, Britain's unions have been greatly weakened by Conservative legislation. Although trade union membership is now only two-thirds of its level in 1979, it still stands at 8.5 million. Unions still negotiate wages and conditions for nearly half the workforce. Those affiliated to Labour have a large if falling share of the vote at the party's conference. They retain two-thirds of the seats on the National Executive Committee and provide a substantial proportion of the party's annual income (£4.7 million of £8.8 million in 1993) and almost all of its general election funds.

A Labour leadership determined to win the hearts and minds of former Conservative voters has agreed that the Winter of Discontent and the Miners Strike were misguided, destructive and are never to be repeated in any form. Well before the advent of the Blair leadership, neo-liberal legislation designed to prevent the effective prosecution or escalation of disputes was firmly endorsed. On issues like strike ballots and secondary action, Conservative reforms to which Tony Blair is personally committed, there will be no easing of the new legal environment. As Labour's leader insisted to the 1995 TUC conference: 'There will be no repeal of all Tory trade union laws. Strike ballots are here to stay. No mass or flying pickets. All those ghosts of time past, they are exorcised, leave them where they lie ...'

Further reductions in the weight of the trade union vote at Labour Party conference are likely to be accompanied by the removal of direct sponsorship of MPs and increased emphasis on membership ballots.

Britain's trade unions appear to have been placed on a political Death Row. As institutions, they are being gradually but irrevocably excluded from direct representation in the national political process. They are being forced back into the workplace and forward into Europe. They will be reprieved only if they are able to relegitimise themselves in eyes of the public and new Labour's newer members. As the legal reforms to which new Labour is committed are the precondition for such a renewal, a period of self restraint can be expected from their leaderships. As the introduction of state funding for political parties may also reduce the burden on their political funds, the unions will have both the time and the opportunity to deal with this threat to their collective citizenship in innovative ways.

They may have other things on their mind. Labour in government will be looking for ways to articulate Britain's decentralised wage bargaining system with what promises to be a rather austere macro-economic policy, prioritising control of inflation and constrained by the Maastricht criteria for European Monetary Union. The party will need a pay strategy even if it doesn't think an incomes policy is feasible, and the current definitions of social partnership could be stretched to the limit rather quickly. The remnants of a trade union left still waits in the wings, a more aggressive agenda to hand. It opposes 'business unionism' and the social partnership philosophy of the TUC. It insists on the right of trade unions to define their own decision-making procedures and constitutional arrangements.[26] Their voice should not be considered marginal. After all, at its 1995 conference, the partnership-oriented TUC still voted for the repeal of all Conservative trade union laws and the re-introduction of the right to solidarity action.

NON-CONSERVATIVE PARTIES AND CONSTITUTIONAL REFORM

Soon after Blair took up the leadership, the Liberal Democrats abandoned their public stance of equidistance between the two major parties and publicly announced that new Labour was their preferred partner in government. For that reason, and despite regular by-election frictions and policy differences, they must now be regarded as part of Labour's coalition of support.

As both parties converge in the centre ground of British politics, the opportunities for co-operation have never been greater. A common agenda has emerged on the issues of Europe, investment in public services, democratic reform, fair taxation, the minimum wage, and the Social Chapter. Lords Jenkins and Rodgers regarded the new Clause Four as a vindication of their formation of the SDP to oppose old Labour. 'A good start,' acknowledged Jenkins. 'Thirty years late,' said Rodgers.[27] Centre left intellectual David Marquand declared that Labour had 'reinvented itself' and taken 'a giant step towards the recreation of a progressive coalition'. He promptly rejoined the party he had already resumed advising. 'Labour,' he argued, 'has a chance to embody the entire progressive tradition in British politics instead of only part of it'.[28]

After a decade of urging – stretching from the tactical voting initiative TV87 to the call of cross-party magazine *Samizdat* for a 'Popular Front of the Mind', the *Whatever Next* conference in 1994 and the formation of the Labour Initiative on Co-operation (Linc) in 1995 – a degree of strategic and day-to-day co-operation between Labour and the Liberal Democrats has at last been established. In the summer of 1995 Blair was speaking of a 'proper dialogue of ideas.'[29] Electoral pacts, mergers and preparations for coalition government are rarely acknowledged as desirable on either side. In any case, they are probably beyond the reach of the respective leaderships: their memberships are by and large too adversarial. This may change as much of the new momentum for convergence is bottom-up, based on the growing number of joint administrations in local government, and long-standing co-operation north of the border in preparation for a

Scottish assembly.

The crowded centre ground of British politics is likely to produce as much jostling as camaraderie. As soon as Labour felt it was again capable of winning an outright majority, the party rediscovered its appetite for centralised power in an unreformed two-party system. Hungry for sovereignty, it began to lose its taste – so recently cultivated – for electoral reform. Although the momentum of convergence keeps the need for new, pluralist and decentralised institutions high on the political agenda, ambiguities proliferate. Is this challenge to Conservatism about a change of government or a change of system? Does the main opposition party wish to seize power or share it out?

New Labour is not presenting electoral reform as an essential step towards a stakeholder society. It will simply be an issue of conscience for individual MPs. There will be no collective cabinet responsibility on which way to campaign in the promised referendum. It is not at all clear how urgent the referendum, itself a deferral of the issue, is felt to be. A Labour whip suggests there is no hurry.'We have a number of constitutional issues, the most important are devolution and reforming the House of Lords. PR will have to take its place in the queue.'[30]

Ken Livingstone has a keener sense of the point at which electoral reform will seem important to a Labour government. When it feels that a second term of office may be slipping from its grasp, the party will rapidly remember the case for changing the electoral system. 'I suspect that a couple of years lagging behind the Tories in the mid-term polls and the prospect of a Redwood/Portillo government may help to clarify thinking'.[31]

These uncertainties over policy, relevance and timing exist because Labour retains a tactical attitude to constitutional reform. Before returning to the party from the Liberal Democrats, David Marquand pointed out that Labour's commitments to constitutional reform seemed to be disconnected from the rest of its programme. 'There is a curiously makeshift air about it. No coherent vision informs it; no spine of theory or analysis holds it together or links it to the rest of Labour's programme. Above all, its implications for the fundamentals of British statehood – and theirs for it – do not seem to have been explored'.[32]

One of the founders of Charter 88, Anthony Barnett, also suggests that Labour has at least two minds on the issue. 'Labour's programme for constitutional reform will be decided by one of two competing philosophies ... The first seeks to preserve, the second to transform the constitutional system. The first wishes to improve, not remove, the inherited monopoly of sovereignty, to tackle each reform piecemeal so as to retain traditional centralism in a modern setting, and prevent our writing down our constitution. The second will seek to create a pluralist instead of a centralist state ... and will try to link each reform together to inspire a new constitutional settlement.'[33]

On constitutional issues, a politics of hesitation has already deferred electoral reform and devolution to a referendum and cancelled the party's commitment to the introduction of regional government. This strategy of wait and see – also a feature of debates about taxation, European Monetary Union and the minimum wage – leads to confusion, contradictory assumptions and mutual suspicion in Labour's coalition of support. It is a guarantee of trouble and demoralisation in the future. In contrast, a thoroughgoing democratisation of the British state – and its own procedures as a party, of course – would make new Labour's diversity and impermanence a strength, opening the door to pluralist coalition-building in its image at every level of society, re-invigorating our political life.

SQUARED WITH THE SQUARE MILE?
LABOUR'S ECONOMIC DILEMMAS

The collapse of sterling in the autumn of 1992 was a watershed for the economic policies of the government and the opposition. There has been an unwritten fiscal consensus ever since. This has allowed new Labour to secure the toleration, if not the active support, of a number of City firms and private sector companies.

City strategists and pension fund managers long ago introduced assumptions about a change of government into their forward planning. They priced the possible impact of new Labour into their bonds and equities and found that they could live with the consequences. As a result many are prepared to consider a cautious partnership with Labour in government. Blair's identification of inflation as the main enemy of the incoming government – 'the essential prerequisite for achieving the social and political aims of the Labour Party'[34] – reassured them further and greatly reduced the likelihood of hostilities on the scale of 1974.

Of course, Labour's accommodation to the City, the decision to regulate rather than renationalise the utilities and its attempt to appease social partners with a preference for low taxation all mean that it will have to discover ways of creating jobs – and of making its objective of full employment seem less than ridiculous – without significant public expenditure. The price of failure will be the loss of trade union and popular support.

The reconciliation with the Square Mile is far from complete. Many sources of friction remain. The City fears dividend restrictions and the impact of tighter regulation of the privatised utilities. It dislikes the prospect of curbs on executive pay and share options and it is also uncomfortable with Labour's proposed crackdown on takeover bids.[35] The private sector is also hesitant. It will be forced to accept a minimum wage and the Social Chapter. In return Labour promises to become the party of enterprise, the provider of long-term investment strategies, higher standards of education and training and a modern transport and communications infrastructure.

The accommodation with the City makes the task of holding Labour's coalition together all the more difficult. One of the time bombs planted deep within the party's new unity is the personal commitment of senior party figures – John Prescott, Robin Cook, Margaret Beckett and many trade union leaders – to Keynesian full employment strategies that will require cash from a parsimonious, City-sensitive Chancellor. New Labour's deflationary stance also places major restraints on its ability to reverse the public spending cuts and reorganisations of the welfare state that have propelled new constituencies into support for the party. Supply side economic interventions are unlikely to generate the resources being sought within one term of office.

A major determinant of New Labour's economic policy, and a constraint on the deal that it can broker with employers and the City, is the timetable for European integration that it will inherit. A decision on the speed of Britain's re-entry to the Exchange Rate Mechanism (ERM) will be required very early in the life of the Labour government. It is extremely unlikely that the party will be able to take that decision and sustain its unity, even with the distancing mechanism of a referendum on monetary union. The seriously conflicting views in the party over the form and pace that European integration should take may have been overshadowed by the Conservative Party's divisions on the issue, but they are just as irreconcilable.

It's not just that there are a large number of Euro-sceptics in the PLP: Labour's MEPs are far more federalist in outlook than

Euro-tentatives like Blair and Cook, and more recalcitrant figures like Prescott and Beckett. Apart from a willingness to consider the extension of majority voting on the Council of Ministers and a determination to strengthen the European Parliament and end the opt-out from the Social Chapter, there is often little to distinguish the caution of Blair from the hesitations of Major. Fortunately for the leadership of new Labour, Major's negotiation of a delayed entry to EMU gives them breathing space too. If they decide to meet the Maastricht criteria for the convergence of currencies – including a spending deficit of no more than 3 per cent of GDP – this will drive their macro-economic strategy, severely limit the concessions that new Labour will be able to offer its supporters and increase the likelihood of industrial and social conflicts of the kind that broke out in France in 1995. This has led influential commentators like Will Hutton and Martin Kettle to argue that the right of veto will have to remain in the near future, that full European monetary union is not on the horizon and that the admittance of new members is out of the question.[36] If the French scenario were to threaten, the barely suppressed conflict between Euro-sceptics, Euro-tentatives and Federalists would turn into a battle for the soul, resources and direction of the new government. This issue has broken the governing coalition first assembled by Thatcher, and it retains sufficient force to unsettle and derail new Labour.

WHITE LIES FOR MIDDLE ENGLAND?

Middle England is a fashionable shorthand term for a diverse body of professionals, skilled workers and business people who voted for the Conservatives but whose confidence in the Thatcher and Major governments was severely damaged by financial pressures, the erosion of the welfare state, the restructuring of the professions, and, more generally, competitive pressures exerted within the global economy. These detached voters took new Labour seriously. As their support was decisive in winnable seats, the party responded in kind.

These settled communities, urban and rural, have had their local authorities disempowered, their education budgets curbed, and the number of unemployed in their midst rapidly increased. They vote for the party that seems most likely to conserve their culture and lifestyles. New Labour's economic orthodoxy and low taxation policies were therefore given a moral spin and wrapped in an appropriately conservative social policy. Blair addressed the rise of crime and the fall of education. Jack Straw promised to clear the streets of winos, graffiti and 'squeegee merchants' and to imprison noisy neighbours.

This appeasement of Middle England reinforced the party's restricted pluralism and cultural inertia. It also impaired new Labour's relationship with Britain's black communities, overwhelmingly but not exclusively Labour voters.

By the time the activist struggle to introduce Black Sections into the party came to an end, in the 1980s, Labour had developed an identity that was sovereign, top-down and overriding rather than one reflecting a coalition of autonomous interests. The politics of race were subordinated to the more immediate agenda of the party. In Birmingham, Tower Hamlets, Manchester Gorton, Bradford, Ealing Southall and Govan a series of bitter disputes over the process by which parliamentary candidates had been selected – particularly in the absence of Muslim representation in the House of Commons – served as an index of the limits of Labour's transformation and pluralism.[37] The criminalisation of black politicians is a related and deep-seated political reflex common to both parties.[38] Racialised codes link it to Labour's wider crusade against crime, single parents and drugs, which are interpreted – by visible minorities and Middle England – as, in part, a promise to police rather than appease Britain's black communities.

Can the support of Middle England for Labour be sustained, or will the relationship reproduce the pattern established by the Conservatives? Certainly some of the toleration will erode in proportion to the degree to which Labour finds itself forced to raise taxes. Anthony Giddens suggests that the impact of globalisation and detraditionalisation (processes for which black people risk serving as a convenient code) on the security of the professional and commercial middle classes makes it almost inevitable.'I myself doubt ... that Blair will be able to sustain an effective hold over Middle England – and for the very same reason that the Tories themselves are experiencing difficulties there. No political party is going to be able to paper over what is effectively an unresolvable paradox at the core of the middle-class experience of the world'.[39]

LEFT OUT OF THE PICTURE

Loyalty to the party and fear of another spell in the wilderness have prompted many soft left politicians to protect Blair's social authoritarianism, reconciliation with the market and the City and indifference to electoral reform for the Commons from criticism. The fact that they are 'biting their tongues' – to use Robin Cook's memorable phrase – will not long prevent the realignments and renewal that are needed on the left.

The PLP showed it was keen to exercise a check on the leadership when the number of votes cast for non-Blairite figures like Beckett, Davis, Meacher, Lestor and Taylor rose heavily in the shadow cabinet polls in October 1995. But apart from the occasional show of resistance, does the left have anything distinct to say about the social dynamics and opportunities being addressed by Blair? Is an alternative response being formulated? A multi-author Manifesto which appeared in *Tribune* in 1995 suggests not. It offered an unremarkable combination of Keynesian measures accompanied by a minimum wage and a bout of nationalisation.[40] Although the scope for state intervention and the nature of our political culture is being radically transformed, the residue of the Bennite left is clearly unwilling to keep pace with it. However, before his absorption into the Whip's Office, the wide-ranging and radically democratic voice of Peter Hain acted as a surrogate for many who did not dare speak out. In *Ayes to the Left* he offered a non-deferential, Keynesian, Euro-tentative project based on a participatory activist culture and an all-round democratisation of the unions, party and state.[41] It is a marker to which the left will one day return.

On the hard left there have been many discussions about whether to leave the party. Most have decided to hold on to their membership cards. Whether Leninist or corporatist in outlook, these activists are in the Labour Party because of its link with the trade unions, which they see as the guarantor of socialist possibility. Like Militant Labour before it, Arthur Scargill's breakaway Socialist Labour Party holds no attraction for them. Only if the major unions begin to break with Labour would this left seriously consider packing its bags. Even then, many would still consider electoral reform to be the precondition for entering into political competition with Labour.[42]

As a result Bevanites, Bennites and Stalinists are very much alive – if rarely kicking – in the constituencies. In the main, they have held on to their roles and avoided relinquishing the party to newer members. An enduring component of the party's coalition, they will make their presence felt when new Labour's project begins to stall, as it must.

For the last decade the left outside the Labour Party has been involved in political Punch and Judy, a disembedded melodrama in which nothing real is any longer at stake. The disappearance of the

Communist Party has pulled the extensive network of activists it once organised in the trade unions from beneath the feet of the Labour left, which depended on it to a greater extent than is usually acknowledged. In the political space to the left of Labour the Socialist Workers Party has started to fill the shoes left by its bigger Stalinist brother. Buoyant in the universities, strong in UNISON and the NUT, prominent in industrial and anti-fascist conflict, Tony Cliff's miniature mass party doubled its membership, which now stands at 10,000, in the three years 1992–5. It is now well placed to embarrass the trade union and town hall partners of a parsimonious Labour government.

Newer protest movements, experts in direct action, are sceptical of parliamentary and party politics, mainstream and marginal.[43] These Do-It-Yourself political cultures confront the roadbuilders, animal abusers and legislators with an imaginative and effective zeal long missing from the political sphere. Although Reclaim the Streets, the Dongas Tribe at Twyford Down and the activists of Wanstonia also won support from Middle England, they are outside Labour's communitarian pale. From the vantage point of Blair's ethical authoritarianism, the anti-roads movement, rave culture and animal rights movement are reduced to emblems of community decay.

Gordon Brown intends to withdraw 40 per cent of the state benefits paid to any young person shirking their economic responsibility to the nation by not taking part in the training schemes that will make Britain competitive. There may be trouble ahead. For the last decade their older brothers and sisters – experts at tree sitting, legal representations and locking on – have shown them how to deal with multinational interests far less divided and beleaguered than a Labour government promises to be.

STANDING STILL IS NOT AN OPTION

In 1979 the Conservatives arrived in government at the head of a new consensus but light on policy. For more than a decade they won new partners to their project through tax policies, privatisations, council house sales and, of course, the Falklands War. After more than a decade the coalition finally exfoliated as a result of job insecurity, collapsing house prices, the poll tax, excessive privatisation and sterling's exit from ERM. Thatcher herself was removed and the Conservative Party was soon paralysed by division.

In office new Labour will have to move even faster in order to remain viable. Assisted by a much less populist overarching theme than Mrs Thatcher's coupling of freedom and the free market – Blair's stakeholder society – Labour will have to manage a similar process in less promising circumstances. Neither its membership nor its wider support has been prepared. Most of new Labour's energies have been spent repositioning the party for the election rather than developing a consensus on the hard choices that it will face in government. As a result there will be disputes and dissent over public spending and public sector pay, over the pace and scope of European integration, on the relevance of electoral reform, on the appropriate derogation of powers to local government, and perhaps, on the differing programme adopted by Scottish Labour. If new Labour holds to its commitments on Maastricht, taxation and the City, the immediate fruits of victory will be meagre. In the absence of an authentically shared vision or ready cash, its social partners – Middle England, the City, the trade unions, the unemployed and youthful DIY activist cultures – are unlikely to remain one nation for long. There will also be tensions between Labour's civil libertarian tradition and the new emphasis on responsibility and compulsion. At this point, Blair's ability to retain the command of his party may depend on further internal reforms, underwritten by the introduction of state funding.

These are a few of the more predictable crises and challenges, external and internal, that new Labour will have to address. The balance of power between the political partners in its coalition will undoubtedly shift. On the direction it takes, and the response of the left, rests the shape and form of political representation for a generation, as well as the continuing viability of the Labour Party as the vehicle through which the interests and aspirations of major sections of the British polity are negotiated and expressed. The only thing that can we can be sure of is that new Labour, as it is presently constituted, is not a permanent formation. It will not – indeed cannot – be allowed to stand still.

REFERENCES

1 Interview with Chrissie Iley, 'A Team Player Who's Biting his Tongue for Tony', *Sunday Times*, 10 December 1995.
2 J. Krieger, *Reagan, Thatcher and the Politics of Decline*, Polity Press, Oxford 1988, p186.
3 See Gerry Hassan's account elsewhere in this volume.
4 See Chris Harman, 'From Bernstein to Blair: One Hundred Years of

Revisionism' in *International Socialism* 67, summer 1995, pp17-36; John McIlroy, 'The Roots of Blairism', *Workers Liberty*, September 1995, pp16-18; Tony Benn, 'Stay Tuned: the Worst is Yet to Come', *Tribune*, 13 October 1995; Louise Lang, 'New Labour and the New Broad Left', *Socialist Action*, October-November 1995, pp13-17.

5 For a debate on the example set by the Australian Labour Party see Martin Kettle, 'On Top Down Under', *Guardian*, 8 November 1995; Dennis McShane, 'The leftwing wizards of Oz', *Guardian*, 4 September 1995, and John Pilger, 'Deals made in Paradise', *New Statesman & Society*, 20 October 1995. On the appeal of communitarianism see Paul Anderson and Kevin Davey, 'Import Duties', *New Statesman & Society*, 3 March 1995, pp18-20. The relevance of the Asia-Pacific economies was explored in 'The Age of Asia: Learning from the Sunrise Societies', *Demos Quarterly* 6, 1995 and Chris Smith, 'Tigertents', *New Statesman & Society*, 26 January 1996. For a brief overview of all the models drawn upon, see Paul Anderson, 'Those we have loved', *New Statesman & Society*, 24 November 1995, pp22-24.

6 Perry Anderson, 'Introduction' to Perry Anderson and Patrick Camiller (eds), *Mapping the West European Left*, Verso, London 1994, p10.

7 Philip Gould's memorandum, 'The Unfinished Revolution', was reprinted in the *Guardian*, 12 September 1995.

8 *Tribune*, 30 June 1995.

9 Tony Benn, 'The Way Forward', *New Left*, no.2, June 1995, p6.

10 Mark Seddon, 'Labour mints a clause with a hole in it', *Guardian*, 30 March 1995.

11 Hugh MacPherson, 'Tory Solutions are the Problem', *Tribune*, 19 May 1995.

12 Hugh Macpherson, 'Old Grandees and Smart Alecs', *Tribune*, 13 October 1995.

13 John Pilger, 'Hail to the New Tories', *New Statesman & Society*, 5 May 1995, pp17-18.

14 John Pilger, 'What is Labour for?', *New Statesman & Society*, 29 September 1995, p16.

15 Arthur Scargill, *Future Strategy for the Left*, Discussion Paper, 4 November 1995.

16 Kevin Davey, 'Waking up to New Times: Doubts and Dilemmas on the Left', in Mark Perryman (ed), *Altered States: Postmodernism, Politics, Culture*, Lawrence & Wishart, London 1994, pp195-217.

17 The best comparative account of the issues raised by the state funding of political parties can be found in Martin Linton, *Money and Voters*, Institute of Public Policy Research, London 1994.

18 Tony Benn, 'Democracy is on the Edge of a Precipice', *Tribune*, 26 May 1995.

19 Peter Hain, *Ayes to the Left: A Future for Socialism*, Lawrence & Wishart, London 1995, pp61-3, pp230-9.

20 Patrick Seyd and Paul Whiteley, *Labour's Grass Roots*, Clarendon Press, Oxford 1992, p199 and p11.

21 Quoted in the *Guardian*, 13 April 1995.

22 See, for example, Paul Richards' call for the party conference to become a

presentational rally in *Tribune*, 25 August 1995 and Patrick Wintour's overview, 'Blair backers force pace of change', *Guardian*, 22 August 1995.

23 Roger Liddle and Peter Mandelson, *The Blair Revolution*, Faber and Faber, London 1996.

24 Ivor Crewe, *Observer*, 7 May 1995.

25 *Renewing Democracy, Rebuilding Communities*, The Labour Party, London, September 1995.

26 See John McIlroy, 'New Labour and the Trade Unions', *New Left*, no.2, June 1995 and his *Trade Unions in Britain Today*, Manchester University Press, Manchester 1994.

27 'What Labour MPs Think of Their New Clause 4', *Independent*, 14 March 1995.

28 David Marquand, 'Escape to the future', *Guardian*, 1 May 1995 and 'Joining the "New" Ship', *New Statesman & Society*, 6 October 1995 pp18-9.

29 'Nearly There', in *New Statesman & Society*, 28 April 1995 pp24-5.

30 Geoff Hoon to *Tribune*, 14 July 1995.

31 Ken Livingstone 'Memo to Mr Blair', *New Statesman & Society*, 20 September 1995.

32 David Marquand, 'Vision wanted', *Guardian*, 18 September 1995.

33 Anthony Barnett, *The Defining Moment*, Charter 88, London 1995, p11.

34 Tony Blair Mais Lecture at City University, 22 May 1995.

35 Dan Atkinson and Patrick Donovan, 'Putting a price on the Blair factor', *Guardian*, 8 April 95.

36 Will Hutton and Martin Kettle, 'Winds Over the West', *Guardian*, 2 November 1995. See also John Palmer's response, 'Let's have no EU retreat', *Guardian*, 3 November 1995.

37 On the changing relationship between Labour and the Asian community see Keenan Malik, 'Party Colours', *New Statesman & Society*, 14 July 1995.

38 John Solomos and Les Back, *Race, Politics and Social Change*, Routledge, London 1995, pp99-101.

39 Anthony Giddens, 'Unstuck in Middle England', *Guardian*, 27 February 1995.

40 'The Tribune Manifesto', *Tribune*, 9 June 1995, pp4-6.

41 *Ayes to the Left, ibid*, and Kevin Davey, 'Libertarian Democrat', *New Times*, 30 September 1995, p2.

42 See Kevin Flack and Jon Rogers, 'Is the Party pooped?', *Labour Briefing*, June 1995, p10; Kevin Davey, 'From King Coal to Crown Prince', *New Times*, 25 November 1995, p5; Hilary Wainwright, 'Not yet, Arthur', *New Statesman & Society*, 24 November 1995, pp20-21; Ken Livingstone, 'The party's not over', *Guardian*, 18 January 1996.

43 See Camilla Berens, 'Generation X', *New Statesman & Society*, 3 February 1995, pp22-3 and 'How Labour Blew the Youth Vote', *Red Pepper*, October 1995, p20. A valuable inside account can be found in *Schnews Reader*, Justice?, Brighton 1995.

Section Three: Theses for a New Labour Government

DANGEROUS BUSINESS: REMEMBERING FREUD AND A POETICS OF POLITICS

Wendy Wheeler

One of the almost immediate results of Tony Blair's election to the leadership of the Labour Party was to effect the naming of a split. Since the attempt to cover over its manifestations throughout the 1980s – or, rather, to disavow it – had by no means fooled the British electorate, its naming was a sign of health. Once named, this division could enter into symbolic life; once there, it could be understood more thoroughly and some form of integration could be attempted.

The split goes, now, under the terms 'new Labour' and 'traditional Labour'. During the 1980s, it was probably most clearly manifested in the differences of understanding, analysis and inclination between a significant number of Labour Party activists and the wider membership. The achievement of One Member, One Vote was undoubtedly a crucial stage in the declining influence of these traditional activists.

What the split names is not simply something of the present (the need to change in response to historical change, and a different emphasis on what constitutes a collectivity), but also a history. As far as the Labour Party goes, it is actually more of a pre-history since it is a history whose terms were organised – in the face of the alienating effects of industrial capitalism – at the beginning of the nineteenth century rather than at the beginning of the twentieth century when the Labour Party was formed.

At the risk of simplification and caricature, we could say that the concerns of the activists of traditional Labour are that the Labour Party was conceived to represent the collective interests of the working masses against the selfish individualism of capitalists and the property-owning bourgeoisie. This, for the traditionalists, is the historic mission of the Labour Party, and it is what it should still be doing – as NUM President Arthur Scargill's attempt to re-establish the old terms of Clause Four at the 1995 Labour Party Conference indicated. In other words, at the end of the one hundred years or so during which British society was transformed from a society based on distinctions of birth, land and rank to one based on the new distinctions of class resulting from the relative social mobility of capital, the Labour Party came into being to protect the interests of the working class under industrial capitalism by promoting a decisive shift in the ownership of capital. For the traditionalists, a hundred years later nothing has really changed.

Labour's modernisers – undoubtedly more in sympathy with both the broader, non-active, membership and with general anxieties about social breakdown in the country at large – argue, on the contrary, that things have significantly changed. Against the 'scientific' socialism of both Marxism and Fabianism, the Blairites seek to return the Labour Party to earlier nineteenth-century and early twentieth-century socialist thought in which collectivity, or community, is thought of in broader terms than those of antagonistic class interests alone. Questioned about what he means by 'community', Blair has said, 'The notion of community for me is less a geographical concept than a belief in the social nature of human beings'.[1] This is an organicist view of community and culture.

The opposition, or difference, between traditionalists and modernisers remains, thus, close to the terms described by critics of industrialism at the end of the eighteenth and the beginning of the nineteenth centuries. The terms and the oppositions remain those of the values of collectivity and social relatedness versus the values of individualism and its close relation, individual competition. It is, broadly, an opposition between an organicist view of society and a utilitarian and atomistic one. At Oxford in the early 1970s, Blair was deeply influenced by the anti-utilitarian arguments of the Scottish philospher John Macmurray and, as John Rentoul points out, these were close to the views argued by other ethical and Christian socialists of the turn of the century such as T.H. Green and L.T. Hobhouse.[2]

The philosophical and theoretical emphases and trajectory of the Labour Party since its early days under the influence of Sidney and

Beatrice Webb has, however, been decidedly utilitarian and 'scientistic'. There have, of course, been earlier critics of this tradition within the Labour Party. Writing in 1956 on socialism's need to be able to think about the virtues of art, beauty and pleasure, as well as the virtues of utility and 'hard facts', Anthony Crosland said:

Much of this can at least claim the sanction of one powerful stream of socialist thought – that stemming from William Morris; though other, Nonconformist and Fabian, influences wear a bleaker and more forbidding air. For one brought up as a Fabian, in particular, this inevitably means a reaction against the Webb tradition. I do not wish to be misunderstood. All who knew the Webbs have testified to their personal kindliness, gentleness, tolerance and humour; and no one who reads *Our Partnership* can fail to be intensely moved by the deep unaffected happiness of their mutual love. But many of their public virtues, so indispensable at the time, may not be as appropriate today. Reacting as they were against an unpractical, utopian, sentimental, romantic, almost anarchist tradition on the Left, they were no doubt right to stress the solid virtues of hard work, self-discipline, efficiency, research and abstinence: to sacrifice private pleasure to public duty, and expect that others should do the same: to put Blue Books before culture, and immunity from physical weakness above all other virtues.

And so they spent their honeymoon investigating trade societies in Dublin. And so Beatrice could write that 'owing to our concentration on research, municipal administration and Fabian propaganda, we had neither the time nor the energy, nor yet the means to listen to music and the drama, to brood over classic literature, to visit picture galleries, or to view with an informed intelligence the wonders of architecture.'[3]

Anyone doubting that it is in the terms of this opposition – between romanticism, art and organicism (Matthew Arnold's 'seeing things steadily and seeing them whole'[4]) on the one hand, and utilitarianism and atomistic scientism on the other – that the modernisers' view of socialism is framed, need only to peruse the writers assembled in Gordon Brown and Tony Wright's *Values, Visions and Voices*[5]: G.D.H. Cole, P.B. Shelley, D.H. Lawrence, Matthew Arnold, Raymond Williams, Charles Dickens, William Cobbett and William Morris are all there. Brown and Wright's anthology is undoubtedly a cultural manifesto by quotation of new Labour.

The greatest change of contemporary (or postmodern) times is that the idea of what constitutes a collectivity has changed: it is, for contemporary radicals, no longer a collectivity which is based in, or can be understood solely in terms of, class-interest. As Roy Hattersley argued in 1995, the modern Labour Party must return to its historic roots in principled arguments about the importance of social justice for all.[6] Doing this, Hattersley claimed, involves the enunciation of a positive philosophy of the collective life and of justice which makes clear its distinction from, and opposition to, the Tories' narrowly utilitarian 'politics of accountancy'.

The roots of this shift away from utilitarianism and towards romantic organicism clearly lie in the enormous cultural and philosophical changes of the post-World War II period. Fifty years ago, the Labour Party was responsible for instituting one of the most humane national institutions of the twentieth century. The effects of this great success – the post-1945 welfare state – were greatly to diminish many of the very worst inequalities, especially in terms of access to healthcare, to education, and to decent housing, of the British class culture within which, and in response to which, the Labour Party – designed to combat these inequalities – was formed. This is not, of course, to suggest that huge inequalities and injustices do not remain. Under the Conservatives since 1979, these inequalities have been increased. But the effects of the welfare state were both to make differences less visible and to change the popular view of the *extent* of misery.

Thatcherism was able to build on popular perceptions of structural change, and also to further the self-interest of its own interest groups, by mounting a critique of 'laziness' and 'dependence'. The ideological success of this critique allowed the Tories to shift resources away from the majority in favour of the minority. A deathly combination of ruthless self-interest and Nonconformist and utilitarian conviction – with a broader than merely party-political appeal – made possible the new right critique of state paternalism as something conducive to a passive (i.e. un-energetic and unproductive) 'culture of dependence'.

The new right aim – of turning everyone into property-owning consumers with an individualistic stake in 'getting on' – has, at the level of popular imagination at least, partially worked. The old pre-World War II culture of deference, and the post-war culture of 'dependence', has largely gone; more or less everyone, regardless of class, is now very keen on their rights as consumers of everything – at least in terms of aspiration, if not in terms of actual access, to goods. Thatcherism was able to build upon the experiential gains of the post-war settlement, even as it undid them. Its gamble – that enough people would benefit, or imagine that they might benefit, from voting Conservative – has paid off for close on seventeen years.

We, in Britain, now live in a more widely and aggressively individualistic society than ever before. Attempting to count the costs of Thatcherism's 'politics of accountancy' in terms of a left utilitarianism has, however, proved inadequate. This is because, firstly, the identifications with the interest groups concerned (ruling class and working class) no longer hold for the majority of the electorate. Secondly, it is because any argument from a narrowly utilitarian basis of interest is now widely seen as suspect. Where broader utilitarian arguments still prevail, they are increasingly those more enlightened ones which recognize that individual self-interest can best be served by the preservation of the healthy collectivity of society and culture as a whole. It is in the terms of this opposition – between unfettered individualism and the organicism of the whole culture – that Blair and the modernisers cast new Labour.

Whatever British society now is, or is in the process of becoming, it can no longer be thought of in precisely the same terms of class division which grew during the nineteenth century, and which still pertained when the Labour Party's 'historic mission' was first institutionally conceived. The politics of the last seventeen years have only been possible because the older class divisions were already changing rapidly after World War II. As much as the traditionalists of the old left might still want to think about themselves as radicals, they are, in fact, now conservatives who seek to conserve a tradition of labour and class division which has more or less passed.

Poverty and distress – potential and actual – now cross earlier class divisions. The middle classes are now just as frightened by the spectre of want as the working classes have always been. 'Middle classness' no longer means safety: we are all – except the very rich – now exposed to danger and social disrepair. As Tony Blair noted in his 1995 party conference speech, despair, cynicism and a sense of wide social and cultural breakdown is the common experience of the majority of people. Radicalism now consists in trying to think through the terms and oppositions of a post-industrial, but still technological, and still alienated, culture.

Strangely enough, it is in the shedding of its own utilitarian and 'scientific' accounts of the world (whether Fabian or Marxist) in terms of self-interest and narrowly-based class interest that the Labour Party – at least in the modernisers' view – can best offer a meaningful opposition to the utilitarian self-interest of new right individualism and economic *laissez-faire*. Even if the economics of *laissez-faire*, in terms of government policy, have now (in 1995) actually passed, they remain as a spectre haunting social life. The ideological roots of a narrow utilitarianism have gone deep, and confidence in the national economy remains weak as far as long-term investment is concerned. This is true of both public and commercial, and also of individual, private and affective, relations: social and market relations bleed, painfully, into each other. At the end of the twentieth century, neo-liberalism has achieved a condition of perpetual reform and change of institutional procedures – in which no-one can any longer be at peace – undreamt of by earlier proponents of permanent revolution.

In many ways, the idea of the welfare state was an attempt to put political flesh on the old romantic ideal of social relatedness as opposed to the socially disintegrating effects of competition. The welfare state didn't simply improve things in fact; it also embodied practices of civic virtue – such as the highly symbolic gift of blood in the free donor system – which were emblematic of an ethical, as opposed to merely utilitarian, social commitment.

Thatcherism's dismantling of this was partly a matter of means (freeing resources), but it was also a matter of commitment to the Protestant ethos of salvation by individual effort. To use the language of psychoanalysis, one could say that Thatcherism embodied the conviction that too much 'parental' binding (too much 'safety' and not enough 'danger') produced an infantilized culture of over-dependence and passivity expressed in the form of the infant's vast, unceasing, and actually unmeetable, demand for more. The prescription was, thus, that the nation should be exposed to the difficulties of reality. In this way it would 'grow up', become responsible, and learn to 'get on' on its own two feet as it were.

'Dependence', however, can be thought of in more than one way; it can be thought of (as the new right did) in infantile terms, but it can also be thought of in terms of the necessary interdependencies of any human society. There is a genuine problem here. It consists of being able to think about a collectivity in terms of necessary degrees of dependence and independence. To use a word I think preferable, it consists in being able to think about the need for, and the necessary limits of, 'holding'. A society has to agree about who, or what, needs to be 'held', and about the limits beyond which forms of 'holding' prevent individuals or institutions from facing the challenges of autonomy and freedom which are an essential part of modernity and democracy. These are, of course, precisely the terms in which Kant cast Enlightenment modernity as an 'exit' (*Ausgang*) from immaturity: freedom imposes obligations.

Nevertheless, the extents of freedom, and thus of obligation, are unequal. Human societies are collectivities in which not all people, at all times, have the same access to free acts. Sick people, or people who are charged with the care of others, or people who suffer from the burdens of discrimination against them on any number of scores, are not as free as those fortunate individuals who are able, unfettered, to pursue their own interests and freedoms. A humane society recognises this.

New Labour appears to consist of those who believe that – within the constraints of a capitalist mass democracy ethically enfeebled by the utilitarian pursuit of self-interest – the genuine interests of collectivity must include the interests of those who, for whatever reason, cannot, at present, help themselves. Collectivity means that *all* reasonable interests must be protected. What constitutes a reasonable interest is, of course, a matter of ongoing debate and democratic political argument and appeal. What constitutes a collectivity is as much about what is (politically, culturally) made as it is about what is inherited, but the modernisers recognise that collectivity can no longer be thought about simply in terms of class identifications and formations. In other words, for new Labourites, the sense of what constitutes the collectivity has changed. It is no longer a class-based grouping, but is closer to the organic model of a culture as a whole which informed earlier, nineteenth-century, critiques of the disintegrating effects of capitalist industrialism.

As Raymond Williams's extensive argument in *Culture and Society*[7] demonstrates, the effects of utilitarian rationalism combined with emergent capitalist industrialism at the end of the eighteenth century were to give form to a debate – about the importance of a sense of society as an organic whole in the face of the disintegrating forces of individualism and self-interest – which continued throughout the nineteenth century. Often expressed in terms of an opposition between Art and Science, or between Romanticism and Mechanism, by the middle of the nineteenth century the terms were shifting to become an opposition between Culture on the one hand, and Anarchy on the other. In this debate, 'Culture' meant the sense that society is a collectivity of relatedness; 'Anarchy' stood for the socially disintegrating and alienating effects of industrial capitalism.

Of course, many of the most important nineteenth-century critics of mechanism and utilitarianism could not be said to have been, in any modern sense, on the side of the people – conceived of as a political force. Few of them had any faith in the emerging idea of mass democracy, because the mass meant simply the ignorant mob and mob rule. Nevertheless, they were all firmly on the side of a vision of society as a collectivity in which everyone must be able to experience, in William Morris's words, 'a thriving and un-anxious life.'[8]

At least one of the traditions which informs socialism as an emphasis on society as a living whole, rather than as a mere (and deathly) aggregation of competing individuals, is this nineteenth-century argument about the importance of art (understood widely as the affective expression of the life of a culture) as embodying the spiritual, or loving, values of a collectivity which is threatened by the pursuit of narrow or individualistic self-interest. The latter is seen as the preserve of the imaginatively narrow middle classes (Matthew Arnold's 'philistines' in his 1869 book *Culture and Anarchy*) in whom a Nonconformist ethos, and the utilitarian habit of mind, is strongest.

Neither should the importance of religious affiliations be overlooked here. English Nonconformist evangelicism, with its economical view of salvation, turns the Christian ideal of *caritas* – which means the love, respect and concern for others as others by which human groups are held and bound – into the more limited sense of love as that which is due within small, atomised, individual groups (the bourgeois family) and, as far as those beyond the family are concerned, into the charitable acts by which the individual salves his conscience and also buys his way into heaven. In other words, a sense of the cultural whole, and of love and relatedness generally, is opposed to atomism and calculation.

Although, by the end of the nineteenth century, utilitarian habits of mind had generally won the day, the broad terms of the nineteenth-century argument are still very familiar to us. Culture (with a capital 'C') is still felt to be important, and our sense that its neglect is somehow generally injurious (even if the number of people who think Shakespeare should be on the school curriculum is far larger than the number who read him) slides easily into a similar sense that culture more broadly – the culture of care and relatedness, and of the whole – should be sustained.

The structure of feeling which animates Tony Blair and those who support him is one which is probably only possible, in its strongest effects, for post-World War II generations. It is probably strongest for Blair's generation itself which grew up in the seemingly unshakeable safety of the welfare state, and which came to maturity with the utopianism of the 1960s counter-culture. Indeed, the romanticism of the 1960s 'Love Generation' can easily be seen as yet another attempt to reaffirm relatedness after the terrible experience of the effects of instrumental uses of reason witnessed during the Second World War. This was the same generation which was old enough, when Thatcher came to power in 1979, to feel – and increasingly so during the 1980s – the full weight of the disintegrations of which a reaffirmed utilitarianism and unfettered political economy are capable.

It is not surprising that the responses of this generation, and of Blair and his supporters in particular, have so much in them of the flavour of much earlier, nineteenth-century, responses to utilitarianism. Blair's social-ism is a recasting of the earlier emphases on the importance of organicism, community, and the reasonable life. It takes place, however, within a Labour Party whose own historical emphases have not generally been upon the importance of culture, and cultural life, as a whole. The last real socialist romantic (the term is not intended pejoratively) was probably William Morris. The Fabianism of Beatrice and Sidney Webb was utilitarian through and through. Of the Webbs' evolutionism, and of Fabians generally, Morris said that they:

> ... very much underrate the strength of the tremendous organization under which we live ... Nothing but a tremendous force can deal with this force; it will not suffer itself to be dismembered, nor to lose anything which really is its essence, without putting forth all its force in resistance; rather than lose anything which it considers of importance, it will pull the roof of the world down upon its head.[9]

In other words, and as Williams points out, 'Webb's mistake, for Morris, was to "overestimate the importance of *the mechanism* of a system of society apart from the end towards which it may be used." '[10]

This, then, is the context in which Blair finds himself: that of a Labour Party which, for many years and in its essentials, bought into a view of the world which believes in the utilitarian calculation of facts and interests (all be they class ones in this case). This is by no means an unworthy method of proceeding. Vague romantic appeals to virtue, without any grounding in the facts and figures of economic disadvantage and its relation to social inequality and investment, were unlikely to find much purchase in the rough soil of the predominantly pragmatic and positivistic culture of late nineteenth- and early twentieth-century England. When Beatrice Webb undertook her social investigations it was both unprecedented and necessary. But Morris's and, later, Crosland's criticisms of the utilitarian habit of mind stand: too great a focus on mechanism may lead to an inability to keep the eye on the larger scene or to grant value to aspects of life which, because mobile, affective and non-calculable, are unamenable to empirical analysis and mechanical reduction.

Blair has chosen the path of socialist (rather than liberal) democracy. In essence, this means a rejection of the liberal idea of an incommensurability, and thus relativity, of values, and an affirmation of the idea that a society involves a commitment to some shared values and the rejection of others. In this sense, commentators who see Blair as conservative, rather than liberal, are thus correct. He does set down a challenge to the twentieth century's uneasy marriage of liberal individualism and socialist collectivism. He opts for an organic, collectivist, view of society in which the task of repairing the tattered social fabric bequeathed by Thatcherism's championing of nineteenth-century *laissez-faire* lies in the pursuit of social justice for all those who may *reasonably* lay claim to it. 'Reason', here, is simply the political consensus which can be constructed around social-ism. Since the collectivity this latter imagines is very wide, it is not yet clear how a socialist concern with economic redistribution fits into Blair's social-ism.

In its organic view of society, this is close to the recommendations of earlier, nineteenth-century critics of utilitarianism; although it is clothed, in ways impossible for those earlier thinkers, in the very real difficulties of the democratic commitment. For Blair, as for any leader and party committed to preserving a sense of collective integrity against the fragmenting tendencies of the unfettered individualism which capitalist competition promotes, the democratic commitment involves convincing voters that self-interest lies also in the support of the common weal. This means at least two things: firstly, that Blair must find a language of integrity capable of giving imaginative form, as well as political substance, to the thinking whole of contemporary British culture, and, secondly, that this language must be informed by a strong theoretical sense of what a culture *is*.

. Inasmuch as this renewed vision of the cultural whole forms the core of Blair's position, it probably places him as more firmly opposed, in practice and in personal inclination, to utilitarian political economy than any other previous leader of the British Labour Party. To anyone who has a developed suspicion of the doleful precepts and methods of utilitarianism – however often seemingly reformist, Millite, and benign – this can only be a cause for celebration. Where not viciously imposed upon others in a prejudicial way, a commitment to the life of spirit – to something which is beyond mere self, and which embraces life as a commitment to 'relationship and love'[11] – cannot be a bad thing. But if Blair finds himself on the side of what came, during the nineteenth century, to be called 'culture', and opposed to the anarchy of unfettered individualism and the utilitarian calculation of interests, what kind of an understanding of 'culture' – and particularly of the ways in which culture is made and made anew – will a Blair-led government have?

One very obvious danger of an organic view of culture is that it always runs the risk of a stultifying conservatism. Current criticisms of Blair's 'conservatism' recognise this danger. The binding forces of a community necessarily work to enforce normative values; this is the 'safety' and homeliness that one experiences in a community of more or less shared meanings. But, equally, such a community implies exclusivities which are often cruel and unjust. A healthy modern society would have to be one which is able to recognise the need for a constant play of binding and unbinding in regard to social institutions, and one which is also able to accommodate such play – always a dangerous business – by remaining adaptive.

IMAGINING CULTURAL RENEWAL

In the lecture jointly organised by the Fabian Society and the *Guardian* in June 1994, in what was, essentially, his inaugural statement as Labour leader, Tony Blair said that, in order to reconnect with, and carry out, its historic mission in British life, the Labour Party must be certain to occupy 'the intellectual high ground'.[12] In other words, he called for an intellectual renewal on the democratic left of British politics which would, in turn, lead to a much-needed renewal of British society and culture.

Promisingly, he called for an understanding of the relationship between tradition and progress in terms of the critical and political traditions which have informed a part of British socialism. These are those organicist traditions, referred to above, which have taken the form of critiques of the deadening effects upon cultural life of capitalism and industrial and technological modernisation. Blair tied this culture of new Labour (remembering the past and imagining the future) to the desire for political and cultural renewal in the country generally. In other words, what new Labour is about is the work of cultural making, re-making and re-newing – both for itself and, as a result, for the country.

But what does culture, and cultural remaking, consist in? There is, of course, a series of semantic relationships which indicate the different levels and modes in which culture exists and is made and made anew. These range from the sense of culture as the worship and tilling of the land (and we still worship our cultural icons, of course), through tilling, husbandry and seed-sowing, and on to the sexual and economic registers of sowing and spending. All these meanings link together the many different strands of what cultural production is. Cultural production includes all the different senses of the verb 'to make'. It is linked both to money-making and to the older sense of making as poetic fabrication. In its turn, fabrication is both making goods (philosophical and material) *and* telling stories. All these senses of making – being on the make, making out, fabricating, telling stories, making it up, making things – tell us what sorts of things cultural making can be. It consists in the making of art, the making of love, the making of children, the making of money, and the making of narratives in which we make sense of our lives.

If society is the complex and many-layered network of relations that binds individuals into groups, culture is the thing that makes the network live, change and have a future. So when Tony Blair calls for cultural renewal, he calls for the possibility of a benevolent environment for all this making and growing of things, relationships, and meanings. If Blair's present position in the history of modern British politics is, as suggested above, that he represents a new democratic socialist engagement with the question of cultural life thought as a whole, one of the most important questions that a Blair-led administration will have to be able to address is the theoretical one which asks: what sort of a thing is culture?

Without some clear guiding sense of what the life of a culture is, the commitment to cultural renewal alone is not enough. Margaret Thatcher was undoubtedly thus committed, and the effects of her commitment have been socially devastating. Blair's modernisers may desire, and speak of, cultural renewal, but they require a model of culture – of what cultural life and experience *is* – which will enable them to understand why the project of renewal can so easily become, as it did for Thatcher, dangerous and deathly.

At the centre of what follows is the argument that the space of culture, and of cultural making, is essentially an uncanny one. Modernity is the experience of ceaseless movement and change, and this is always dangerous. Understanding the nature of what is involved may, however, increase the possibilities of a healthy culture and politics and – Morris's words will do – of everyone living 'a thriving and unanxious life'.

UNCANNY GOTHIC DREAMS

In June 1995, BBC 2 broadcast an extraordinarily insightful and prescient film – the third in Adam Curtis's trilogy *The Living Dead* – entitled 'The Attic'. The film traced the development of the new right vision of England as dreamt by Conservative MPs Airey Neave and Keith Joseph during the 1970s, and as given substance in the political life of Neave's protegée Margaret Thatcher throughout the 1980s. According to Patrick Cosgrave, one of Thatcher's political advisers, this dream turned out to be Thatcher's dream of Churchill's dream of England. It was, thus, a kind of uncanny double dream of a place and time that had hardly existed in fact at all. Perhaps best caught in the fabled image of the last Edwardian summer before the Great War – tea in china cups on a gently sloping lawn; warm beer and cricket on the village green – its reality, like that of Christminster in Thomas Hardy's *Jude the Obscure* (1895), can only have been lived as the dream of a remarkably privileged few: both utterly phantasmatic and also endlessly seductive for the vast majority who desired, but could not have, it – as was the case for Jude.

And yet this nostalgic dream of England, reconjured by Churchill in the desperate early years of World War II, and raised again by Thatcher forty years later, was the haunted dream that the British people have now lived through, at huge cost, for upwards of a decade and a half. When the interviewer in Curtis's film said 'But it's a dream!', Cosgrave replied 'But of course! All dreams are, in some sense – remember your Freud – reality.'

I use Curtis's film, and its illuminating reference to Freud, because its complex view of both present and past, and the ways in which haunting repetitions can inflect political life, was clearly also shared by the people it interviewed, such as Patrick Cosgrave and Alan Clark, who were close to Thatcher. The film thus usefully makes the point that this way of understanding political and social life – the view that reality is not an easily knowable thing, and is endlessly conjurable and strange – is not restricted to the fanciful academicisms of Anglo-American relativism, or to Continental Philosophy and literary and critical theory; it is also shared by a significant number of influential politicians and image-makers, at least on the right.

On the left, the dominance of scientist accounts of the world (in which romanticism, where it returns, returns as the romanticisation of the working class, whose Coleridgean 'unity from diversity' will provide the moment of transcendent overcoming) has led to an increasingly limited ability to offer political analyses of either depth or popular appeal. The Labour Party's idealists have too often been, in the main, materialists with little or no time for a non-didactic politics of pleasure and 'picture galleries'. Yet the project of thinking a culture whole requires a wider grasp of life than that afforded by just thinking about 'facts'. The utilitarian cast of mind which has, historically, dominated the British Labour Party, has no way of thinking about – because it has no language for – things which cannot be weighed, calculated and decisively known. Yet who would want to say (aside from Margaret Thatcher) that there is no such thing as society: that inter-relatedness, affection, emotional investment, are not just as important as more mechanical forms of communication? In fact, Thatcherism did have a romanticism, but it was one which despised the present and remained tied to a fantasy of the past. In other words, it was melancholic.

The driving force which animates the Labour Party modernisers is the attempt to formulate a language of more comprehensive cultural experience. But will this language be one which is able to think cultural remaking positively – as a form of healthy mourning? Or will it be one which falls prey, as Margaret Thatcher's did, to those more problematic expressions of grief which Freud called melancholia?

UNCANNY CULTURAL SPACES

In Curtis's film, there was a strong sense of the uncanniness of Thatcher's attempt to re-imagine England, but it was one in which the idea of cultural making was confined to a nostalgic and melancholic sense of re-making the past.[13]

The space of cultural making is – in the psychoanalytic sense – certainly an uncanny space. It is neither absolutely bound, regulated and known (homely), nor absolutely strange, unbound, unknowable, sublime and lawless (unhomely). In the sense which the German word *das Unheimlich* (the uncanny, the unhomely) conveys better than the English, the uncanny space is both homely and familar (*heimlich*) and alien, strange and frightening (*unheimlich*) at the same *time* and in the same place. In fact, and as Freud's discussion in his 1919 paper 'The Uncanny' makes clear,[14] *Unheimlich* means both familiar and homely and unfamiliar, strange and frightening at the same time. This uncanny space is neither inside nor outside the net of social life; it is what makes that net move: contract, stretch, grow and change. It is the space of the processes – always hopeful, always uncertain and fraught with real dangers – of 'coming-to-be'. It both marks the boundaries of the social, and of collective and individual identities whilst, at the same time, changing and rearranging them, and making new ones.

But if this is the sort of space where cultural making happens, it should be clear that it does not inevitably do so. The space of culture is uncanny because it is also the space of loss and mourning. No new things grow without the loss of the old. But, as with individuals, cultures can get caught on the dark and dangerous side of mourning – which psychoanalysis calls melancholia – in which no sane story of the future is possible.[15] The successful mourner gradually finds symbolic consolation from loss, and thus builds a narrative of renewed selves and worlds; but, for the melancholic, no story that is not a story of a richer time 'before' is possible.

Melancholia means mistaking just one aspect of making (its preoccupation with things lost) for the whole thing. In other words, the unsuccessful mourner remains nostalgically trapped in danger and loss – and in the melancholias of repeated attempts to recapture the past. The strength of Margaret Thatcher's appeal to the British people lay in the fact that she undoubtedly had an instinctive grasp of the uncanniness of the space of cultural renewal; this was the strength of her famous 'conviction', and it informed the feeling-tone, or poetics, of her imaginative address to the British electorate. But her vision – a calling up of the 'Victorian values' of nineteenth-century liberalism and individualism, in which an ethics and an economics were intextricably intertwined – remained melancholic and, where denial of loss and change is deeply pathological, close to something psychotic.

BURYING OUR DEAD

The image of the unburied dead in the 1978–9 Winter of Discontent is one which has haunted Labour through four successive general election defeats. It is an image of great barbarism and power. The party which is associated with a refusal to allow the performance of last rites is, perforce, associated with the refusal of mourning. It, itself, will have a great deal of mourning to do. In the spring of 1994, the Labour Party was at last able to give symbolic recognition to that task.

The death of Labour leader John Smith in April 1994 was uncanny in the extent of the shock it generated. The country was more shocked than anyone might have expected. It was, as it were, shocked at its own shock. But there is, I think, an explanation for the force of the collective unconscious identifications that Smith's death released.

Smith's leadership of the Opposition had been, quite evidently and determinedly, a huge work of reparation in a party riven by divisions ideological and actual and, throughout the 1980s and after 1989 especially, haunted by a massive loss of identity and a consequent failure to come to terms with a profoundly politically changed world. As such, Smith's work as leader began, for the Labour Party, the consoling reparations of a radically altered identity which we associate with the effects of loss and its self-shatterings, and also with the work of mourning which must follow from that. It signalled the possibility that the Labour Party might have the will to think itself as mourningfully, elegiacly, transformed, and also the will to take up its responsibility of offering an alternative to the deathly havoc that free market Conservatism was wreaking – both upon the British economy and upon the fabric of individual and collective life.

Smith's death shot this mourning-work into a remarkable collective focus, so that it was able to symbolise – in this extraordinary constellation of events – precisely what had been collectively struggling for articulation in the melancholic nostalgias of the 1980s and early 1990s. Smith's repair of the Labour Party offered, first, a glimpse – in non-pathological form – of healthy mourning and then, when he died, its symbolic actuality.

It is, thus, unsurprising that Smith's sudden death had the uncanny effect it did, since it gave specific form to a longer history of grief in which he, himself, had become first a benevolent political actor and, secondly, and with stunning symbolic coherence, a decent man who had died too soon. It is equally unsurprising that public life across the political spectrum found itself compelled (with all the force of unconscious motivations) to extensive expressions of grief, and that Smith's burial on Iona – the remote burying place of ancient Scottish kings – took on mythic resonances. In the sense that myth gives symbolic expression to experiences which cannot be articulated with their full affective force in other ways, Smith's death was mythic. The extraordinary, Chaucerian, talk of pilgrimages to Iona the following April was absolutely of a piece with the symbolic meanings released.

REMEMBERING FREUD

What does it mean, then, to remember Freud? And especially, what does it mean to remember Freud in the context of politics? In the first place, it means to remember, as Patrick Cosgrave reminded the viewers of Curtis's film, that fantasy and reality are not entirely separate or separable things. This means understanding that politics requires a language of the imagination – of the importance of symbolic, poetic, meanings, and of our affective investments in them – as much as it requires a language of utilitarian 'facts'.

We must all, eventually, find our way to becoming social beings. The way that Freud told this story was to say that we relinquish the narcissism of infancy via the experience of symbolic loss which psychoanalysis calls castration. In place of what is lost (undifferentiated joy in the mother), the father – which is to say the figure which symbolises the laws by which social identities and meanings are more or less fixed – offers us the possibility of social life as users and makers of symbols. Language, and its complex organisations of life in the form of recognisable social institutions, is what binds us up as human selves in human societies.

Modernity – especially in the form of industrial capitalism – is characterised by a terrific sense of social and psychical unbinding. As Marx said, 'All fixed, fast-frozen relations, with their train of ancient and venerable prejudices and opinions, are swept away, all new ones become antiquated before they can ossify. All that is sold melts into air, all that is holy is profaned ...'[16] As readers of the industrial novels of Dickens and of Mrs Gaskell will know, the industrial city of the mid-nineteenth century is represented in terms redolent of the terrible sublimity of Satan's Hell in *Paradise Lost*. The awesome and terrifying experience of social and psychical unbinding which these images reveal is not something that can be dispensed with: change, loss, renewal are the very motors of modernity itself.

Nonetheless, there has to be some place where modernity's dialectic of unbinding and binding – the ceaseless dynamic of loss and remaking – can be safely played out. This is the place of art and of the creativity of cultural experience generally; it involves the creation of a space which allows of playfulness, and of the instability of meanings and of identities, whilst at the same time binding them up in the affirmation of relatedness. At best, in the experience of culture and cultural life, we stage our pleasures and our pains, our losses and our remakings, as shared: as a sort of collective 'holding' of modern alienation and grief.

What, then, is the role of the father, of authority, here? The father of utility – J.S. Mill's own father, close friend of Jeremy Bentham; or Dickens's Thomas Gradgrind in *Hard Times* (1854) – is a panoptic father. With him, everything is fact, every detail is organised, no stone is left unturned, every moment is known. But, of course, this radical rationalist demystifying of the world has no way of weighing, calculating and knowing the affective investments which make human creatures social beings: hence Gradgrind's antipathy to circuses; hence Lousia Gradrind's lost cry to her father, 'Where are the graces of my soul?'.[17]

THE LOCATION OF CULTURAL EXPERIENCE

In a move which is historically symptomatic (that is, after the Second World War, when the virtues of instrumental uses of reason, and of the authority which sanctioned it, were subjected to increasingly anxious scrutiny), the psychoanalyst D.W. Winnicott described cultural experience in a way which offers a different account of authority. In his account, both authority (the handing-on of inherited meanings) and its failures (what Winnicott calls 'localised spoiling': the intentional and necessary moments of unbinding which make changes in meanings possible) come together in one space. This is Winnicott's 'transitional space' and, in it, both binding and unbinding are made possible by a maternal-paternal capacity for 'holding' rather than absolute mastery.

For Winnicott, writing in the 1960s, what can now count as a good form of authority has undergone a change. It must have something in it which is less characterised by a penetrative and rational mastery of the world, and is more characterised by 'maternal' forms of regulation; these latter are apparently almost entirely contingent (they are rules for which no general rule can be given) and are, thus, unamenable to detailed rationalisation. 'Holding' is a form of binding which is extremely fluid, responsive and adaptive to change. The values which it implies are not those of mastery; they are, rather, those of the constant negotiations and renegotiations of human identities, identifications and relatedness.

In 'The Location of Cultural Experience',[18] Winnicott asks: where can we find the space of cultural experience in Freud's topography of the mind? His answer is that it lies in the 'neither one thing nor another' which forms the boundary condition – a 'separation that is not a separation but a form of union'[19] – of transitional spaces and phenomena. Winnicott's spaces of 'neither one thing nor the other' are clearly uncanny.

The first space of cultural experience is precisely that space in which we first come-to-be as individuals. We can say that the experience of cultural making generally recapitulates the features of that first finding and making of ourselves as makers and users of symbols. In transitional space, and via the use of 'transitional objects', the infant learns to lose something precious and to take and make something new which will, elegiacly, stand in for what is gone. In other words, 'transitional objects' mark the infant's first use of symbols for something lost.

There are no fathers present in Winnicott's account of cultural experience. The 'good enough' mother, who is central to Winnicott's account of cultural experience, fulfils both maternal and paternal functions; the space she creates and holds for infantine coming-to-be is both bound and unbound by her.

Transitional spaces are characterised by play between two entirely different kinds of economies: one (the part played by the mother) works within the symbolic meanings of inherited traditions (what is found), the other (the part played by the infant) is entirely creative: it is an economy of inventing meanings. Winnicott says: 'An essential part of my formulation of transitional phenomena is that we agree never to make the challenge to the baby: did you create this object, or did you find it conveniently lying around?'.[20] In other words, while the mother knows that she works (although not, strictly, legally) with inherited material, the infant's mourning will only be successful if his or her play in this space is entirely creative. He or she must be allowed to experience the making of meanings for him- or herself. He or she must be allowed to build. Both infant and mother play creatively with the cultural inheritance but, whilst the mother knows it, the baby does not. The infant's creative mourning-play is, says Winnicott, a form of playing which does not yet know games.

In Winnicott, the mother works within the realm of inherited traditions and meanings, and ethical valuations, which, twenty years ago, the French feminist Hélène Cixous referred to as the 'masculine' realm of the proper,[21] but she does so 'illegally' and, thus, within Cixous's other realm: that 'feminine' realm of the gift. The gift affirms giving to the other as an open-ended and unbound act – like free blood donation.

The realm of the proper is the realm of the symbolic law, of the father, of prohibition, restriction, and a closed economy of bounded exchange and of fixed and calculable returns – whether of money or meanings. In distinction, the realm of the gift is a realm in which meanings are mutable – poetic even – provisional, transformative, good enough for the time being. In the realm of the gift meanings can, Cixous says, 'fly' or 'be stolen'; they are contingent and do not necessarily come back to their place. Here, returns are neither calculable nor fixed but are endlessly transformable. The 'meaning' of a Winnicottian transitional object is a mysterious meaning which the infant makes. 'Holding' suggests a form of relatedness which involves a commitment to cultural experience as the space where inherited meanings are always potentially on their way to other meanings – as a poetics, and a poetics of politics, understands.

DANGEROUS BUSINESS

Adam Phillips suggests that: 'Where Freud is preoccupied with defensive forms of control, Winnicott emphasises something less virile, which he calls "holding".[22] When Winnicott describes a 'father-less' space, and the less virile 'holding', perhaps he gives us a clue: not only to what sort of a space the space of cultural making is, but also about the kinds of values which should characterise it. Whether held and propelled by men or women, these are the (what we have come to think of as more 'feminine' and poetic) values of making time for things to grow, and of waiting for meanings to get to where they're going to, and to change.

'Holding' means knowing how to accommodate yourself to the burdens of difference rather than having an expectation of narcissistic sameness and repetition. ('Holding' describes the early maternal care that makes possible the infant's psychosomatic integration; and holding implies reciprocal accommodations, exactly what one observes in the subtle process of someone's carrying or picking up a child'[23]). It also means 'holding off': knowing when not to penetrate, or to 'know' and to master, all the strange spaces of cultural making. 'Holding' means knowing when it is alright not to know, and when it is alright simply to let strangeness and 'otherness' be what it is without the immediate profit of knowledge for the one who holds or holds off.

Zygmunt Bauman thinks that the postmodern may be about the attempt to 're-enchant' the world, and to grant value to things without the demand for rational justification:

> The postmodern world is one in which *mystery* is no more a barely tolerated alien awaiting a deportation order ... We learn to live with events and acts that are not only not-yet-explained, but (for all we know about what we will ever know) inexplicable ... We learn again to respect ambiguity, to feel regard for human emotions, to appreciate actions without purpose and calculable rewards. We accept that not all actions, and particularly not all among the most important of actions, need to justify and explain themselves to be worthy of our esteem.[24]

What Bauman writes of involves, of course, a different sort of strength, that of holding to the commitment to an ethical relation to others, and to their value, as an end in itself. This sort of holding and holding off from immediate mastery – in which cultural making is possible – neither fetishises the means nor expects or calculates any immediate, or indeed any *knowable*, rewards.

Tony Blair's emphasis, in his inaugural lecture, on the ethics of socialism as a broader commitment to the importance of social and symbolic life, rather than as simply economic determinism, is promising. The attempt to shift the Labour Party from the more narrowing effects of its utilitarianism, and to encourage a wider sense of collective goods, is hopeful. Equally, Blair's identification with Christian life suggests at least some form of commitment to the importance of 'mystery' in human experience.

At least some of the available evidence suggests that Blair's 'project' articulates a conceptual return to the roots of the engagement with loss (of a certain way of being in the world) which characterised the experience of modernity in the late eighteenth and early nineteenth centuries, and a return to the particular forms in which such alienation was lived under early nineteenth-century capitalism. It does so, especially, in the ways in which – as in earlier nineteenth-century critiques – it opposes an organic view of culture to a fragmented, atomized and mechanistic one. It signals a return to, and a re-engagement with, the terms in which loss, alienation and cultural grieving are experienced in modernity. It is not an exaggeration to say that these terms – marked and unmarked, acknowledged and disavowed – are those which have significantly defined the intellectual and creative experience of the last two hundred years of Western European history.

If conscious political and cultural engagement with this modern problematic defines the 'intellectual high ground' and history to which Blair recalls the modern Labour Party, this would bespeak an extraordinary and historic seriousness of intent. If Blair is asking the Labour Party both to understand its own part in the much larger story in which it was formed, and also to recognise that its contemporary responsibility lies in meeting politically those challenges whose terms were laid down so long ago, then there is genuine cause for hope. Cynicism is a luxury only affordable to the personally secure. Individuals or groups whose daily lived experience is traumatic must have hope born of social solidarity and collective witness.

If all this is the case, then those whose responses to the 1995 Conference speech by Blair were to call him a Tory or a Liberal Democrat are very wide of the mark. On a hopeful, rather than a cynical, account, Blair's modernisers are not working within either the terms or the identities which those words name; they are returning to the anterior conditions of such namings and identities in order, one assumes, to make a new political language and new political identities.

There are a lot of 'ifs' in what I have just said. All identities contain, are made of, ambivalences: things which seem good and hopeful can, under pressure of events, tip over into rigidly defended positions in which identity is maintained at the cost of creative remaking. Perhaps it would be more accurate to say that there are, uncannily, two 'Blairs': one gives some cause for hope; the other is potentially disturbing – a new conservative in the worst, blinkered, sense. But commentators and critics do not simply describe a reality that already exists; they are also a part of what forms perceptions and of what brings a reality into being. We may get the goverments we deserve, but this is only because we get the goverments we spin into being.

Tony Blair's, and new Labour's, identity is no more finally formed –

provided we remain creative beings – than yours or mine is. Just as, with a child, we seek to affirm the positive things in the hope that this is what the the child will become, so – with the politicians we make – we must spin them according to the thread we wish them to be. The 'Blair' I wish to spin is the one who remembers his early influences in the 'mutuality' of John Macmurray's philosophy, and who is not so distracted by the malign mechanisms of *realpolitik* that he forgets that 'mutuality' – as in Dickens' *Our Mutual Friend* – is forged by the open heart. As John Macmurray said, we can only be wholly creative and human when we 'soak ourselves in the life of the world around us … [and thus] … act with the whole of ourselves.'[25] Let us hope that the approach to high office and power does not make Blair forgetful, mechanistic and narrow.

In a world that is shattered by loss, the mourner's task lies in making new meanings from old forms. One of the most ancient tropes of elegy is the spinning of new threads which bind.[26] Renewal means that what is inherited must always be capable of being re-made as something – a new social fabric and fabrication – which is slightly different. The challenge is to learn how, creatively and politically, to mourn and make. For Zygmunt Bauman, postmodernity is 'modernity without illusions':[27]

> The illusions in question boil down to the belief that the 'messiness' of the human world is but a temporary and repairable state, sooner or later to be replaced by the orderly and systematic rule of reason. The truth in question is that the messiness will stay whatever we do or know, that the little orders and systems we carve out in the world are brittle, until-further-notice, and as arbitrary and in the end as contingent as their alternatives.[28]

Postmodernity returns us to the conditions of modernity but without the solutions, and the identities, which were subsequently offered. More strongly, postmodernity sees the melancholic terms of modernity – the romantic fantasy of a final overcoming in the whole and the one, and the utilitarian fantasy of complete and sufficient knowledge of detail (both of which may turn out to have been the same thing) – as a pathological refusal of the contingency of solutions and of making do.

Despite the dinosaur rumblings from the butch left which Blair provokes ('hard and 'soft' are such tellingly gendered terms here; being right-on about feminism doesn't at all mean rethinking the terms and values of one's politics apparently), it is the case that the future must be different. The politics of the twenty-first century *will* be different. Only time and office will tell whether the Blairite 'stakeholder' promise to 'hold' in mutuality and community, rather than to master, will be made good. Only time and office will tell whether the modernisers have a grasp on the pleasures and dangers of the uncanny.

A little Utopianism, a little hope, is essential to mourning and imagining the future. Only the melancholic sees cultural wealth as entirely in the past and lost, or all hope for the future as ridiculous. If the Labour Party has managed to produce a politician capable of meeting the challenges of the postmodern creatively and not, as contemporary Conservatism has done, in terms of a *failed* mourning, then a little cautious hope should not be seen as incompatible with proper traditions of critique.

Needless to say, the creative rearticulation of the past – in the present and for the future – means making meanings fly and change. It means stealing meanings. It is – and should be – a dangerous business; but, against the *dangerous business* of narcissistic individualism and unrestrained utilitarian capitalism, it is, hopefully, one of a very different, *social*ist, kind.

REFERENCES

I would like to thank Carolyn Burdett and Beatrix Campbell for helpful conversation and comments on an earlier draft of this chapter, and also Steve Baker, whose own inspired use of the work of Hélène Cixous sent me back to read her again with fresh eyes.

1 John Rentoul, *Tony Blair*, Little, Brown & Co., London, 1995, p420.
2 *Ibid.*, p42.
3 Gordon Brown & Tony Wright (eds.), *Values, Visions and Voices*, Mainstream, Edinburgh, 1995, pp128-9.
4 Matthew Arnold, 'On the Modern Element in Literature', M. Arnold, *Selected Prose*, ed., P.J. Keating, Penguin, Harmondsworth 1970, p67.
5 Brown & Wright, *Values, op.cit.*
6 Roy Hattersley, 'End the politics of accountancy', The *Guardian*, 30 September 1995.
7 Raymond Williams, *Culture and Society: Coleridge to Orwell*, Hogarth Press, London 1987.
8 *Ibid.*, p150.
9 *Ibid.*, p183.
10 *Ibid.*

11 William Wordsworth, quoted in *Culture and Society, ibid.*, p41.
12 Tony Blair, 'Socialism', *Fabian Pamphlet*, 565, Fabian Society, London, July 1994.
13 For a more detailed discussion of the relationship between nostalgia and melancholia, see my 'After Grief? What kinds of Inhuman Selves?', *New Formations*, summer 1995.
14 Sigmund Freud, 'The Uncanny'(1919), PFL 14: *Art and Literature*, Penguin, Harmondsworth 1985.
15 Sigmund Freud, 'Mourning and Melancholia'(1917[1915]), PF 11: *On Metapsychology*, Penguin, Harmondsworth 1984.
16 Quoted in Marshall Berman, *All That Is Solid Melts Into Air: The Experience of Modernity*, Verso, London 1983, p21.
17 Charles Dickens, *Hard Times*, Penguin, Harmondsworth 1969, p239.
18 D.W. Winnicott, 'The Location of Cultural Experience', *Playing and Reality*, Routledge, London 1991.
19 *Ibid.*, p98.
20 *Ibid.*, p96.
21 Hélène Cixous, 'Sorties', in *The Newly Born Woman*, tr. B. Wing, Manchester U.P., Manchester 1986.
22 Adam Phillips, *On Kissing, Tickling and Being Bored*, Faber & Faber, London 1993, p42.
23 *Ibid.*
24 Zygmunt Bauman, *Postmodern Ethics*, Blackwell, Oxford 1993, p33.
25 John Macmurray, *Reason and Emotion*, Faber and Faber, London 1995, p23.
26 Peter Sacks, *The English Elegy: Studies in the Genre from Spenser to Yeats*, Johns Hopkins University Press, London 1985, p18.
27 Bauman, *op.cit.*, p32.
28 *Ibid.*, pp32-3.

NEW LABOUR,
NEW ENGLAND?
Leighton Andrews

'New Britain' is already one of Tony Blair's better known themes. His speeches are suffused with the language of national renewal, promising not only new Britain but a new Union, wanting us to become 'a young country again'.[1] He has, says one supporter, woven patriotism and national pride 'into a promise to rejuvenate and inspire a divided nation'.[2] Blair's message is positive, and upbeat, promising a new land of economic, social, political and technological opportunity, in a rhetoric that marks a real confrontation with the fatalistic approach to Britishness – and its dominant component, Englishness – which has dogged Labour and the left since the end of Empire. One commentator has even related the explosion of interest in Britpop (essentially an English popular music phenomenon) to 'Blair-ism in action'.[3]

Blair's new Britain proposition has to be seen against the background of a widespread feeling that the dominant image of Britain is one of a country trapped in its past: a heritage country, seeming to have little to offer a modern information society.[4] This is not simply an analysis limited to think-tankers and sectarians: Britain's 'brand image' has become increasingly of concern to those responsible for marketing British business.[5] Images which reflect Britain externally seem bound up with Britain's institutions: but while they reflect images of the British state, their provenance is invariably English in derivation, and often it is hard to separate images of Englishness and Britishness, not least for the English.[6]

Modernising those images of Britishness may be more necessary than daring, but no-one could pretend that it will be an easy task. Blair's promise of a more open, more mobile, more modern Britain cannot be achieved by simply willing it: winning an election is one thing but winning a second and turning around deeply-imbued cultural beliefs quite another. So Blair has set out to amplify his patriotic view of new Britain. He has said that the challenge of developing a coherent view of the nation state will be one of the central political questions of the next few decades. He recognises that many on the left have feared a debate about nationhood, confusing it with 'a narrower nationalism'. Blair sees the nation as being at the heart of new Labour. He proclaims his patriotism as one 'born not of nostalgia but of an understanding of the changing nature of the world and a determination to secure our place within it, confident, influential, with a real sense of identity, finally breaking out of our imperial shadows'.[7] In a sense it has three focuses – a more open, tolerant and flexible Union, based on devolution to Wales and Scotland; reassurance to English opinion; confidence about Britain's place in Europe and the world.

Blair's new Britain philosophy can be read directly in the context of longstanding debates on the left about the nature and formation of the British state, the relation of state formation to culture, to Britishness and Englishness, and to the constitutional reforms necessary to enable a more tolerant, progressive and modern civil society to grow and develop. Labour recovery in England has been central to Blair's political strategy, and Englishness and Britishness form one of the most contested areas of analysis. A positive, open and optimistic approach to Englishness will be an important element of Blair's challenge to Conservative political domination of England and thus to long-term structural reform of the British state. That challenge must also overthrow the determinedly pessimistic and naively romantic approaches to Englishness which have dogged the British left for decades.

TRADITIONAL LABOURISM AND THE NATION

The constitutional agenda has challenged the Westminster nationalism of old Labour, and Blair has been sensitive to this. Since its creation, Labour's approach has largely focused on the centralised state as the mechanism of social and economic reform. With a belief in the inevitability of progress inherited from the Whigs, this approach assumed the state will deliver the gradual amelioration of conditions.

Will Hutton has said that Labour

> has sought to empower trade unions, extend public ownership, build a welfare state and organise a viable British Keynesianism as a means of transforming Britain but has left the wider social and political order intact, together with its value system. In effect social democracy has been bolted on to a fundamentally conservative constitution and wider institutional structure, which has blocked Labour's objectives ... The state and its institutions were simply means to economic and social ends, whether in the form of public ownership or Keynesian tools of demand management.[8]

The object was to capture the state, and use it for planning economic and social change in a form still evident in Labour's alternative economic strategy and 'suicide-note manifesto' of 1983.

It was a form of activity derived from the organisational necessities of trade unionism, and the gradualism of Fabian reformers. It depended on the absolute sovereignty of Parliament, best expressed by Aneurin Bevan: 'Parliament is a weapon and the most formidable one we have in the struggle.'[9] Bevan saw Parliament as a popular vehicle, lined up against Property: 'If there is one thing we must assert, it is the sovereignty of Parliament over any section of the community.'[10]

That tradition, albeit with its own great strengths and achievements, marginalised or ignored concerns about constitutional reform. It saw Britain as a unitary state in which structured constitutional reform was a diversion and perceived the British parliament as the focus of all meaningful political action. This conviction drove Labour anti-Europe feelings in terms that sound more like the Conservative leadership of today: as Gaitskell said in 1962: 'European federation means the end of Britain as an independent nation; we become no more than "Texas" or "California" in the United States of Europe. It means the end of a thousand years of history.'[11]

That doctrine of parliamentary rather than popular sovereignty, allied to a traditional belief that class was more important than nation, underpinned the opposition within Labour to devolution in the 1970s, leading one anti-devolution leader to tell the Commons in 1977, 'I believe that the emancipation of the class which I have come to this House to represent, unapologetically, can best be achieved in a single nation and in a single economic unit, by which I mean a unit in which we have a brotherhood of all nations and have the combined strength of working-class people throughout the UK.'[12] This kind of commitment inevitably bound patriotism to the defence of the existing institutions, so calls by some on the left for a new patriotism after the Falklands were inevitably seen by many as raising the Union Jack in defence of unreformed state institutions.[13] Subsequently, the constitutional debate, expanded away from its core Liberal caucus by Charter 88, has enabled a separation of patriotism from the defence of the existing settlement to take place. It is that new political momentum which gives Blair's 'new Britain' patriotism its clarity and radicalism, promising clear reform of the British state and a new, inclusive sense of national identity derived from the people as citizens rather than from the ancient and mystical traditions of the British constitution.

NEW BRITAIN OR NEW ENGLAND?

When the English debate Britishness they are really debating Englishness: and even if they aren't the boundaries are hard to define. Welshness and Scottishness, perhaps reflecting more longstanding debates within Wales and Scotland about national identity and culture, tend to be seen in writings on culture and politics as more clearly distinct from Britishness.

There is plenty of day by day anecdotal evidence which confirms the general confusion between England and Britain in England. Reading almost any cultural commentary in a London broadsheet will throw up this confusion. Like Shakespeare's John of Gaunt, some see England as an island. Others attribute to Britain icons and traditions which are deeply English. Some seem to think that we have a tripartite system of national affiliation: there is Scotland, and there is Wales, and there is Britain. England is entirely absent. Great Britain in everything on this island except Wales and Scotland: but England is a silent sleeping partner. This view is frequently encountered amongst the metropolitan elite, whose conception of society tends to be a highly universalist one, in which their own – itself provincial – society is capable of standing for all other societies. It is never entirely malevolent, however: in some cases, using 'Britain' for 'England' represents an attempt to find a term that sounds more pluralistic than England, as Raphael Samuel suggests.[14] But to those of us with Welsh or Scottish origins, it often feels rather like a reversal of the famous *Encyclopaedia Britannica* entry which recorded 'For Wales, see England': today we have, for England, see Britain.

The New Debate on Englishness

More positively, almost coinciding with Blair's rise to leadership of the Labour Party, there has been a spate of writing about Englishness on the left which could not have been entertained even a couple of years ago. It is itself a sign of a new confidence that the theme is even being raised. At an intellectual level, it has resulted in the left engaging with the question of Englishness, in ways that move beyond the automatic and sterile assumption that Englishness is owned by one political party only, the Conservatives as the national party of England.[15]

In most cultures, a pessimistic analysis seems to dominate debates around national identity. Debates on Englishness, like debates on Scottishness and Welshness, revolve around similar themes: despair at political defeat; self-disgust; pessimism; historical and cultural analysis of imagery and icons; disentangling of national feeling from state-identity; desire to create a more progessive and usable national identity; demands for political and cultural reform. The debate around heritage has been particularly intensive in all three countries.[16] Industry, active work, has been replaced by museum-culture, for example as the framed heritage of mining museums.

Welshness and Scottishness have been more and more confidently expressed since the late 1980s – though the debates within Welsh and Scottish political culture remain deeply contested – and debates over their meanings have gone on far longer. The debate on Englishness is more hesitant and more recent. The concepts 'English' socialist or 'English' liberal are not found on many lips, whereas socialists and liberals in Wales or Scotland appear to have no difficulty combining national identity and political affiliation.

So the growth in recent times of positive statements of Englishness by a variety of radical writers is a real departure from the national traditions of old Labour. It is principally of course a consequence of the growth in support for the constitutional reform agenda which has enabled people to disentangle Englishness from the images and icons of the British state. It suggests a real prospect for a new intellectual grounding for Blair's new Britain: one in which Englishness, for so long seen as a Conservative project with racial overtones, can flourish in England, alongside other identities.

DEBATING ENGLAND

Jack Straw has summed up the debate on Englishness as follows: 'For the left, it is time to end the right-wing ghetto in which public feeling for England has been for too long corralled'.[17] While the new debate has principally been a debate of elites, not one across classes,[18] its influence on the alignment of politics remains fundamentally important. Until recently, there have been two streams in the debate on Englishness on the left: the romantics, who subscribe to a belief in an alternative radical England; and the pessimists, who believe England is irreconcilable to any ideology other than Conservativism. Yet more recently, we have seen the emergence of a third strand, more in keeping with the general direction of Blair's own new Britain philosophy – what I would call the new realists, who see a need for the left to come to terms with England.

The romantics stand for the attempt to recreate what Philip Dodd calls the 'United Radical People': the 'Freeborn Englishman' struggling to overcome this or that Yoke in a long family tree of radicalism stretching back into the middle ages.[19] There may be some therapeutic power in rekindling memories of popular power and activity, but there are real dangers of taking the Fantasy Football League approach to labour history, enlisting the radical names which sound the most inspiring and lining them up in defence of the latest cause. At best anachronistic, at worst it means substituting one version of the past for another, in order to strengthen one's resolve about the present.

The pessimists have had most of the best songs over the last fifteen years. There has been a long-standing culture of defeatism on the left, at its sharpest after the Conservative election victories of 1987 and 1992. It has shown itself repeatedly in the belief that England is lost for good. Such a view has been called national nihilism – 'the settled conviction that all is hopeless in one's own country.'[20] This defeatism is sometimes articulated as snobbery, the belief that England is becoming a theme park, that there is no culture outside a small metropolitan elite; that there is no longer any English culture – it has all been taken over by the Americans. Clearly, for some intellectuals, England is outside themselves, it is something other.

The new realists have a strong element of romanticism within them. Even realist narratives need some mythology after all. But their analysis does not rely on the belief in substituting one history for another. It relies on a new pluralism about English identity. It takes from the romantic analysis the belief that people can make change themselves; but it recognises, as with the pessimists, that the structures of English society and the British state are significantly biased against change and require fundamental reform. Billy Bragg has written, 'although the British Empire has officially ceased to exist, the machinery that ran it is still mostly intact'. He warns that by letting the right set the agenda on Englishness the patriotic majority who believe in equality and accountability will be alienated.[21] It is this combination of determination to achieve constitutional reform and optimism about the possibility of change that is at the heart of Blair's new Britain.

THE ROOTS OF THE DEBATE

Disputes between the romantics and pessimists have found different forms down the years, but are still going on today, almost thirty years after they first started. For these analyses of England are not of particularly recent origin. There has been a debate on the nature of England – though it would have confused the terms England and Britain – since the first post-war Labour government. In other words, from the end of Empire. On the left, the debate began in the late 1940s and early 1950s with the Communist Party Historians' Group and the first New Left. This movement gave birth amongst other things to the creation of the History Workshop movement and its particular approach to labour history, with the emphasis on recovering popular history and social movements from what Edward Thompson had called 'the enormous condescension of posterity.' This movement emphasised activity and the capacity for spontaneous political action.[22]

But the debate became fiercer in the 1960s. Under Perry Anderson and Tom Nairn's tutelage, what became known as the second New Left drastically modified the themes of the debate, confronting what it saw as the sterile vacuous empiricism of a British labourism that exalted Parliament and resisted more robust theoretical work. Their emphasis on the linkage of historical development, state-formation and political culture was ground-breaking, but elitist and top-down in its theory of the state and its analysis of popular movements. Thompson, in particular, disputed their analyses on both historical and theoretical grounds.[23]

Post 1968, New Left thinking was modified further by the Centre for Contemporary Cultural Studies (CCCS) under Stuart Hall's directorship, disputing the analyses of both these groups. The work of the CCCS led to the analysis of the crisis of the British state and Englishness set out in the book *Policing the Crisis*.[24] This sought to deconstruct the ideology of the state and analysed the 'authoritarian populism' of what was soon to be called Thatcherism. Like Nairn and Anderson, this group of writers retained the emphasis on the analysis of the state rather than on popular movements, but switched attention towards the active ideological mobilisation of opinion by Conservative forces. The intellectual framework set out here was heavily influential, and gave rise to a subsequent generation of writing ostensibly on Britain but really on England, in the pages of *Marxism Today*, and latterly the writings of Patrick Wright and Paul Gilroy.[25] It is important to record that these analyses of the British state were formed at key moments of intellectual disillusion with Labour governments – with Wilson in the 1960s and Callaghan in the 1970s. They derived from and appealed not only to a new generation of political radicals to the left of Labour, but also to many within the emerging nationalist movements in Wales and Scotland, for whom they provided a fundamental understanding of the nature of English domination of the British state (although it is interesting to note that the ideological focus of the CCCS theorists meant that they, unlike Nairn, saw constitutional change as a liberal irrelevance).[26]

In all these analyses, there is no real dispute that the political culture of 'Britishness' is rooted in long-standing practices and culture which exalt one form of 'Englishness' as standing for the whole. The institutions which make up the British state – what Anthony Barnett calls the 'Empire State'[27] – constitute that very Conservative culture which helps to sustain them. Today, the agenda of Charter 88 may be seen to be considerably in debt to the writings of the New Left and to the thinking of Liberal and nationalist theorists – and some exceptional Labour theorists like John P. Mackintosh and David Marquand[28] – developing over the same period.

Historical development is central to these analyses of the British state. Indeed, most recently the New Left-inspired debates have become the stuff of mainstream historical debate, with the development of the Four Nations school of history which sees British or UK history as properly the study of England, Scotland, Wales and Northern Ireland.[29]

According to Tom Nairn[30] England was the first self-aware nation. The Elizabethan settlement was the first expression of a modern nationalism: its bookends were the full incorporation of Wales in 1536 and the Stuart Accession of 1603. The concept of the British Empire – coined by a Welshman – occurred in this period. The English revolution of the next century, which occurred before industrialisation, before the creation of a real bourgeoisie, before the creation of a language of rights, institutionalised the ancien regime. The doctrine of sovereignty which derived from the Crown rather than the people was thus firmly ingrained. Englishness – or Britishness – as the defining ideology was further reinforced by hostility to others down the years: the French, the Irish, the Spanish, the Dutch, the Germans, latterly blacks and Asians. Linda Colley, however, argues that it was more complex than that: Britishness was not substituted for Englishness in the eighteenth and early nineteenth century in opposition to the external enemy but rather 'Britishness was superimposed over an array of internal differences in response to contact with the Other, and above all in response to conflict with the Other.'[31] Later still, class, religion, the new discipline of English literature, codified at the height of Empire between 1880 and 1920, and the new broadcasting media, all played their part in reinforcing and constituting the settlement.

In these theories, it is actually Conservative ideology that has linked the texts of Englishness and Britishness and confused them. If there is one thing in this analysis that stands above all else for Englishness, it is territory as heritage. The heartland of England has been the heartland of Conservatism. Call it 'Greater England'[32] or 'Deep England',[33] one part of England has been allowed to stand for England and for Britain as a whole. Nairn calls it 'This Disney-like English world where the Saxon ploughs his fields and the sun sets to strains by Vaughan Williams.'[34] 'To be a subject of deep England', says Patrick Wright, 'is above all to have been there – one must have had the essential experience, and one must have had it in the past to the extent that the meaningful ceremonies of deep England are above all ceremonies of remembrance and recollection.'[35] Deep England has no love of outsiders and lives in fear of encroachment; by the masses, the suburbs, outsiders, industry, others. It relies on notions of the authentic. 'It is a particularistic England in which belonging is mystical and intuitive', says Wright. To be English one's family must have been there for generations. Being English means being against outsiders. As Gilroy notes, 'The language of national belonging has acquired a series of racial referents that cannot be spontaneously dislodged by a pure act of will.'[36] Even its landscape has apparently become part of the ideology.[37]

Reclaiming England From
the Pessimists

What the pessimists have done is to take certain elements of the analysis, and turn it into something immutable. There is strength in the historical analysis and power in its critique. Yet in its very particularity, it fails to tell the whole story. Too often intellectuals on the left are so transfixed by the weight of their own historical analysis that they are unable to think beyond it: that there might be other Englands, beyond and against the one they have analysed. Speaking from Wales, Raymond Williams once made the telling point 'It won't help, either side of the border, to mistake the state for the real identity, or the projections for the people.'[38] Arguing against the tenets of Four Nations history, Linda Colley has contended that it can be as inappropriate to analyse England in terms of one national culture as it it can be to try and disaggregate Britishness into four components of Welshness, Scottishness, Irishness and Englishness.[39] Perhaps, as Fielding, Thompson and Tiratsoo comment in analysing the Labour governments of 1945 to 1951, often intellectual critics on the left are in danger of interpreting events and histories in the light of their own hopes for the future.[40]

It is notable that the most positive alternative uses of Englishness today come from those on the left whose identity is rooted in an Englishness and in another identity as well: the west-country identity of Michael Foot; the Yorkshire identities of Sheila Rowbotham and Roy Hattersley; the Forest of Dean border identity of Dennis Potter; the black English identity of Paul Gilroy.

It is time to face people with their own provincialisms. This is an intellectual culture which has turned in on itself: it is guilty of what Raymond Williams and Kenneth Morgan have called 'metropolitan provincialism'.[41] As Philip Dodd has noted, metropolitan intellectuals 'have given up the struggle to imagine a usable national identity: They are part of the problem. Above all, it is they who are dispirited, who have gathered up the sense of loss and decline.'[42]Metropolitan political and literary culture can be highly parochial and inward-looking, driven by the latest idea or fashion, insufficiently rooted in more complex communities which require daily negotiation and confrontation with disagreeable ideas. Some have found solace from their own metropolitan disillusion in the belief that a republican nationalism in Scotland and Wales will be their salvation. Some will no doubt object that Blair's is a unionist project: but so too is Charter 88 – indeed in its early days Charter 88 gave insufficient recognition to the demands of Wales and Scotland for devolution. Will Hutton's agenda of civic republicanism – and earlier writings by David Marquand – has at last given some coherence to a radical constitutional programme not constructed in a nationalistic idiom.[43]

A realistic approach to England and Englishness requires jettisoning romance and leaving behind pessimism. For many, it may mean accepting and embracing their own Englishness before they can recognise and respect the identities of other people. Pluralism in England requires an expansion of the vision of what it is to be English. The concepts that are useful here may be closer to the 'double consciousness' that Paul Gilroy writes about in his *The Black Atlantic*.[44] There is a double consciousness about being both Welsh (or Scottish) and at the same time British or indeed Welsh and European. Maybe in someone like the athlete Colin Jackson, one hears the language of triple consciousness, of being black, Welsh and British. The double consciousness of English and British should not be too hard, even for the English! Indeed Colley has argued that it was common in the eighteenth century to think of oneself in dual nationalities: 'Nationalities are not like hats. Human beings can and do put on several at a time'.[45] Paul Gilroy has argued for an end to people having to choose between different facets of their identities. 'I make no apology for the fact that this shift in my own thinking arises from a desire to be recognised as being both black and English in addition to everything else that I am'.[46] This approach has been echoed by the writer Mike Phillips, who says 'I think of myself as a black English person and that's somewhat provocative'.[47] This possibility of loyalty to dual identities has also been explicitly recognised by Blair. Indeed, Blair's 'young country' is in some senses directly counterposed to Patrick Wright's 'old country'. Blair's new Britain would be a place in which it is possible to change things, where it is possible to hold, value and reconcile separate identities.[48]

ENGLISHNESS AND THE NEW BRITAIN PROJECT

Blair often speaks of his 'project' – and he is a more strategic politician than many on the left of politics give him credit for – carefully assessing and assembling his positions before identifying routes forward. That has been as true of his approach to the politics of England as it has been to any other aspect of policy.

First, there has been the challenging of pessimism about political progress in England; next the necessary reminders to intellectual opinion in Wales and Scotland that – outside London and certain regions like the North East – England has had little to say about devolution either for itself or in reaction to devolution in Wales and Scotland; then the negotiation of traps which the Conservative Party might set, in relation either to regional government in England or in relation to Europe; throughout carefully balancing competing interests, but ruling little out. Finally, he has underpinned all this with a deepening rhetoric about an inclusive, communal, tolerant new Britain.

In challenging pessimism, Blair has achieved rather more with his own party than with intellectual opinion. At a political level, the new confidence about England is reflected in his determination that there will be no no-go areas for Labour, even in Southern England.[49] Blair has sought to broaden Labour's appeal beyond its traditional heartlands. Labour had become an increasingly Celtic party, and had relied on Scotland and Wales for a disproportionate range of Parliamentary seats. England, as Andrew Adonis reminds us, accounts for 80 per cent of the UK's Parliamentary seats, and the Conservatives have never polled below 40 per cent of the English vote.[50] Indeed, if census projections are accurate, England, and Southern England in particular, is set to grow significantly and disproportionately to the rest of Britain. The English population is expected to grow by 3.4 million over the next twenty years, with a higher growth in the shire counties than the metropolitan counties, and little growth in the North.[51] This need not be a disincentive to Labour, since while the number of Labour MPs in England dropped by two-fifths between 1974 and 1983, Labour gained around forty seats in England in 1992.[52] Unparallelled political successes in England in the 1995 local and 1994 European elections have given Labour activists in England a new confidence.

Intellectual opinion is however a different matter. Blair's camp has been frustrated at the failure of intellectuals to engage with his agenda. The truth is that the left in general has found it hard to engage comfortably with the idea of England. This can be attributed to particular formulations of the libertarian political culture developed by the later New Left in the 1960s.

Increasingly during the 1980s and 1990s left-wing intellectuals working in traditional academic institutions have moved further and further away from influencing politics. There certainly seems to have been a divorce between theory and practice. Anne Showstack Sassoon says that intellectuals 'face a constant danger of being cut off from reality.'[53] There has been plenty of pessimism of the intellect, but precious little optimism of the will. Plenty of commentary on the necessities and difficulties of pluralism, but less on the possibilities and difficulties of building political structures which radiate pluralism. Increasingly, as the opposition parties penetrate further into deep England, the debate on England needs to be rescued from the intellectuals who've dominated it. Theirs has become almost an entirely apolitical agenda.[54] Blair has had to build his political project in the face of an active remaking of a Conservative Englishness mobilised in defence of the *ancien regime*.

A NEW ENGLAND IN A NEW UNION?

Balancing the political imperatives of England, Scotland and Wales may, however, mean balancing radically different interests, as it has often done down the centuries for the parties or interests attempting to manage the state. Blair was surely right to say that the constitutional debate has not penetrated so far into England as it has into Wales and Scotland.[55] Without a wider debate in England, the risk of real popular – and party – resistance to proposals for regional government is significant. Poll findings regularly record little genuine support for English regional government outside London and possibly the North East. In any case, it has never been entirely clear that the way to balance the national aspirations of Wales and Scotland is through regional government in England. Many people in Wales and Scotland feel that only a metropolitan elite could make the assumption that national identity can be equated with regional identity; that Wales and Scotland are the same as the regions of England; that constitutional politics is a question of the size of population. Wales and Scotland have their own regions too: Scotland, after all, occupies about one third of the landmass of the UK. Those of us born in South Wales are well aware of the difference between there and the traditional Welsh-speaking heartland of North West Wales.

So, while polls demonstrate a huge measure of consensus in Wales and Scotland about devolution, England needs a debate about its own constitutional requirements. It is a debate which Labour found too problematic by half last time round in 1976. The White Paper issued then on devolution in England was concerned to avoid any challenge to the sovereignty of Westminster.[56] In that period interlocking sovereignties could barely be imagined in the political culture of the British Labour Party outside Wales and Scotland (and scarcely there either). A year after a referendum on membership of the EEC, perhaps that wasn't so surprising. Has the political culture today matured in its understanding of sovereignty?

Proposals for regional government in England have in the past had the job of meeting two different objectives: answering the West Lothian question, on the one hand (why should Scottish MPs at Westminster vote on English issues when neither they nor English MPs at Westminster can vote on Scottish issues?) and the need for an active devolution of power in a centralist England. These objectives are separable. Labour's proposals for a staged move to greater devolution in England (rolling devolution) may not satisfy constitutional purists, but constitution-building often suffers from an excess of Utopian ambition. Clarity of vision is essential but popular endorsement is also critical, as recent challenges to elite opinion on the future of the European Union have demonstrated throughout its Member States. The building of new constitutional frameworks is too important to be left to the constitutional lawyers.

Is an English consciousness essential to the devolution of power in England away from Westminster? Not necessarily, if regional identities are stronger. Today English identity seems mainly focused around indifferent sporting performances, with the 1966 World Cup Final standing, for part of the population, as a defining moment. But in the context of the creation of a Scottish Parliament and Welsh Assembly, the development of English institutions, including quangos, may be required alongside devolved assemblies in England. Some, like the Arts Council of England, may already exist: others will have to be created, hopefully with more democratic credentials. These could provide a basis for the growth of a more popular English consciousness, less bound up with the icons of the British state.

It may be too late: English identity may by now be so bound up with what we know as Britishness that we have gone past the moment when a positive Englishness could be a real development. But it is more likely that with a Scottish Parliament and Welsh Assembly in existence the English question will come more sharply into focus. Some argue[57] that the English themselves will want to open the constitutional debate in that context. For Labour, it is arguable whether this is a short, medium or long-term threat. In the short-term, Labour needs to do well in England, and there is no doubt that the Conservatives will target English fears about loss of influence deriving from the break-up of the Union, and Euro-federalism, as a major political theme. In the medium term, there is the question of building devolution in Scotland and Wales while remaining sensitive to concerns in England. There is also a question of whether Labour success in England in a general election will itself dissipate the energies for constitutional reform in Wales and Scotland: if England comes into line with its neighbours, how urgent will be the popular demands for change? There will be some who will want to give up on the constitutional agenda. Blair himself is aware of this, and he has warned that it is easy to be pluralist in opposition, but harder to give up power in government – but he is determined to do so.[58] In the long term, there is always the danger that English discontent could threaten Blair's hopes of removing the Conservatives for a generation.

In fact, it may well be the success of devolution in Wales and Scotland which provokes support for regional assemblies in England. Economic development and investment issues already give rise to considerable competition (and often suspicion) between different nations and regions within the UK, and the success of elected, accepted institutions in Wales and Scotland could be a key motivator of popular support for devolution in England.

The important issue is that constitutional change should be viewed as a dynamic process of continuing modernisation, rather than the purchase of an off-the-shelf model, already solidified into a mould according to an elite blueprint. This is not an argument against a written constitution but in favour of maintaining popular support. In any event, it is hard to see how a process of constitutional reform, once begun, can easily be stopped. Understandably the focus in preparing Labour for government has been on the legislative feasibility of change. Some appear to want to limit commitments and measures, fearing that too many commitments could see a Labour government running into difficulties. Others are clearly opposed to the constitutional agenda and would like to withdraw from it. Some, not necessarily all opposed ideologically to Labour, are already finding problems with the party's existing proposals.

Realism may suggest that there is no ideal state where the perfect constitution is found. Business today reels to the incantation of the inevitability and dynamism of change, and change management has become an art in itself. Constitutional change is likely to produce its own dynamic, and this has been recognised in Labour's plans for the English regions.[59] It may have to become a motor for the constitutional agenda as a whole. The danger, of course, is that some might use flexibility as an excuse for inaction. In the longer-term, Labour needs sustained intellectual input to help generate a popular-political culture more sympathetic to Blair's new Britain agenda.

THE CONSERVATIVE AGENDA IN ENGLAND

Commentators from a variety of backgrounds see English nationalism as a key battleground for the next election. In the last week of the 1992 election, John Major focussed his attack on the opposition parties very precisely.[60] His attack on constitutional reform was that it would mean the weakening of government and the break-up of Britain. Britain's strength abroad was founded on the authority of its government in Parliament. It is an attack to which John Major has returned since, arguing that 'You cannot shake your constitution around as though it were a cocktail at an Islington dinner party.'[61] This Conservative attack is aimed precisely at what the Conservatives see as their heartland. Major knows his supporters, and believes, not without reason, that he can make this agenda matter.

The debate on England is also likely to intensify, rather than diminish, because of the Inter-Governmental Conference on the future of the European Union and moves towards a single currency. Debates on national sovereignty and the role of national parliaments will inevitably be under intensive examination. A lot of this debate of course is about England: some believe that for the English sense of national identity, it is important that the UK is powerful – through membership of the G7 or the UN Security Council. Others suggest that Brussels represents the same bogey for the English as Westminster does for the Scots.[62]

Conservative Englishness and Britishness provide a core philo-sophic underpinning to a diverse range of positions.[63] These have ranged from well-known attacks on devolution as the break-up of Britain to invocations of the countryside as reflecting 'the character that is especially British'. Englishness and Britishness have also raised their heads again in the context of the treatment of the history curriculum in schools in England. The teaching of history of course was a subject of controversy throughout the 1980s. In two key speeches the Government's Chief Curriculum Adviser Dr Nicholas Tate set out an agenda, first for the teaching of Britishness (actually Englishness) and then called for the reinstatement of heroes and narratives into the teaching of history. He said 'pupils need a sense of the nation as an entity which stretched back through time and through whose continuing existence past and present are linked.'[64] David Marquand, however, believes that it could be difficult for the Conservatives to continue to forge a nationalism in England: 'Heroic nationalism is like drug addiction: each fix has to be bigger than the last'[65]; and the result is destabilising.

These arguments are not simply about identity but 'about the form of representation and the distribution of power within the political and economic system.'[66] However, Conservative Englishness is well-grounded and reflected through a variety of institutions. Engendering a positive sense of Englishness can no more be willed into existence than can a 'new Britain'. But it may be not only a requisite for the deeper cultural change which Blair wishes to see, but also a real opportunity.

FORGING NEW ENGLAND IN A NEW BRITAIN

England is for the English to make up their minds about. But Raymond Williams was right when he wrote that 'Until they solve it, there will not be much peace for the rest of us'.[67] Once the demonisation of England stops, it may give space for a less romantic and nostalgic vision of Wales and Scotland, one which gives less ground to more extreme nationalisms in those two countries.

The historian Gwyn Alf Williams said of Wales, 'There is no historical necessity for Wales; there is no historical necessity for a Welsh people or a Welsh nation. Wales will not exist unless the Welsh want it. It is not compulsory to want it ... If we want Wales, we will have to make Wales'.[68] So too with England – if the English want it, they will have to make it. Reclaiming it from the pessimists would be a start. In coming to terms with England, the English are coming to terms with political change. What we are looking at is an identity politics for the English.

'Britishness', Raphael Samuel reminds us, echoing Gwyn Alf

Williams, 'instead of being a secure, genetic identity, can be seen as something culturally and historically conditional, always in the making, never made.'[69] Some see Blair's new Britain philosophy as being an attempt to remake a sense of Britishness, after the dislocations of the 1980s, with which the Scots and Welsh can feel comfortable[70] – not unlike the model of Britishness in the eighteenth century which Linda Colley has descibed.[71] It also seeks to make the English more comfortable with Europe. Some others see Blair's Britishness as being about the well-being of its citizens, not about flags.[72] Others may argue it should go further than Labour seems prepared to do, losing the remaining imperial and defence commitments, taking a more active environmental stance and tackling the monarchy, the Lords and private schools.[73] Neal Ascherson believes, 'It's not hard to see what's being attempted, and it's something very English. The aim of social justice, which must surely be radical and disruptive to the existing order, is being dressed up in the old uniform of Ancient British patriotism.'[74] Blair's constitutional agenda is more radical than any a previous Labour government has promised. For many, it is too cautious in terms of actual commitment – particularly on electoral reform, so critical to a pluralist society – not just in party terms but also in terms of social composition. But Blair's new Britain represents the best prospect for real reform of the British state there has been.

It is an incremental agenda – and must be a dynamic process of reform. The test will be what is ultimately ruled out: and whether the dynamic actually makes it feasible to rule anything out. Does 'a new union' mean the long-term endurance of Westminster sovereignty? It is a question that cannot be tested in the abstract. On the other hand, if Labour fails to implement a coherent constitutional agenda, more radical questions may come to be asked of the British state, and of the Labour Party. If Labour does succeed, the question of forging new Britain will have only just begun. New Britain cannot be willed into existence: and if it is to have any chance of growth, let alone survival, it will need a new, more confident, tolerant and democratic England to allow it to develop. A positive Englishness should certainly not mean defence of the existing constitutional settlement.

Tony Blair's conception of new Britain fundamentally challenges the conclusions of decades of cultural thinking on the left of British politics. Alternatively romantic and pessimistic in turns, that cultural theorising has blocked the evolution, until recently, of a positive and dynamic Englishness conceived independently of the institutions of the British state. In a context of radical constitutional change, a positive sense of Englishness may be one element needed within the culture of Labour and the left to entrench that change and enable Blair's 'new Britain' not only to develop, but to survive.

RERENCES

1 Tony Blair, 'Speech to the 1995 Labour Party Conference', Brighton, 3 October 1995.
2 Geoff Mulgan, 'Patriotism is not enough', *The Spectator*, 14 October 1995, and 'A new sense of Britishness' in *Welsh Agenda*, August 1995.
3 The former Scottish Nationalist and songwriter, Pat Kane, quoted in *The Times* Magazine, 2 December 1995; see also Cosmo Landesman, *Sunday Times Culture Section*, 5 November 1995 on Englishness and Britpop.
4 Robert Hewison, *The Heritage Industry*, Methuen, London 1987. Patrick Wright, *On Living in an Old Country*, Verso, London 1985.
5 Anneke Elwes, *Nations for Sale*, BMP DDB Needham, London 1994; S.Richards, 'UK plc: trapped in a timewarp', *Sunday Times Culture Section*, 30 October 1994; and Patrick Wright, 'Wrapped in the tatters of the flag', *Guardian*, 31 December 1994.
6 Demos, 'Open Letter to Tony Blair', *Guardian*, September 1994. Geoff Mulgan, 'Political Strategy in an anti-political age', *Renewal*, October 1994; Bernard Crick, 'The English and the British', in Crick (ed), *National Identities*, Blackwell, Oxford 1991. Opinion polls suggest that identification with 'England' is as strong as identification with 'Britain' (MORI *Socioconsult*, September 1994), but that the Welsh, and even more so the Scots, are more likely to feel more Welsh – or Scots – than British, while a higher proportion of the English are more likely to feel equally English and British (*Scottish Public Opinion*, MORI, Edinburgh, September 1995) and *Scotsman*, 11 September 1995.
7 Tony Blair, 'Speech to the *Time* Magazine Distinguished Speakers' Dinner', 30 November 1995. Visiting Scotland a week later, he told the Glasgow *Herald* that New Labour stood for 'a New Union', *Herald*, 8 December 1995.
8 Will Hutton, *The State We're In*, Jonathan Cape, London 1995; see also Neal Ascherson, *Games With Shadows*, Radius, London 1988.
9 Aneurin Bevan, *In Place of Fear*, Heinemann, Surrey 1952.
10 *Hansard*, 9 February 1948.
11 Quoted in Philip Williams, *Hugh Gaitskell*, OUP, Oxford 1982. For responses, see Tom Nairn, *The Left Against Europe?* Penguin, London 1973, and Raymond Williams, 'The Culture of Nations' in *Towards 2000*, Penguin 1983.
12 Neil Kinnock, quoted in Robert Harris, *The Making of Neil Kinnock*, Faber, London 1982.
13 See for example, Eric Hobsbawm, 'Falklands Fallout' and Robert Gray 'The Falklands Factor' in Stuart Hall and Martin Jacques (eds), *The Politics of Thatcherism*, Lawrence & Wishart, London 1983; only Tom Nairn in the

same volume, 'Britain's living legacy' and Anthony Barnett, *Iron Britannia*, Allison and Busby, London 1982 provided a more structural approach.

14 Raphael Samuel, Preface to *Patriotism*, Vol 1, Routledge, London 1989. Neal Ascherson makes a similar point: Prospect, May 1996.

15 Bernard Crick 'An Englishman considers his passport', *Political Thoughts and Polemics*, Edinburgh University Press, Edinburgh 1990 and 'The English and the British' in Crick (ed), *National Identities*, Blackwell, Oxford 1991; Beatrix Campbell 'Recline and Fall', *New Statesman & Society*, 30 September 1994; Billy Bragg, 'England made me too' in Anthony Barnett (ed), *The Power and the Throne*, Vintage, London 1994 and 'Looking for a New England' in *New Statesman & Society*, 17 March 1995; also 'Billy Bragg Among the British', BBC Radio Four, 10, 17 and 24 January 1995; special issue of *New Statesman & Society*, 6 March 1995; Dennis Potter, *An interview with Dennis Potter*, Channel Four Television, London 1994; and Neil Spencer's interview with the English folk singer Liza Carthy, 'Folk springs eternal', *Observer*, 4 February 1996.

16 See David McCrone *et al*, *Scotland The Brand*, EUP, Edinburgh 1995; J. Geraint Jenkins, *Getting Yesterday Right*, University of Wales Press, 1992; G. Rosie, 'Museumry and the Heritage Industry' in Ian Donnachie and Christopher Whatley (ed.), *The Manufacture of Scottish History*, Polygon, Edinburgh 1992; Hewison, *op.cit.*

17 Jack Straw, 'Reclaiming the Flag' in *New Statesman & Society*, 6 March 1995.

18 Kim Howells, 'Identity: Real or unreal', *Welsh Agenda*, August 1995.

19 Philip Dodd, *The Battle over Britain*, Demos, London 1995. Anyone who doubts this should re-read Tony Benn's introduction to Tony Benn (ed), *Writings on the Wall*, Faber, London 1984.

20 Tom Nairn, *The Enchanted Glass*, Radius, London 1988.

21 Billy Bragg, 'Looking for a New England', *New Statesman & Society*, 17 March 1995.

22 E.P. Thompson, *The Making of the English Working Class*, Penguin, London 1975; Bill Schwarz, 'The People in History', *Making Histories*, Hutchinson, London 1982; David Eastwood, 'E.P. Thompson, Britain and the French Revolution', *History Workshop Journal*, 39, Spring 1995; Raphael Samuel, *A History Workshop Collecteana 1967–91*, HWJ, Oxford 1991; Michael Kenny, *The First New Left*, Lawrence & Wishart, London 1995.

23 Perry Anderson, 'Origins of the Present Crisis' and Tom Nairn, 'The Nature of the Labour Party' in *Towards Socialism*, Fontana, London 1965; Perry Anderson, 'Components of the National Culture', in *Student Power*, Penguin, Harmondsworth 1969; E.P. Thompson, 'The Peculiarities of the English' in *The Poverty of Theory*, Merlin, 1979; see also Raphael Samuel (ed), *People's History and Socialist Theory*, Routledge, London 1981.

24 Stuart Hall *et al*, *Policing the Crisis*, MacMillan, Basingstoke 1978.

25 Wright, *op.cit.*; Paul Gilroy, *There ain't no black in the Union Jack*, Routledge, London 1992.

26 Hall's scene-setting essay 'The Great Moving Right Show', *Marxism Today*, January 1979, made no mention of the devolution debates then

fiercely underway in Wales and Scotland; see also Richard Johnson, 'Barrington Moore, Perry Anderson and English Social Development' in Stuart Hall *et al*, *Culture, Media, Language*, Hutchinson, London 1980, and Tom Nairn's commentary on this in *The Enchanted Glass*, Radius, London 1988. Neal Ascherson has also noted the linkages between these movements: 'The state we've been in for fifty years and how a book could change it', *Independent on Sunday*, 4 February 1996.

27 Anthony Barnett, 'The Empire State', in Anthony Barnett (ed), *The Power and the Throne*, Vintage, London 1994.

28 J.P. Mackintosh, *The Government and Politics of Britain*, Hutchinson, London 1977 and J.P. Mackintosh, *The Devolution of Power*, Penguin, Harmondsworth 1968; David Marquand, *The Progressive Dilemma*, Heinemann, London 1991; David Marquand, *The Unprincipled Society*, Cape, London 1988.

29 Raphael Samuel, 'British Dimensions: Four Nations History', *History Workshop Journal*, 40, Oxford, Autumn 1995.

30 Tom Nairn, 'Introduction' to the Second Edition, *The Enchanted Glass*, Vintage, London 1994.

31 Linda Colley, *Britons*, Yale, London 1992.

32 Osmond, *op.cit.*

33 Wright, *op.cit.*

34 Tom Nairn, *The Break-up of Britain*, Verso, London 1981.

35 Patrick Wright, *op.cit.*

36 Paul Gilroy, *op.cit.*

37 Stephen Daniels, *Fields of Vision*, Polity, Cambridge 1994.

38 Raymond Williams, 'Wales and England' in John Osmond (ed), *op.cit.*

39 Linda Colley, 'These Islands Now', BBC Radio 3, 8 July 1995. Robert Crawford makes a similar point about Scottishness (*Scotland on Sunday*, 7 January 1996).

40 Stephen Fielding, Paul Thompson, Nick Tiratsoo, *England Arise!*, M.U.P., London 1995.

41 Raymond Williams 'Decentralism and the Politics of Place' in *Resources of Hope*, Verso, London 1989; K.O. Morgan, *Wales in British Politics*, Welsh University Press, Cardiff 1963.

42 Dodd, *op.cit.* See also D.J. Taylor, 'A few cheers for England', *Guardian*, 5 January 1995.

43 Hutton, *op.cit.*

44 Paul Gilroy, *The Black Atlantic*, Verso, London 1993.

45 Linda Colley, *Britons, op.cit.*

46 Paul Gilroy, *Small Acts*, Serpents Tail, London 1993.

47 On 'The Disunited Kingdom', *BBC Radio Four*, 21 October 1995.

48 Tony Blair, Speech to *Time* magazine dinner, *op.cit.*

49 Tony Blair, Speech in Bournemouth, February 1995.

50 Andrew Adonis 'England: The West's One-Party State', *Financial Times*, 30/31 July 1994.

51 *Daily Telegraph*, 8 September 1995.

52 Peter Riddell, *The Times*, 7 August 1995.

53 Anne Showstack Sassoon, 'Equality and Difference' in David MacLellan

and Sean Sayers (eds), *Socialism and Democracy*, Macmillan, Basingstoke 1991.

54 David Marquand and Tony Wright, 'Engaging the Eggheads', *Guardian*, 11 December 1995.

55 *Western Mail*, 19 November 1994.

56 *Devolution – The English Dimension*, HMSO, 1976.

57 David Dimbleby, 'The Disunited Kingdom', BBC Radio Four, 23 September–21 October 1995; 'Don't forget English views, says Dimbleby', *Herald*, 22 September 1995; David Dimbleby, 'Scotland? It's one of England's colonies', *Daily Telegraph*, 22 September 1995. See also, Boris Johnson, 'Sauce for the Scots is sauce for the English too', *Daily Telegraph*, 14 December 1995.

58 Blair, Speech to *Time*, *op.cit*. This manuscript was completed months before Labour's plans for referendums in Wales and Scotland were announced.

59 *A Choice for England – A consultation paper on Labour's plans for English regional government* (Labour Party, London, July 1995). See also Stephen Tindale, *Devolution on Demand – options for the English regions and London*, IPPR, London, May 1995.

60 Sarah Hogg and Jonathan Hill, *Too Close to Call*, Little, Brown and Co, London 1995.

61 *The Times*, 3 December 1994.

62 'The Disunited Kingdom' *op.cit*.; Iain McWhirter, 'Nationhood: a counter in the electoral game', *Observer*, 10 September 1995. The beef war happened too late for this manuscript.

63 Speeches by Ministers at the 1995 Conservative Party Conference.

64 See *Daily Mail*, 18 July 1995; Suzanne Moore, 'Flying the Flag of convenience', *Guardian*, 20 July 1995; *Independent on Sunday*, 23 July 1995; *Daily Telegraph*, 19 September 1995; *Sunday Telegraph* leader 'Heroic Virtues', 24 September 1995.

65 David Marquand, *Guardian*, 'Flagging Fortunes' 5 July 1995.

66 Dafydd Elis-Thomas, 'How many identities', *Welsh Agenda*, August 1995.

67 Raymond Williams, in Osmond, *op.cit*.

68 Gwyn A.Williams, 'When was Wales', in *The Welsh in their History*, Croom Helm, Kent 1982.

69 Raphael Samuel, *op.cit*.

70 Kenny Farquharson, 'Tactical moves to put the brakes on Britain's break-up', *Scotland on Sunday*, 5 November 1995. For an alternative view, see Melvyn Bragg, 'Patriot Games', *Observer*, 7 January 1996.

71 Colley, *Britons*, *op.cit*.

72 Peter Kellner, *Sunday Times*, 8 October 1995.

73 Martin Kettle, *Guardian*, 7 October 1995.

74 Neal Ascherson, *Independent on Sunday*, 8 October 1995.

BEYOND PESSIMISM OF THE INTELLECT: AGENDAS FOR SOCIAL JUSTICE AND CHANGE
Anne Showstack Sassoon

> Cynics inside the Labour Party and in abundance beyond in the media like to prove their independence and powers of professional scepticism by scoffing ... to display enthusiasm, interest or understanding is to depart from the unwritten code. All politicians are knaves and propagandists; all their ideas are confused, inadequate or boil down to the same old left/right divide in the end.[1]

In the absence of understanding clearly the complex analysis which lies at the bottom of the new directions of so much new Labour policy, most critics do not have much more than soundbites. This reflects the enormous gap which exists between policy announcements and a more profound understanding of the analysis which underpins them. Consequently, the desire for change easily turns into diffidence and suspicion that what is being advocated is just electoral calculation. Yet it is also obvious that much of the country has been impressed by Blair's leadership of the party and transformation of Labour's policy agenda. The negativity of so many academics, journalists, pressure group campaigners and others on the left is therefore all the more striking.

Prior to putting the notion of a stakeholder society on the agenda in early 1996, Blair reflected on the widespread suspicion and dismissal of his ideas as a move to the right. An interview with him in the *Observer* just before the 1995 Labour Party conference, noted that,

> One of the remaining problems is to persuade the liberal-left

intelligentsia ... to abandon their pessimism of the intellect and adopt some optimism of the will. 'There (is) a very great defeatism that (grips) the left intelligentsia. If I can put it politely, there is a distinction between the *Guardian-Observer* left and what I would call the broader Labour supporters in the country ... What I would like to see more of on the left is genuine intellectual debate.'[2]

This was referring to the oft-quoted phrase which Antonio Gramsci, the Italian Marxist, used on the masthead of *l'Ordine Nuovo*, the radical newspaper he edited in Turin after the first world war.[3] The original phrase, 'pessimism of the intellect, optimism of the will', meant that clear, hard-headed analysis, undistorted by any illusions, had to inform the determination to make the world a better place. But it also meant that realism on its own without political will can lead to resignation to the status quo.

SHAPING CHANGE

The roots of this dialectic between human knowledge and the capacity to intervene in nature can, of course, be traced all the way back to the Greeks. It is certainly found in Machiavelli's depiction of the interplay between princely 'virtù', or what we might today call leadership skills, on the one hand, and 'fortuna' or chance, on the other. In *The Prince* Machiavelli joins incisive analysis of the attributes needed by a political leader to overcome the chaos existing in the Italian peninsula to a passionate plea for a united Italy. It is no accident that later, writing in a fascist prison in the 1930s, Gramsci builds on this Italian tradition and uses the term 'Modern Prince' to challenge Mussolini's claim to follow in the footsteps of Machiavelli's Prince, and to be the heir of the Risorgimento, as the *duce*, or the leader who can complete Italy's imperfect unification and modernise Italian society.

In *The Prison Notebooks* Gramsci writes that modern society and twentieth century politics are so complex that no one individual could provide the leadership needed to transform society. The Modern Prince could only consist in a political party able to forge a collective will to transform society in a progressive direction.[4] Gramsci describes a particular kind of party and politics capable of analysing social and historical development as it reaches out to learn from the experiences of the widest possible cross-section of society and from what we would now call the cutting edge of socio-economic change. On the basis of what is *possible* and what is *necessary*, the aim is to develop a strategy to achieve what is *desirable*, and in so doing provide a focus for gaining widespread and continuous popular consent.[5] Whereas Lenin was most concerned to establish doctrinal correctness and party discipline,[6] Gramsci was much more worried about political isolation when a party loses touch with reality and when unity becomes purely mechanical.[7]

The first key to retaining consent to a party's policies was to make sure that they reflected the real needs of the vast majority as they actually lived and not as some political ideology or political force wished that they did.[8] This was why the party had to be deeply rooted in the society. Secondly, these policies could only succeed if they were based on the understanding that historical development was not a mechanical, inevitable, mystical process. Rather, it was the product of human activity. But neither was it within the control of any single political force. Referring again to Machiavelli, Gramsci examines the complex relationship between analysis of the situation confronting a political organisation – a reality in which, he argues, the aims of that organisation are themselves an element – and the attempt to transform that reality in line with new political priorities to influence the direction of change.[9]

Historical change could not be stopped, but it did provide opportunities for progressive politics as it brought both advances and losses. That was the lesson Gramsci drew from the impossibility of simply opposing one of the major challenges of his period, what he called Fordism, that is, assembly line production as developed by Henry Ford, and the 'scientific management' of Frederick Taylor. Some American trade unions and, indeed, some conservative elements in Europe, had tried to oppose these trends but had been defeated. Nor, for a progressive politics, was it possible simply to endorse the productive potential of these developments as representing 'progress' and 'rationality' as did a wide range of people from the fascist right to the Bolshevik left.[10] Any progressive potential could only be fulfilled by a fundamental re-think about the enhancement of the skills and knowledge of the majority of the population. This was the pre-condition for a creative contribution to a democratic discussion about the uses to which expertise and technological advancement could be put in relation to a progressive political agenda.[11]

Just as Gramsci himself was clear that Lenin and the Russian

Revolution provided no model for the West European Left,[12] much of Gramsci's writing is not relevant for us today. What still is absolutely relevant, however, is Gramsci's special insistence on the need to base politics on a clear understanding of the nature of change and the experiences of the widest possible sections of the population in order to unite people and to earn their support for a progressive transformation of society. This is what Gramsci meant by hegemonic politics.

Fortunately, our situation today is quite different from the traumatic post-World War I period. However, we are living through major political, social and economic transformations that are leading to a level of political confusion unprecedented in recent times. As the century ends, it is getting harder and harder to determine what is progressive and what is not. How often today the word 'left' seems to connote 'leftover' or indeed at times reactionary. This is meant in the historical, post-French Revolution sense of reacting to a major change by looking backward to an *ancien régime*. On the other hand, claims by the 'right' to be radical, for all the changes which have been initiated, are hardly borne out, at least if we understand the word as a fundamental reorientation of society.[13] As Ross McKibbin has commented in the *London Review of Books*, Conservative government policies have in fact preserved significant aspects of British society, for example, the Beveridge welfare state, but 'in an utterly degraded form'.[14] There is no shame, then, in feeling anxious because the old goal posts not only keep moving, but the boundaries of the political football pitch seem so blurred.

SOCIAL JUSTICE IN A CHANGED WORLD

Indeed, anxiety and confusion have marked the reception given to the most ambitious attempt since Beveridge to redefine and to reorganise provision for the social and economic well-being of the British people, Labour's Commission on Social Justice Report.[15] 'The size of the problem,' the report states in the introduction, is so great that there is 'no "quick fix", for the UK's difficulties'.

> If politicians or others suggest that there is, no one should believe them
> … Our world is so different from that which William Beveridge
> addressed fifty years ago, and it is now changing so fast, that there is no
> way in which the prescriptions that suited an earlier time can merely be

renewed, however much goodwill, money or technical sophistication one might hope to call up in their support.[16]

Echoed subsequently in Blair's idea of a stakeholder society, the report maintains that in addition to social justice being an ideal in its own right,

> Economic success requires a greater measure of social justice ... Squalor and crime carry enormous economic as well as social costs; unemployment uses resources simply to sustain people who might sustain themselves and contribute to the economy ... Social justice stands against fanatics of the market economy, who forget that a market is a social reality which itself requires trust, order, goodwill and other forms of support ... Social justice does indeed attend to the needy ... but in doing so it can be an enabling force for everybody ... something that society requires because everyone's quality of life is dependent in part on a high degree of social well-being. This conclusion, that social justice is not simply a moral ideal but an economic necessity, is at the heart of this report.[17]

The dimensions of the change which the report's perspective depicts and the dramatic nature of the UK's predicament which it describes require a leap of imagination to reformulate the very terms of the debate. This has confounded people and led to no little anxiety. The UK's problems, it argues, 'are not simply the product of Conservative mistakes. The causes reach back well before the onset of the Conservative administration in 1979, and they will not be tackled by trying to recreate the country that existed before that ... The reality was that the foundations of the post-war settlement had been destroyed by national and international change the tragedy of the 1960s and 1970s was that the Left, which had created the successful post-war settlement, failed to come to terms with change 'the Right, which grasped the need for change, failed to understand what was really needed.'[18]

Agreeing with the statement made to the Commission by Bill Morris, General Secretary of the Transport and General Workers' Union, that 'many of the principles on which the post-war welfare state was based still hold good today,' the report argues that:

> If the values of the welfare state – opportunities, security, responsibility – are to have real meaning in the future, then they will require new

institutions and policies to give them practical effect. We have no option but to engage with the three great revolutions – economic, social, and political – which are changing our lives, and those of people in every other industrialised country.[19]

The UK has been left behind by the global economic revolution of 'finance, competition, skill and technology', while neither government nor employers have caught up with the social revolution which has taken place 'of women's life chances, of family structures and of demography', even though 'social change has been faster and gone further in the UK than in most other European countries'. Nor do political institutions escape the challenge, particularly 'the UK's old assumptions of parliamentary sovereignty and ... its growing centralisation of government power.' The political revolution 'involves a fundamental re-orientation of the relationship between those who govern and those who are governed'.[20]

DOUBTS, CONFUSION, AND NEGATIVITY

Reflecting on the period since the publication of the Commission on Social Justice report in October 1994, what is striking in the general response by academics and others on the left, is the negativity of most of it. As Christopher Pierson has written, 'The Commission's Report has faced that mixture of weary cynicism, vested interests and quack cures which seem to greet any attempt at deep-seated welfare reform. It finds itself condemned in just about equal measure for having been both too bold and too timid.'[21]

It would be worthwhile considering some of the reasons for this negativity. It is one thing to feel pessimistic confronting the scenario of economic mismanagement and institutional arteriosclerosis depicted by Will Hutton in *The State We're In*.[22] It is another to give up all hope of influencing change for the better and to mistake the attempt to depict the nature of current trends, in order to ground policy in a clear assessment of the dynamic of contemporary reality and the way millions of people live their lives, with an outright endorsement of those trends.[23] Weary cynicism, or pessimism of the intellect without optimism of the will, leads to defeatism. After all, as Gramsci also argued, the way to undermine the old is to construct the new.[24] But if this optimism of the will is to result in real change, it cannot be based on what we would wish but what we endeavour to construct in the difficult conditions we face, conditions which are not of our choosing. Wishful thinking by another name is ineffectual utopianism.[25]

The problem is determining what is indeed new, and progressive, and how to achieve it. If this cynicism and negativity are understandable, they are ultimately a self-fulfilling prophecy. Valid reasons for being doubting Thomases (and Thomasinas) are certainly not hard to find. There is, of course, the collapse of old certainties in this postmodern, post-fordist, and post-communist yet still socially unjust and violent world. There is also the habit – strongest in academia perhaps, but which, as Will Hutton notes, marks a whole style of polemical debate – of a type of critique which tells us what is wrong but often does little to draw out what is positive or useful in the contributions of others or in policy proposals which do not conform to favoured prescriptions in which individuals have an intellectual, political or professional investment.[26] Here, too, are vested interests of a sort which need to be taken into account, especially as the depth of psychological investment must not be underestimated.

Yet, if this psychological investment is at the root of much of the confusion, perhaps most importantly some of the political messages coming from the Labour Party have been no less confusing, to say the least. Mixed with soundbites, by-election leaflets and comments which seem recycled from the Conservatives' dustbin of black propaganda, are radical policy proposals like abolishing the assisted places scheme and GP fundholding, transforming the House of Lords, establishing a Bill of Rights and a Freedom of Information Act, holding a referendum on proportional representation, providing for Scottish devolution, applying a windfall tax on excessive monopoly profits, signing up for the Social Chapter, legislating for a minimum wage – and the list thankfully goes on.

One possible response to what is being proposed is to play the 'up the ante' political game, where it is considered left-wing to oppose any suggestion for change by raising the stakes. Even those of us who have no interest in participating in this particular game[27] are nonetheless still left with the doubt whether the mixed messages from Labour are intentional. What appear – at least from the soundbites which the media pick up – opportunistic moves to win an election, combine with heartfelt and inspiring ethical commitments together with convincing explanations why an up-to-date and realistic analysis of the world requires a different radical strategy today.[28] The desired effect may be to unbalance the opposition, but the result is very often confusion and the closing down of spaces for constructive criticism.

FEARS AND DESIRES

Beyond this confusion, there are genuine psychological reasons why it is easier to make a negative critique than join in constructing a progressive alternative at the very moment that change seems most possible. On the one hand, there is the fear of loss, and, on the other, the anxiety of having to assume responsibility without being able to blame someone else. The familiar is held onto for dear life, however uncomfortable, be it the memories of long, hard-fought battles, and defeats, or cherished beliefs. We hold onto everything for fear of losing something. It may appear highly contradictory, and both politics and individual psychology are contradictory, but going beyond blaming others for defeat, accepting one's own responsibilities, leaving isolated opposition and joining a majority, and after so many years plunging into the unknown, can feel very dangerous. Worries about losing what we know, however imperfect, for what we do not is quite real. Vested interests are not just material but are the result of psychological and ideological investments as well.

Furthermore, a strategy to dampen down expectations given harsh realities, however politically intelligent in the long run, can easily feed widespread cynicism about any possibility of change today. And yet, reaction to the Social Justice report also reveals an enormous desire to believe that Britain *can* be changed for the better. As one respondent put it, 'At first, I was worried about what would be lost, but then I thought, I would be delighted to live in a country with the kind of provision it argues for.'[29] That person was thinking about, for example, universal nursery provision, the possibility to combine part-time work with part-time benefits, a minimum wage, a Jobs, Education and Training programme to ease the transition into work and between jobs, the right to a minimum second pension with pension contributions guaranteed even when unemployed or not employed from choice, for example, while caring for a child – in short the kind of programmes aimed at eliminating the social exclusion that large sectors of British society suffer at the moment. But what is certain is that unless widespread consent is developed around the kind of fundamental reforms that the report calls for, given the very real difficulties of getting a complex society to shift in new directions, much of its promise will be stillborn, even if it is beginning to show through in many of the Labour Party's policy choices,[30] and even with the most optimistic and determined political will in the world.

BEYOND BEVERIDGE

But developing such active consent will not be easy. The Social Justice report comes out of a very different context than the 1942 Beveridge report. An official government document, the product of a civil service interdepartmental committee with Beveridge the only non-civil servant, Ross McKibbin points out that it had 'an "official" character which raised expectations that it would be implemented.' Discussed widely in the armed forces, 'in many ways, and quite deliberately so, it summed up what the Allies were fighting for.'[31] The Beveridge report was a cornerstone of wartime national unity and encapsulated hopes for the reconstruction of peacetime Britain. As McKibbin so well describes, 'The long queues outside HMSOs; the hurried reprintings; the intensity of public discussion and, to judge by wartime diaries, private discussion as well; the enormous publicity given to Beveridge by the *Mirror*: all contrived to give the report a social centrality inconceivable today.'[32]

Fifty years later the situation was dramatically different when the Commission on Social Justice was set up by John Smith from opposition in the wake of Labour's 1992 general election defeat. Created as an independent, broadly based group, chaired by Sir Gordon Borrie, it was at arms length from the Labour Party and far from effective political power. The difference could hardly be greater than the excitement which greeted Beveridge and the way in which its message was spread and its proposals discussed, although the need was hardly less. The Commission was set up in a moment when the argument for dropping the policy of a minimum wage and for targeting benefits such as child benefit was gaining ground. The question was bound to arise then, and is still relevant – in a period when even the Nordic welfare states, often looked to as providing a model of advance, are facing serious challenges – whether any of the 'principles on which the post-war welfare state was based', referred to by Bill Morris,[33] when Britain itself seemed to many to provide a model internationally,[34] could be adhered to by any party seeking to form a government. The conclusion it came to has to be reiterated: society, and especially its economic performance, cannot do without adequate social provision.

By the time the report was published in the autumn of 1994, after almost two decades of neo-liberal Conservative governments, international economic restructuring and UK decline, and a dramatic increase in social polarisation,[35] the need to go beyond restoration to reconstruction was becoming more and more obvious on the centre left.[36] The Commission on Social Justice report was the most ambitious amongst several important publications from the centre and left of the political spectrum addressed to reconstructing the British welfare state and the economy. Although they vary in perspective and policy prescriptions, their very proliferation is a manifestation of a widespread conviction that it is impossible to go back to the *status quo* from before 1979 nor would it be particularly desirable. There are real differences in perspective, but there are also real points of contact and overlaps both in analysis and prescription. Indeed, James McCormick and Carey Oppenheim argue that far from Labour filling in a blank sheet, there is a broad left-of-centre consensus on which to build.[37] However much this is true, there still remains the fact that as long as debate focuses on details without a wider understanding of the underlying analysis, there is a danger that the opportunity for a radical, progressive reconstruction will be opposed by those who feel the loss of what they know and fear the unknown more than anything else.[38]

A REPORT LITTLE READ AND LESS UNDERSTOOD

The Social Justice report sparked widespread press coverage, but the changes in the Labour Party's Clause Four soon came to dominate debate, and discussion about the report quickly died out. Yet, without the process being very clear to anyone not involved, and without it being the only source, the report's impact is gradually becoming evident in a range of Labour Party policy proposals and pronouncements. But because of its length, wealth of detail, and breadth of scope, going well beyond Beveridge, few Labour Party members have read it. Those who have are faced by a document which steadfastly refuses to be organised into the kind of categories, policy proposals, frames of analysis or concepts which most people are familiar with, and which describes an expansion of choice which is lacking at the moment and which many people find hard to imagine.[39] The report goes well beyond Labour's traditional, and simple, commitment to a redistribution of financial resources, while still highlighting the costs to individuals and to society of increasing poverty. To grasp what is radical in the report requires an investment of time, good faith, hope, and optimism – qualities which far too few people will have.

The report has not been backed by any campaigning organisation, at least until the founding of the Labour Campaign for Social Justice and of the Social Justice Group (a network affiliated to Unions '95 and linked to Democratic Left) more than a year after publication. The negative reaction of sincere doubt, weary cynicism and vested interests noted by Pierson plus backward-looking leftism consequently expanded to fill the political vacuum. As Blair's concept of a stakeholder society begins to fill out,[40] the analysis in the Commission on Social Justice report, even if not cited, has regained a greater prominence. The very desire to get rid of the Tories has tended to silence most outright opposition from the centre and left, but the doubt remains whether most people really understand the radical nature of the changes suggested.

POLITICAL CONVICTION ROOTED IN ANALYSIS

So on what grounds can it be argued that this report is radical, progressive, and deserving of support? First, it puts women at the very centre of its analysis and their life chances at the core of its proposals. We are well beyond tokenism here.[41] Secondly, it puts overcoming poverty and providing the conditions to achieve greater social justice at the very top of the agenda. And thirdly, it is convincing because of its mode of arguing from the grain of change that it is possible to influence it for the better. It all adds up to a fundamental and welcome shift in perspective. Its ambition is no less than to refound the welfare state in Britain considered in a world perspective, posing questions for the next two decades. It is a radical document not just because of its concerns, but because of its mode of analysis: it joins pessimism of the intellect with optimism of the will. It goes well beyond Labourism where the old left/right divide so often ran between grand rhetoric and resigned pragmatism covered with a gloss of moralism. With few exceptions Labour programmes, whether influenced by the Labour left or the right, have never been derived from an analysis of contemporary trends in order to shape the future. What is emerging here is an attempt to ground conviction in analysis. The Social Justice report has contributed to that process.

A NEW DEAL FOR WOMEN

The debate has certainly come a long way since the early 1980s when *Women and the State*[42] was published. At that time very few analysts focused on the dramatic social changes taking place as more and more women were entering formal, paid work at the same time as having major family responsibilities, or on the implications of these changes for the organisation of the welfare state, in the broad sense, the world of work, and the household – all of which still assumed the primacy of a male-breadwinner.[43] Today all these spheres still continue largely to operate according to a logic which ignores the fact that very few women are full-time housewives for more than a short period in their lives, and that most households depend fundamentally on their income from paid jobs to keep above the poverty line.[44] That is, major social institutions operate in a way which is in contradiction with the way millions of people in fact live. One of the main reasons the Social Justice report is so progressive is that it defines the social revolution which has been taking place, above all, with regard to 'women's life chances, family structures and demography.'[45] Indeed, the preconditions for eliminating poverty and transforming the economy are organically linked in the report to establishing what has been called in the Nordic countries and elsewhere a new gender contract[46] in which the relationship between work and family needs changes, and in which women, and men, are given the possibility to live more flexible and productive lives with greater freedom of choice and fewer constraints.

More concretely, to give just one example, counting part-time work for pensions and other benefits without penalising the partners of the unemployed, backed by a minimum wage and guarantees of employees' rights, would especially help women and their families.[47] Analysing trends does not mean endorsing them, but understanding change is the pre-condition for developing policies to influence outcomes for the better. The report does not advocate part-time work. Rather, it recognises that part-time work is convenient for many people at different times in their lives.[48] As it argues,

> Full employment in a modern economy must recognise that, for both men and women, the world of work has changed fundamentally. In the 1950s, full employment involved full-time, life-time employment for men; in the 1990s and beyond, it will involve for both men and women frequent changes of occupation, part-time as well as full-time work,

self-employment as well as employment, time spent caring for children or elderly relatives (as well as or instead of employment) and periods spent in further education and training. Forty years ago the typical worker was a man working full-time in industry; today the typical worker is increasingly likely to be a women working part-time in a service job. Already, there are more people in Britain employed as childcare-workers than as carworkers.[49]

Far from endorsing those labour market trends and management strategies which make part-time work a synonym for insecurity, and flexibility the equivalent of marginalisation, or those social policies which encourage some households to be 'work rich' with two, exhausted, partners in employment, and others kept 'work poor' because benefits are withdrawn if either works even part-time, the report describes a series of inter-related policies which will facilitate women, and men, to combine family, education and training, and paid work in ways which suit new living patterns. For example, an immediate priority is placed on free, universal nursery education, which is considered the 'first goal' of investment,[50] and on a learning bank to be drawn upon over the life cycle.[51] Justice across genders, a greater contribution by men to household responsibilities, minimising the current loss to the economy and society more generally of women's skills, better educational opportunities for all social groups at different ages are some of the aims of the report. These are connected to its radical perspective in arguing for a redistribution of time and not just money between the genders and over the life cycle and the clear influence of feminist debates on social policy, economic organisation and citizenship.

TOWARDS A SOCIAL STRATEGY OF INCLUSION

The report's damning critique of poverty and of the increasing inequalities in British society has contributed to putting social exclusion back at the centre of the political agenda. Describing the state of Britain, it explains:

> In January 1994, a 28-year-old Birmingham engineer sent us his payslip. He earns £2.50 an hour – £101 a week. 'I am scared to put the heating on as I would not be able to afford the electricity bill,' he told us. 'Please do

not tell my employer I wrote to you as I would be straight on the dole'
... For those at the top, these are the best of times. For those at the
bottom, horizons are even narrower than they were a decade ago and the
gap between rich and poor is greater than at any time since the 1930s.
For most people – those in the middle – insecurity and anxiety are rife.
Comparison with the past is important ... But the real comparison – the
comparison to shock anyone concerned with the future of this country –
is the one between what we are and what we have it in ourselves to
become, the gap between potential and performance. Most people in this
country are doing less well than they want to and less well than they
could, if only they were able to learn more, work more productively (or
work at all), live more safely, more securely and more healthily. Too
often, opportunities are distributed not on the basis of ability, but on the
basis of ability to pay; not on who you are but who your parents were;
not on the basis of merit, but on grounds of race or gender.[52]

The fact that it speaks in the language of inclusion, considering the
needs of the vast majority of the population, without losing sight of the
situation of those who are excluded, is one of the main features which
recommends its approach. Another is the conviction that expectations
can and must be raised. 'Doing better than we used to is not good
enough when (other countries) set their sights far higher.'[53] The report
talks about a flexible, intelligent welfare state to help people into work
and to enable individuals to change jobs 'upwards' rather than be
trapped in low skill, low pay jobs or no jobs. The object is not to
eliminate uncertainty, which is inevitable, but insecurity, deskilling
and long term unemployment.

In an argument now familiar on both sides of the Atlantic, education
and training, understood widely over the life cycle, are presented as the
necessary pre-condition, if not guarantee, of economic regeneration.[54]
This flies in the face of Tory arguments that the way forward consists
in keeping wages down and in preserving the kind of labour market
flexibility which encourages low investment in skills and suits the
needs of poor employers rather than those who work. Indeed, the
report turns the usual argument on its head: it maintains that social
justice is a prerequisite for economic success.[55]

Throughout the Social Justice report there is a strong argument for
universalism with redistributive consequences. It is important to avoid
confusion here by differentiating between targeting and means-testing.
To take the example of child benefit, if every mother has the right to a

considerably higher child allowance than at present, as the report strongly argues she should, taxing that allowance for those earning at the higher rate signifies targeting the affluent, within universal provision, without a means test for the poor as usually understood. All mothers would receive the same, higher child benefit, but the affluent would repay a proportion as part of the existing taxation system, without increasing costs in any significant way in administration. The same is true of the right to a second, 'topping up' pension for those people whose pension provision falls below a certain level, most likely because they do not have an occupational pension, which would be of particular benefit to women, although the report suggests different ways of calculating this, and also applies to a graduate tax for those earning above a certain amount.[56]

In fact, with regards to redistribution, the report is much more ambitious than the usual definition which relies so heavily on higher income tax. Much can be achieved, it argues, from changes in existing allowances; for example phasing out mortgage tax relief and the married couple's allowances would release, it is estimated, £9 billion to increase substantially child benefit and to help to provide for a second pension, without raising a penny on income taxes, while a minimum wage and facilitating women's contribution to household incomes would help to cut down on the *de facto* welfare subsidies given to poor employers who pay low wages.

The report follows best Nordic practice in linking labour market strategies with family policy.[57] It expands our horizons and demands a new way of thinking as it takes into account life cycle perspectives for women and men to facilitate a better fit between individual and family needs for employment, for care work, and education and training when the likelihood of lifelong, full-time, family wage male employment has almost disappeared. In short, the report argues that a radical rethink is necessary, that tinkering is inadvisable, and a return to the past neither possible nor desirable, since it would be inadequate for today's needs.

There are, of course, problems. More emphasis could have been placed on the need to provide for those who are not able to undertake paid work, for example, the severely disabled.[58] Those not in waged work must be part of the included. The report is not perfect. Racism is named as one of the major evils to be eliminated without being given due prominence. Some issues are fudged. There are some contradictions between helping people now and building for the future. As Ruth Lister writes, 'A new Labour government, committed to social justice and the extension of citizenship, will need to combine the kind of long-term structural strategy proposed by the Commission with some immediate help for those who have been the main victims of over a decade of redistribution from the poor to the rich.'[59]

More fundamentally, the fact that what is presented is a complex package, not a political manifesto, leads to the question of where to start and in what order. Although some things are clear priorities, if Labour chooses to pick some parts but not others, the outcomes may well not be the progressive ones hoped for. What is required is a long time span, at least fifteen years, and the question arises how to organise and maintain consent around such a programme of reform, and how to keep a government in power devoted to this kind of change. This, of course, necessitates consent across a larger section of the population than the Labour Party has traditionally achieved, at least without the horrific experience of a world war to galvanize support. The implication that the electoral system should be changed to some form of proportional representation to allow a more pluralistic form of government is not spelt out. And finally the economic perspective leads to the question of how an expanding economy in Europe can be achieved, and which policies should be pursued to ensure that enough jobs are created or if not created quickly enough, that the door is left open to some type of guaranteed income outside the labour market.[60]

There have been several critiques by political philosophers of the definition of social justice in the report, and the argument in it that those inequalities which are unjust (implying that some are), should where possible be eliminated, suggesting that the elimination of inequality is to some extent contingent on what can be achieved. Certainly there is an ongoing discussion to be had about the conditions which are necessary to bring about greater social justice.[61] But it is desperately short-sighted to miss the contribution the report makes to opening up a wider discussion about social justice because it does not in the abstract provide a perfect definition. These questions are complex in the extreme.[62] One thing is certain, the radical perspectives in the report will never come to fruition unless current cynicism and pessimism are undermined by different narratives of what is possible and needed.

This, then, is an invitation to engage in a much more adventurous and imaginative debate than has taken place so far. The report is aimed at all those who are ill served as things are and who deserve something better, an attempt at hegemonic politics if there ever was one. What is at stake are not just documents or detailed policy proposals, but fundamental questions about how the future can be influenced and how we determine what is worth fighting for, what is feasible, and how to achieve it. In short, how we can construct a version of change which is progressive: for change there will be, as sure as death and taxes. Analysis of society as it *is*, in an international context, for any decent social science or political strategy, can help us to think about what it might be, no less today than for Marx or Gramsci. That is precisely what the report sets out to do.

Certainly many people, inside the Labour Party, including many on the Labour backbenches, and likely some also on the frontbench, remain to be convinced about the validity of the analysis and the policy conclusions to be drawn from it. Even more importantly there is still much work to do to make the analysis intelligible, the policy conclusions acceptable, and the conviction convincing to the country at large. We must not underestimate how difficult it is to convey policy, let alone complex analysis, to those inside or outside the Labour Party, or how necessary for that analysis to exist in dialogue with the widest possible range of ideas and experiences. The Labour Party does not have a tradition of debating the rationale of policy, as opposed to resolutions. It cannot do it on its own inside or outside Parliament. But it cannot do without such a debate either. Tony Blair may talk in terms of common purpose rather than collective will but what is required is a widespread understanding of the nature of the dilemmas facing Britain in order to construct a better place in which to live. The hope, desperation and excitement ensuing from a change of government might make it possible to forge a new hegemony, a widespread consent which will inevitably be full of contradictions and diversity, but willing to unite around a project to renew Britain. We need space, tolerance and acceptance of constructive criticism, to keep people on board, to maintain consent, to construct a hegemonic politics.

As the Commission on Social Justice report argues:

> Ours is a long term strategy, designed not to amend a few policies but to set a new direction. That is what people want, and that is what the country needs. But the fact that change will take a long time does not mean that there is time to spare; it means that we have to get on with it. Ours is a call for urgent action ... When the challenge is so urgent, our

timescale of ten to fifteen years may seem too long. Imagine, however, that fifteen years ago, government had determined to invest the revenues from North Sea Oil in the long-term development of the UK economy; that ten years ago, it had embarked upon a programme to expand nursery education; that a Jobs, Education and Training programme to prevent long-term unemployment had been initiated five years ago, and a welfare-to-work reform was already under way. We would not be living in Utopia, but this would already be a very different country. What we need from government now is willingness to help develop a political and economic culture in which long-term strategies can flourish.[63]

REFERENCES

1 Will Hutton, 'Raising the Stakes', in the *Guardian*, Wednesday 17 January 1996, pG2. This chapter is an expanded version of my inaugural lecture as Professor of Politics, Kingston University, Kingston upon Thames, 26 October 1995. I would like to thank Geoff Andrews, Paul Auerbach,Kate Crehan, Nina Fishman, Jane Lewis, James McCormick, Alan MacDougall, Mark Perryman, Ann Sedley, Birte Siim, Ken Spours, Stuart Wilks, and Michael Young for comments and help.

2 Interview with Andrew Jaspan and Sarah Baxter in the *Observer Review*, Sunday 10 September 1995, p2.

3 See Antonio Gramsci, *Selections from Political Writings, 1910–20*, Lawrence & Wishart, London 1977.

4 Gramsci refers to a piece written by Mussolini in the early 1920s, *Prelude to Machiavelli*. Antonio Gramsci, *Selections from the Prison Notebooks*, Lawrence & Wishart, London 1971, p276. See *op.cit.* pp125-143, pp169-175, 247-252, 266-267, and 413-414 for further references. For a much fuller discussion see Benedetto Fontana, *Hegemony and Power. On the Relationship between Gramsci and Machiavelli*, University of Minnesota Press, Minneapolis 1993.

5 Antonio Gramsci, *Selections from the Prison Notebooks*, *op.cit.*, p171.

6 The classic statement is found in 'What is to be Done?', in *Selected Works*, Foreign Languages Publishing House, Moscow 1946.

7 He writes that one 'of the most important questions concerning the political party (is)the party's capacity to react against force of habit, against the tendency to become mummified and anachronistic ... Parties ... are not always capable of adapting themselves to new tasks and to new epochs ...' Antonio Gramsci, *Selections from the Prison Notebooks*, *op.cit.*, p211. I have a fuller discussion of these themes in Anne Showstack Sassoon, *Gramsci's Politics*, second edition, Hutchinson, London 1987.

8 See, for example, his criticism of the inability of the 'left' in the Italian Risorgimento to develop a programme reflecting popular demands. See Antonio Gramsci, *Selections from the Prison Notebooks*, *op.cit.*, p61 and

p168.

9 See Antonio Gramsci, *Selections from the Prison Notebooks*, *op.cit.*, pp169-172. The question, he writes, 'is one ... of seeing whether what "ought to be" is arbitrary or necessary; whether it is concrete will on the one hand or idle fancy, yearning, daydream on the other. The active politician is a creator, an initiator; but he (sic) neither creates from nothing nor does he move in the turbid void of his own desires and dreams. He bases himself on effective reality...to dominate and transcend it (or to contribute to this).' *op.cit.* p172.

10 See 'Americanism and Fordism' in Antonio Gramsci, *Selections from the Prison Notebooks*, *op.cit.*, pp277-318.

11 See Ken Spours and Michael Young, 'Beyond Vocationalism' in *British Journal of Education and Work*. vol. 2, no. 2, 1988, and Michael Young, 'A Curriculum for the 21st Century: Towards a New Basis for Overcoming Academic/Vocational Divisions' in *British Journal of Educational Studies*, vol 40, no. 3, 1993.

12 See Antonio Gramsci, *Selections from the Prison Notebooks*, *op.cit.* pp237-238 and Anne Showstack Sassoon, *op.cit.*, p93.

13 Radical is defined as 'Original, fundamental; reaching to the center or ultimate source; affecting the vital principle or principles; hence thoroughgoing; extreme.' *Webster's New Collegiate Dictionary*, G. & C. Merriam Publishers, Springfield, Mass., U.S.A. 1961.

14 Ross McKibbin, 'On the Defensive – Ross McKibbin Asks Who's Afraid of the Borrie Report, And Gets a Surprising Answer', in *The London Review of Books*, 26 January 1995, p7.

15 Commission on Social Justice, *Social Justice*, Vintage, London 1994 (*CSJ*).

16 *CSJ*, p16. The Commission's terms of reference were: 'To consider the principles of social justice and their application to the economic well-being of individuals and the community; to examine the relationship between social justice and other goals, including economic competitiveness and prosperity; to probe the changes in social and economic life over the last fifty years, and the failure of public policy to reflect them adequately; and to survey the changes that are likely in the foreseeable future, and the demands that they will place on government; to analyse public policies, particularly in the fields of employment, taxation and social welfare, which could enable every individual to live free from want and to enjoy the fullest possible social and economic opportunities; and to examine the contribution which such policies could make to the creation of a fairer and more just society.' *op.cit*, p412.

17 *CSJ*, pp18-19. In his Singapore speech Blair argued, 'The implications of creating a Stakeholder Economy are profound. They mean a commitment by government to tackle long term and structural unemployment. The development of an underclass of people, cut off from society's mainstream, living often in poverty, the black economy, crime and family instability is a moral and economic evil. Most Western economies suffer from it. It is wrong, and unnecessary, and incidentally, very costly ... The Stakeholder Economy has a Stakeholder Welfare system. By that I mean that the system will only flourish in its aims of promoting security and opportunity across

the life-cycle if it holds the commitment of the whole population, rich and poor. This requires that everyone has a stake'. Press release, Monday, 8 January 1996. See also Tony Blair, 'A Stakeholder Society', in *Fabian Review*, vol. 108, no. 1, February. 1996.

18 *CSJ*, pp62-4.
19 *CSJ*, p64.
20 *CSJ*, pp3. For a summary of each 'revolution', see p64, p77, and p84.
21 Christopher Pierson, 'Doing Social Justice: the Case of the Borrie Commission,' in *Contemporary Political Studies*, vol.2, no. 2, 1995, p240.
22 Will Hutton, *The State We're In*, 2nd. ed., Vintage, London 1996.
23 See the letter from Jim McCormick and Carey Oppenheim in response to John Pilger's article, both cited in note 21 above. For just a few examples of critiques: G.A. Cohen, 'Back to Socialist Basics', *New Left Review*, no.207, September/October 1994 (in response to the Commission on Social Justice discussion documents, 'The Justice Gap' and 'Social Justice in a Changing World' published prior to the report, London: IPPR, 1993); Editorial, 'Labour's Currant Bun', *New Statesman & Society*, 28 October 1994; Ian Aitkin, 'Borrie Ducks Commission to Explore', *New Statesman & Society*, 11 November 1994, p.12; David Purdy, 'Commission Opts for Caution', *New Times*, 12 November 1994, pp.6-7; Anthony Arblaster, 'Don't Follow the Tory Agenda', *Red Pepper*, December 1994, p.30; *Action for Health and Welfare*, Bulletin of the Welfare State Network, no.2, 1994, pp.10-11; Megnad Desai, 'Borrie Is No Beveridge: Citizen's Income Now!', *Citizen's Income Bulletin*, no.19, February 1995; 'A Critique of the Report of the Commission on Social Justice', *Socialist Campaign Group News*, n.d.; Anne Kane, Ann Pettifor, and Pam Tatlow, 'The Hijacking of Feminism', Labour Women's Action Committee, n.d.; John Pilger, 'Emily Wouldn't Like It', *New Statesman & Society*, 7 July 1995; (For responses to Pilger see Letters, *New Statesman & Society*, 21 July 1995, pp.25-6); Miriam David and Dulcie Groves, 'From Beveridge to Borrie and Beyond', in *Journal of Social Policy*, vol.24, no.2, 1995, pp.161-2; Stuart White, 'Rethinking the Strategy of Equality: a Critical Appraisal of the Report of the Borrie Commission on Social Justice', papper for the IPPR 'Back to basics' Seminar, 21 March 1995, unpublished; Peter Townsend, 'Pessimism and Conformity: an Assessment of the Borrie Report on Social Justice', in *New Left Review*, no.213, September/October 1995. For a few examples of more positive discussion, excluding pieces by people who served on the Commission, see: Malcolm Wicks, 'A New Beveridge?', *New Statesman & Society*, 28 October 1994, pp.18-21; Richard Thomas, 'Strong Welfare and Flexible labour? Why Kenneth Clarke Is Wrong'; Chris Pierson, 'From Words to Deeds: Labour and the Just Society'; Fran Bennett, 'Ambition Checked by Caution: the Commission of Social Justice Reviewed'; all in *Renewal*, vol.3, no.1, January 1995, pp.37-61; Shelagh Diplock, 'Recognition at Last. Women Should Not Allow the Borrie Report to Gather Dust on the Shelf', *Towards Equality*, The Fawcett Society, winter, 1995.
24 See Antonio Gramsci, *Selections from the Prison Notebooks*, op.cit., p129; p168.

25 Ibid., pp172-3.

26 See Townsend, *op.cit.* and Peter Townsend and Alan Walker, 'Revitalising National Insurance' in *Fabian Review*, vol. 107, no. 6, December, 1995.

27 I have to confess that I have personally done so in an earlier, youthful Trotskyist incarnation.

28 See Anna Coote, 'A Bit Too Much', in *The Independent*, 3 July 1995. 'In the fine print of his speeches, Blair is often a sophisticated, liberal social analyst. The sound-bites and the silences tell another story.'

29 On a broader note, Will Hutton has written that the report represents 'one step nearer to genuine citizenship ... a remarkable document, for throughout there is the point/counterpoint between the economic, social and political that must be at the heart of any reform programme. And if a *still* intellectually timid Labour Party could be persuaded to sign up wholeheartedly there would be a transformation of British political life – and a genuine threat to sleaze and social injustice at the same time.' Quoted in Ruth Lister, ' "One step nearer to genuine citizenship": Reflections on the Commission on Social Justice Report', in *Soundings*, no. 2, 1996, p193.

30 See, for example, Gordon Brown, 'Modernising Tax, Employment and Benefit Policies', an extract from a speech he gave to the Unions '95 conference, *New Times*, 25 November 1995.

31 Ross McKibbin, *op.cit.*, p6.

32 *loc.cit.*

33 *CSJ*, p64.

34 Ross McKibbin finds the fact that this is no longer the case particularly depressing. *op.cit.*, p6.

35 This is well portrayed in the first two chapters of the report. Peter Townsend's criticism of a lack of attention to increasing poverty and social polarization in the report is not justified. *op.cit.*

36 The bestseller status of Will Hutton's book *op.cit.* and the success of Andrew Marr's *Ruling Britannia*, London, Michael Joseph, 1995 are indicative of the changing mood.

37 James McCormick and Carey Oppenheim, 'Options for Change', *New Statesman & Society*, 26 January 1996, pp18-21. They compare the *CSJ* with two other major reports: Joseph Rountree Foundation, *Inquiry into Income and Wealth*, York 1995 and Dahrendorf Commission, *Report on Wealth Creation and Social Cohesion in a Free Society*, Commission on Wealth Creation and Social Cohesion in a Free Society, London 1995 which was initiated by Paddy Ashdown.

38 It is the lack of depth of analysis which makes Peter Mandelson's and Roger Liddle's *The Blair Revolution – Can New Labour Deliver?*, Faber, London, 1996 much more part of the old labour tradition than they might like to admit.

39 The way the report is organised gives a sense of its general perspective. In the section 'Strategies for the Future', the first chapter is 'Investment: Adding Value Through Lifelong Learning' which expands the notion of education well beyond schooling. 'Opportunity: Working for a Living' goes well beyond Beveridge's definition of full employment as full-time male employment with men earning a high enough wage to cover family

needs (family wage) to consider the need for family-friendly employment practices, a minimum wage, etc. See for example, *CSJ*, p205. 'Security: Building an Intelligent Welfare State' argues for working with the grain of change to develop ways to combine work, benefits, caring, and education in new ways. See for example, *CSJ*, p223. 'Responsibility: Making a Good Society' concerns facilitating local initiatives for community regeneration, investment in children, and housing, whereas 'Taxation: Investing in Ourselves' makes the case for fair and acceptable taxation.

40 See Andrew Gamble and Gavin Kelly, 'Stakeholder Capitalism and One-Nation Socialism', in *Renewal*, vol. 4, no. 1, January, 1996.

41 Of all the recent reports on reconstructing the welfare state and the economy only the Commission on Social Justice report places women's roles at the heart of its analysis. See James McCormick and Carey Oppenheim, 'Options for Change', *op.cit.*, p18.

42 Anne Showstack Sassoon, (ed), *Women and the State*, Routledge, London 1992. The book first came out in 1987.

43 In 'Women's New Social Role: Contradictions of the Welfare State' I talk about a male model of work which assumes that whoever is in fact employed, the premise around which paid work is organised is that another person has the main responsibility for household needs. In Anne Showstack Sassoon (ed), *Women and the State, op.cit.* The term male-breadwinner model is, however, more widely used. See Hilary Land, 'The Family Wage,' *Feminist Review*, no. 6, 1980.

44 See 'Introduction: the Personal and the Intellectual, Fragments and Order, International Trends and National Specificities', and 'Women's New Social Role: Contradictions of the Welfare Sate' in *Women and the State, op.cit.*

45 *CSJ*, p3., also Patricia Hewitt, *About Time. The Revolution in Work and Family Life*, IPPR/River Orams Press, London 1993.

46 This concept derives from an essay by Yvonne Hirdman, 'The Gender System. Theoretical Reflections About Women's Social Oppression' in *Kvinnovetenskaplig tidskrift*, no. 3, 1988 (in Swedish). It attempts to take account of the social agreements which arise around the divisions of labour between men and women and between the state and family-households.

47 It is noteworthy that Townsend, *op.cit.*, and Townsend and Walker, *op.cit.*, despite recognising that poverty in old age is mainly a problem for women, treat these questions almost as asides.One of the contentious issues in the report is the sugggestion that retirement should be equalized between men and women at 65. However, as with many of the policy proposals in the report, it must be taken into account that this is suggested within a perspective of facilitating periods of full-time and part-time work, if desired, of education and training, and of caring work over the life cycle.

48 See the letter from James McCormick and Carey Oppenheim to the *New Statesman & Society, op.cit.*

49 *CSJ*, p154. It should be noted that given that Britain had almost the worst child-care provision in Europe when this was written (see *CSJ*, pp122-3).

50 *CSJ*, pp122-128.

51 *CSJ*, pp141-147. The report argues for the establishment of a learning bank for *all* to enable people to have the *right* over a lifetime to financial support for

education and training, rather than devote government resources so overwhelmingly to the tuition costs of full-time students between 18 and 21 as at present.

52 *CSJ*, pp28-29.

53 *CSJ*, p28.

54 See, for example, OECD Center for Educational Research and Innovation, *Education at a Glance. OECD Indicators*. OECD, Paris 1992; Robert Barrow, Human Capital and Economic Growth' in *Policies for Long-Run Economic Growth. A Symposium Sponsored by the Federal Reserve Bank of Kansas City*, Jackson Hole, Wyoming, 27–29 August 1992; Ray Marshall and Marc Tucker, *Thinking for a Living. Education and the Wealth of Nations*, Basic Books, New York 1992.

55 Andrew Glyn and David Miliband, (eds), *Paying for Inequality*, IPPR/Rivers Oram Press, London 1994. Also David Miliband, (ed), *Reinventing the Left*, Polity Press, Oxford 1994.

56 A learning bank would in part be financed by a progressive graduate tax linked to earnings levels and spread over long periods, and only invoked when people earn above a certain amount. It would be important, of course, to make sure that the funds thus raised were ringfenced. See Ruth Lister *op.cit.*

57 *CSJ*, p223.

58 See Fran Bennett, *op.cit.* and James McCormick and Carey Oppenheim, *op.cit.*

59 Ruth Lister, *op.cit.*, p7.

60 See *CSJ*, pp263-5.

61 See *CSJ*, pp17-22. See also the Commission's interim reports, *The Justice Gap*, and *Social Justice in a Changing World*, both IPPR, London 1993. These latter 2 are criticized by G.A. Cohen *op.cit.* while Stuart White *op.cit.* provides a critique of ideas of social justice in the report itself. For other, earlier contributions to the discussion see Anna Coote, ed. *The Welfare of Citizens. Developing New Social Rights*, London: Rivers Oram Press, 1992, and Raymond Plant, 'Social Justice, Labour and the New Right', Fabian Pamphlet 556, London: The Fabian Society, 1993.

62 There is a clear recognition in the report of the need to invest in social capital and to involve local people to facilitate community regeneration, that is, to invest in creating those conditions which are needed to underpin citizenship rights and responsibilities. Ruth Lister comments that this last point has not received the attention it should. *op.cit.*

63 *CSJ*, p398.

Section Four: Mission Possible – Prospects for New Politics

NEW LABOUR AND THE POLITICS OF A NEW SCOTLAND

Gerry Hassan

New Labour has been in gestation for over a decade, dating back at least to the nemesis of the 1983 election disaster, but only officially born, to much celebration and expectation, with the arrival of Tony Blair in July 1994. New Labour 1994–6 has proven that rare moment, comparable with 1945–6 and the original new Britain' of 1963–4, when Labour briefly articulated and defined the changing political tide of the nation.

Blair challenges and unsettles many people in the Labour Party and particularly on today's left, to the same degree that he offers reassurance and trust to those beyond Labour's traditional communities. He is both a metaphor and living embodiment of failed 80s fantasies and narrowed 90s realities. However, questions remain about the basic character of the Blair project: is it proto-post Thatcherite or an embryonic new realist social democracy?

The prospects for the Blair project will be crucially shaped by the relationship between Blair and Labour, and so far this has not been an easy one. While Blair has won grass-roots respect for his leadership and on Clause Four won party members to change, it is not yet a dynamic, two-way relationship of rapport and understanding in the way Thatcher understood the Tory grass-roots, and vice-versa. This is essential for the Blair revolution to develop a modernisation strategy of governing capable of renewal and adaption in office: something Labour has never previously achieved even under the Attlee administration.

Labour's caution now could have disastrous consequences in office as Stuart Hall has highlighted: 'Labour is *always* more cautious, more conservative, in office than before it. What it does not campaign about beforehand, it will be mastered and driven by afterwards.'[1] It is not a sufficient defence against future charges of betrayal to promise little and deliver little: a Labour Party that catches the political mood of a nation, draws forth further hopes and expectations.

The political trajectory of new Labour has widened differences between Scottish and British Labour. This is in part because of the different political terrains they inhabit: Scottish Labour is part of a majority social democrat, nationalist set of values anathema to contemporary Toryism, whereas British Labour operates on the post-Thatcherite agenda of markets, inequality and the limits of politics. These fundamental differences of trajectory and terrain expressed in different politics and priorities indicate the potential for conflict and disagreement under a future Blair Labour government.

SCOTTISH LABOUR: MYTHS AND HISTORIES

The Scottish Labour Party (as it has been called since 1994) has a very distinctive and selective view of itself which promotes a certain under-standing of its aims, values and history, via the propagation of what can be called 'myths'. The term 'myths' is used here not in a derogatory sense, but in James Mitchell's definition of the 'myths' of 'Scottish political culture' as 'an idea or set of ideas whose importance lies in being believed or accepted by a significant body of people sufficient to affect behaviour or attitudes whether grounded in fact or fiction.'[2]

It is revealing that the party had the confidence to rename itself the Scottish Labour Party, as it was previously clumsily titled the Scottish Council of the Labour Party. The name change reflects the growing autonomy and confidence of the Scottish party over its own organisation and decision-making, rather than being a provincial outpost of Walworth Road. The name chosen itself is significant: for when Jim Sillars left Labour over its foot-dragging on devolution to set up his own party in 1976, the name he chose was the Scottish Labour Party.[3] It indicates a certain self-assuredness in Scottish Labour that it can reclaim a name used by Sillars only twenty years ago, comparable with Blair rechristening Labour, the Social Democrats.

Scottish Labour's myths not only shape its view of itself, but have a wider relevance on both Scottish and British politics. First, it sees itself as a radical party. In this view, it is more connected to radical opinion than Labour in the rest of the UK. This view gained adherents as the 1980s went on and particularly post-1987. It was grounded in Labour's parliamentary dominance and preparedness to engage in cross-party co-operation (when it was fashionable in certain circles of the left in England), and offered as its main evidence the constitutional issue. It ignored the rest of Scottish Labour's tradition (and indeed its actual history on home rule) and policies such as its oligarchical old style practice in Scottish local government.

Second, it believes it is a popular party. This is again a perspective that gained ground in the 1980s and more so, after 1987, based on the unarguable premise that Scottish Labour won elections whereas English Labour lost them. This ignores the realities of Scottish politics: in 1992, Labour won 39 per cent of the Scottish vote and 34 per cent of the English vote – a 5 per cent difference. The difference in contemporary Scottish politics vis-a-vis British politics is not Labour strength, but Conservative weakness. Both Conservatives and Labour have experienced electoral decline from 1955 onwards in Scotland and England, but the Conservatives have declined relative to Labour in Scotland and Labour relative to the Conservatives in England. This has produced a widening Conservative/Labour voting gap between Scotland and England which in 1945–55 averaged 1 per cent (the difference between the Conservative and Labour lead in Scotland and England), rising to 21 per cent in 1979, 35 per cent in 1987, before falling slightly to 28 per cent in 1992[4]. This divide polarises perceptions into a Labour Scotland and Conservative England.

Third, the Scottish question is perceived as a historical linkage of Scottish Labour running unbroken from Keir Hardie through to John Smith and Scottish Labour's spokespeople of today. This is revisionism on an epic scale, rewriting Labour's past to suit the needs of the present. Labour at earlier points in its history merely gave a symbolic attachment to home rule, and the moment it came near power it abandoned any pretence at this, only coming back to it with a thud of realpolitik in 1974 as the SNP advanced on Labour's Scottish heartlands. Labour's current Scottish commitment to a specific Parliament is just over twenty years old.

This is a crucial commitment which still shapes Scottish Labour to this very day, but it is a far cry from the uninterrupted Whig-like history invoked by Labour. For these reasons, Scottish Labour has yet to transcend the limitations of its reconversion to home rule. The

Scottish party was dragged back to this issue by the electoral threat of the SNP in between the two 1974 elections, and by Harold Wilson's concern that the Scottish party and a Labour government would be swept away. This reconversion to home rule in 1974 took place at a special Scottish Labour conference under carefully controlled conditions, with pressure from Wilson and the party leadership, and was designed to be as limited as possible: a Scottish Assembly with legislative powers, the Scottish Secretary's post and number of Westminster seats retained. This is the politics of a Scottish Assembly: while changing as little as possible, grafting it onto the existing structures of the British political system. In the words of the 1974 compromise: 'Within the context of the political and economic unity of the UK.'[5] It is no accident that the parameters of this compromise twenty years ago shape Scottish Labour's deliberations over home rule in the Constitutional Convention and elsewhere to the present day.

These three interconnected assumptions lie at the heart of how Scottish Labour thinks about itself: as the party of Scotland able to speak without equivocation for all Scotland. The reality could not be more different: Scottish Labour is a minority party, as it has always been, its parliamentary majority a product of the same distortive electoral system that produces Tory majorities at Westminster. The Scottish political system has for the last twenty years been a highly competitive four party system with different regional battlegrounds: primarily Labour/SNP in Central Scotland, Liberal Democrat/SNP/ Tories in the Highlands and North East. Despite the Tories up until 1992 being Scotland's second party, in no region of Scotland do Labour and Tories face each other as sole competitors; this only happens in isolated seats: Stirling, Ayr, Aberdeen Central and South, Edinburgh Pentlands and Dumfries.

The complex and pluralist politics of modern day Scotland are often not reflected in the poses and postures of politicians. One example is the mandate argument, most frequently put during the Thatcherite 1980s when it seemed that Labour would never win again. It went along the following lines: Labour had to stress that Thatcher had 'no mandate' in Scotland, and counterpose this with Scottish Labour's 'mandate' to take action. This argument was used as a lever against a cautious, conservative Scottish Labour leadership who then proposed little in the way of action or thought to move Labour out of the Doomsday scenario: Labour always winning in Scotland, but never in the rest of the UK. One fundamental problem about this thesis was that it invoked the problematic notion of 'mandate', and while the left criticised Thatcher's use of mandate to impose unpopular policies not just on Scotland, but the UK, some in Scottish Labour were prepared to invoke a similar style of politics for Scotland.

The 'no mandate' view has fallen silent as Labour's British opinion poll ratings have risen, but the flawed thinking behind it remains: the presumption that Scottish Labour can act as a majority party when, like all Scottish parties, it is a minority one. It is linked to the myth of consensus in Scottish society: the view that a left-wing, anti-Tory consensus exists, supported by the traditions of egalitarianism, radicalism and increasing belief in national homogeneity, whereby England is seen as being synonymous with the Tory government. This Scottish consensus, according to Lindsay Paterson, deflects from a serious study of the divisions between romantic radicalism and paternalism in the anti-Tory majority, which could have a profound impact on the future: 'What will a Scottish Parliament actually do? ... the leaders of the Scottish consensus are ill-prepared for autonomy. They have devoted all their analytical activities to how to achieve a Scottish parliament, and have virtually ignored what they can do when they get there.'[6] Paterson poses the nightmare scenario of a Scottish Parliament arriving, but no one knowing what to do with it because they have been too fascinated for the two decades of uninterrupted Tory rule with maintaining the myth of consensus.

What can Scottish Labour do about this? A Scottish modernisation strategy would begin by acknowledging these realities and dispensing with the deeply held myths that unite the party. However, where would this strategy originate from? Scottish Labour itself is so tightly woven together by these assumptions that to challenge them challenges Scottish Labour's right to exist.

SCOTTISH LABOUR, BRITISH LABOUR: AN UNEASY RELATIONSHIP?

Debates in Scotland and the rest of the UK on the constitutional question have often happened in ignorance of each other, and the same is true of Scottish and British Labour's thinking on the Scottish question (despite an overlap in personnel at the top in both).

Scottish Labour has invoked the language of entrenchment, a Bill of Rights, electoral reform and power sharing, while British Labour has presented the same ground in terms of sovereignty, the West Lothian question and Westminster. It is the philosophical, not semantic difference between home rule and devolution: between seeing the issue as the British question and the Scottish question.

Cross-influence between the two is rare and can often prove troublesome. Jack Straw, Shadow Home Secretary, declared it an impossibility to entrench a future Scottish Parliament, while Kim Howells, then a Labour constitutional spokesperson, attacked nationalism and threw doubt on Labour's commitment to constitutional change:

> I didn't become a Labour MP in order to take part in the Balkanisation of Britain and I am profoundly anti-nationalist. I think that always underlying it is a kind of fascism, whether it is a gentle one or a malign one ... I think the pressure will certainly come off if we win the next election and win it handsomely. There'll be a lot of the demands for constitutional change, and remember devolution is only a bit of it. I think a lot of these things will evaporate and it will be up to Tony Blair and the leadership of the Labour Party to make sure that the changes which now some MPs believe in very passionately are actually carried through.[7]

A more complex example occurred when Tony Blair seemed to unravel one of the key commitments of the Constitutional Convention: the envisaged right of the future Scottish Parliament to raise or reduce income tax by up to 3p, or what has become known as 'the tartan tax'. Blair made it clear only one week after the official launch of the Constitutional Convention that Labour would not use such a power in the foreseeable future, but instead take a self-denying ordinance: 'Parties that are going to raise tax have a political obligation: if we intended to raise tax we would say so when we called an election.'[8]

A report in the *Independent* that Blair was to order a high-powered review of the impact of Scottish home rule on English politics and in particular the West Lothian question illuminates the potential faultlines within Labour. This would 'establish whether an answer could be found to the question posed repeatedly in the late 1970s by Tam Dalyell'[9]: of Scottish MPs voting on English and Welsh legislation, while English and Welsh MPs cannot vote on Scottish issues because they would be the preserve of a Scottish Parliament. The Labour leadership has been quoted as 'open-minded' on the outcome of this review, with one possibility being a reduction in the number of Scottish MPs.

The announcement by Scottish Labour of a two question referendum on a Scottish Parliament and tax raising powers in June

1996 is a product of these tensions and competing agendas. Despite the increasing confidence and autonomy of Scottish Labour, it revealed where ultimate power rests in new Labour. A referendum was always right and potentially radical, but Scottish Labour opposed one because of the experience of 1979, while new Labour's motives are highly suspicious with the tax raising question included due to paranoia over tax and spending, concerns over Middle England, and framed with the hope of voters' rejection. However, opposition to a referendum reveals the complacency of Scottish home rulers – that devolution is, in John Smith's words, 'unfinished business' and 'the settled will of the Scottish people'. The Scottish Constitutional Convention was the ultimate expression of this: set up as the embodiment of popular sovereignty, but opposing the most obvious expression of it: a referendum. Labour's shift prefigures the likely influence of the Convention on a Labour government: reduced to a resource to be drawn on at times and ignored at others.

There are several ways of interpreting these responses: one is of new Labour creatively responding to genuine concerns, while another is of a process of retreat and qualification over previously made commitments. The truth is both more complex and subtle: illustrating the political tensions between Scottish and British Labour and a nervousness in the face of Tory attacks about 'tartan taxes' and constitutional upheaval. These episodes only highlight the potential for future disagreement and conflict.

The debate is not just problematic vis-a-vis English or Welsh interventions in Scotland, but also the other way round: with Scottish Labour's commitment to electoral reform and new government structures proving difficult for a Scottish Labour leadership to sell to the British party because of the lack of a common language or dialogue. These points raise profound issues about the nature of Scottish Labour's proposed plans: are they exceptional with Scotland 'a special case', or a catalyst for wider UK reform? If Scotland is to be constitutionally ring-fenced then the lack of a common language may be less fatal, as long as Scottish Labour has autonomy over home rule plans. However, it does place any Scottish settlement in a constitutional limbo in terms of locating it in an unreformed British political system, and thus, vulnerable to political fashion. A Scotland that acts as a persuader for more fundamental change and as a harbinger for some ill-defined kind of 'new politics' requires as a prerequisite that a serious Scottish and British dialogue is undertaken, within both Labour and society.

Labour is far removed from establishing such a position. In its years of electoral success, British Labour spoke the same language from the Clyde to the Isle of Wight: a centralist state-driven socialism. Labour's popular decline and near two decades in opposition have shifted that, with Labour now presenting different messages to different groups and parts of the country. In many ways, this is a cause for celebration and should be a sign of strength, but Labour developed this approach as a defensive reaction to the years of retreat into its heartlands, and the same approach may not endure as Labour redefines itself as a 'national party' and invokes the language and legacy of 'One Nation' reformism.

Labour's fragmented vision means in terms of Scotland that a common assumption is that modernisation is a southern-driven strategy, deriving from the need to win Labour-Tory marginals in the Midlands and South, attract disillusioned Tory voters and articulate aspirational middle-class values. Such a strategy, the argument goes, has little or no relevance in Scotland, where traditionalism has won Labour every election since 1959.

This misunderstands Scotland and modernisation. The arguments made for modernisation need just as desperately to be put in Scotland as the South. Scottish Labour with its 39 per cent of the popular vote has no room for self-satisfaction, and desperately needs to attract the same groups the southern party is targeting. It is also a party which has traditionally attracted few young people, women, blacks, lesbians and gay men, and has a shameful record of representation of these groups.

Scottish Labour has been built on a local government tradition of 'city fathers' running their municipal city states; Labour MPs were usually taken from the ranks of senior councillors, thus allowing these values to achieve a vice-like dominance over the party whereby both left and right operated within this political culture. Scottish Labour only elected three women out of forty-nine MPs in 1992, rising to four when Helen Liddell won Monklands East in 1994, and has only ever elected thirteen women MPs in the party's entire history. The party's perspective has been more sexist and exclusionary than elsewhere, and lasted longer, and has been infused with a belief in a combination of economism and tokenism on both left and right. In 1978, Scottish Labour abolished the Women's Section on the Scottish Executive as it claimed that the Equal Pay Act and Sex Discrimination Act had brought about sexual equality![10].

Scottish Labour's representation of black communities and issues has been negligent. Local representation has been minisicule, with a few black councillors, while racial equality policies have been seldom prioritised. Lesbian and gay issues were seen as even more beyond the pale, with it taking until 1980, thirteen years after England and Wales, for male homosexuality to be legalised in Scotland. This was partly due to the opposition of Scottish Labour MPs.[11] These areas: women, blacks, lesbians and gays, were perceived by many in Scottish Labour as peripheral issues primarily concerning articulate, middle-class people as opposed to 'bread and butter issues' such as jobs, housing, transport and so on. They were the concern of the London left of the GLC years, and Scotland with its civic traditions of local respectability would have none of that.

This is still an influential view, but cracks are appearing. Labour knows the constituencies it used to appeal to with these assumptions and prejudices are disappearing, and new groups developing which need to be addressed. The SNP's benefitting from high-profile women candidates, particularly in parliamentary by-elections such as Winnie Ewing at Hamilton in 1967 sent shockwaves through Scottish politics and challenged the gender assumptions of Labour.[12] The Constitutional Convention's 50/50 gender proposals could not have come about without this and will send another much needed culture shock through Labour. The campaign of Mohammed Sarwar, for the Labour nomination in the Glasgow Govan seat against Mike Watson, Glasgow Central MP, has proven a landmark. Sarwar's ecentual selection after a bitter contest marked a breakthrough for Asian representation in Scottish Labour.[13] It also signifies the historic decline of the old labourist culture, seeing for the first time the deselection of a Scottish Labour MP. Lesbian and gay issues remain the most sensitive, as the voting of some of Glasgow Labour MPs on the age of consent debate illustrated, voting against sixteen and eighteen,[14] but recent developments such as the funding by Glasgow District and Strathclyde Region of the arts festival 'Glasgay!' and Glasgow Gay and Lesbian Centre show some positive signs.

Scottish Labour has only just begun to address these new groups because previously it had never felt the need to move outside its old, traditional constituencies. The same pattern can be seen in Scottish Labour's relationship with such pivotal groups as young people, owner occupiers, the new middle class and socially aspiring: Labour has succeeded in Scotland where it has managed to update its traditional values of public provision and support, rather than address them in the language of new Labour. This approach carries limitations with it, leaving unquestioned the democratic delivery of services, the need for more pluralism and diversity, as well as issues of fiscal efficiency and accountability.

THE IMPORTANCE OF CONSTITUTIONAL CHANGE

The 1992 election produced an unexpected result: a Tory fourth term and Labour defeat against all the odds and opinion poll predictions. What has been hardly explored is how the Scottish election was lost – and the rise and fall of the SNP, in some ways similar to Labour across the UK: both were characterised by favourable poll ratings, an inability to break through, followed by retreat, disappointment and bewilderment.[15] It could also be added that both parties, British Labour and the SNP, avoided inquests into why in such historical positive times they failed, because to do so would involve asking profound questions about their identity and purpose.

An examination of why the SNP lost in 1992 would reveal wider truths about the nature of the SNP's appeal and character, the constitutional question and its place in Scottish politics. The Scottish election run-in began in earnest with the Tories losing the Kincardine and Deeside by-election in November 1991 to the Liberal Democrats and becoming Scotland's third party in terms of Parliamentary seats; this gave extra impetus to the arguments about the Doomsday Scenario and a Tory government with no mandate governing Scotland. This was then followed by a *Scotsman* poll in January 1992 indicating a historic all-time high of 50 per cent of respondents indicating support for independence; with this the Scottish election campaign was truly declared open.[16]

Media coverage of Scottish politics, or more accurately the constitutional dimension, reached massive heights as the British press, TV and radio fell over themselves to dust down their Scottish cliches. SNP support rose dramatically to 30 per cent: entering the election at the critical mass needed to make an electoral breakthrough. With the SNP gaining mass media publicity, much of it sympathetic, with constitutional change at the forefront of the campaign, the SNP bandwagon seemed primed for a historic victory.

Events did not quite go to plan. The 50 per cent independence poll proved to be a rogue, and further surveys placed support in line with previous surveys at 30–35 per cent. Whereas in the earlier poll, 50 per cent of Labour voters supported independence and 28 per cent devolution, by April 1992 this had reversed to 55 per cent of Labour voters for devolution and 27 per cent for independence. As David McCrone put it: 'In the midst of a general election campaign, especially one in which the government sought to make political capital out of the Union, party affiliations seem to have won out'.[17] This does not, though, address the changing nature of party allegiances as the SNP momentum, instead of gathering apace, stalled and went into reverse. The final Scottish results at first shocked people: Labour 39 per cent, Conservatives 26 per cent, SNP 22 per cent, Liberal Democrats 13 per cent. The SNP vote had risen by 7.5 per cent but no seats were gained, Govan was lost and they could not even win second place in votes; while the Tories against all predictions marginally increased their vote and representation (claiming this as a watershed victory for the Conservatives and Unionism).

Several explanations have since been proposed to explain this. One is that there was a widespread belief that Labour was going to win at a UK level, and this reduced the SNP vote to the role of a lever on a future Labour government. Another is that the SNP vote is a protest vote, like Liberal Democrat by-election victories, which vanishes the moment change becomes a reality: this was certainly one of the post-election lessons drawn by Scottish Labour politicians – that yet again they had survived the SNP bandwagon. The third is that the possibility of constitutional change played into the fears raised by the pro-Union campaign of the Conservatives and others.

All these explanations have some elements of truth, but more profoundly at work is the ambiguity and uncertainty about who the SNP is and what it stands for. The SNP fought a triumphalist and belligerent campaign: a nationalist version of Labourism's style with Thatcherism's certainty. Fought under the slogan 'Free by 93', the SNP presented the complexities of change as simple, straightforward and existing in a debate of two extremes: independence or nothing. This concealed the SNP's own uncertainties about future strategies between gradualism and fundamentalism which have lain at its heart since the party's origins.[18]

The SNP's bellicose language was a model case of concealing the truth by shouting louder to prevent it noticing its own doubts: a form of denial and lack of self-confidence. It had the opposite effect from that intended because it worked against the SNP, actually estranging it from the wider currents of Scottish nationalism which had grown in the 1980s, by talking a fundamentalist language at odds with the spirit of the Scotland that had emerged. The SNP still talked in old nationalist terms: of rewinning our nationhood, implying it has been lost, with the evocative 'Rise Now and Be A Nation Again'.

CULTURAL NATIONALISMS: FROM JAMES KELMAN TO THE SOARAWAY, SCOTTISH *SUN*

The SNP's campaign was launched with the benefits of two cultural allies: one was the wider cultural nationalism and confidence which had sprung up in the 1980s, and the other was the *Sun* newspaper which had recently switched in Scotland from English to Scottish nationalism and the cause of independence. Two more opposite cultural forces it would be hard to imagine: one reflecting diversity, doubt and ambiguity; the other promoting certainty, polarity and xenophobia; but representing in their ways the twin sides of the SNP – the inclusive and exclusive aspects of nationalism.

The wider cultural nationalism grew up in the 1980s in the aftermath of disillusion with devolution, conventional politics and the arrival of Thatcherism. Writers, artists, film-makers, playwrights and painters created an 'imagined Scotland' of the mind. This movement was not merely a middle-class art school creation: the writings of James Kelman, Alasdair Gray and William McIlvanney touched on the changing nature of working-class experience, de-industrialisation and often a very male sense of loss.[19] Pop stars such as Hue and Cry, Deacon Blue and the Proclaimers sang about Scotland's experience and identified themselves as nationalists leading to the formation before the election, of 'Artists for Independence', modelled, in spirit at least, on 'Artists against Apartheid'.

The SNP's failure in 1992 led many commentators to wonder what all this fuss about cultural nationalism was for if it could not deliver the votes. This inquest usually led on to lament the SNP's lack of an organic relationship with cultural nationalism, beyond setting up various 'front' organisations: a common view being that because of this failure the SNP is not a 'real' nationalist party. The dilemma for the SNP was hardly examined from the opposite perspective: that the SNP's distant and nervous relationship with the wider nationalisms might be as much to do with the latter as the former, and that issues of ambiguity, difference and diversity which are central to cultural politics, hardly make for the easiest translations into the narrow world of party politics. The impact of cultural nationalism seems not to have benefitted one party; but the broader 'Scottishing' of Scottish society and politics, and the association of Scottish distinctiveness with democracy and home rule, did accelerate the continuing marginalisation of the Scottish Conservatives and the widespread perception that they are somehow 'unScottish'.

It is also worth acknowledging that this wider cultural nationalism was limited in its impact, because it did not have Scotland to itself. It did not operate as a coherent set of beliefs, but a disparate, diffuse set of discourses located in an environment where the old Scottish discourses still had much influence.

As experienced an observer as McCrone commented in 1992: 'Unlike many forms of nationalism, the cultural content of the Scottish variety is relatively weak.' This recognised the old discourses of tartanry and kailyard as 'the dominant discourses on Scottish culture',[20] without mentioning the new discourses of cultural nationalism; the nearest McCrone gets is a discussion of the discourse of 'Clydesidism', which Colin McArthur and John Caughie defined as drawing from images of working-class life and experience, but carrying connotations of socialist realism and male heroicism:[21] these notions can be seen in the work of Kelman, Gray and McIlvanney. The political repercussions of the *Sun*'s shift in Scotland have yet to be studied. While in the rest of the UK, the *Sun*'s claim that 'It's the *Sun* Wot Won It' has been examined by David McKie and Martin Linton and given substance, no comparative research has been undertaken in Scotland[22]; indeed, research on the political effect of the *Sun* at the 1992 election is really about the English *Sun*, completely ignoring the Scottish *Sun*. The *Sun*'s conversion was thought by many as short-term and opportunistic, commercial not political, but the *Sun*'s change of editorial line and lack of SNP breakthrough raise questions about why the *Sun* 'won' in England, but not in Scotland. The Scottish *Sun* experience throws up issues about the power of newspapers and the relationship between a paper's politics and its readers' politics, which may throw light on the power of the English *Sun* and other papers. The Scottish *Sun* did have an effect: its newspaper sales increased, while the SNP's vote at the 1992 election became more young, male and working-class, mirroring the *Sun*'s readership: although whether it is a causal relationship is unclear. It also reproduced a Scottish nationalism that is easy to dismiss because of its source, but plays into the prejudices of many Scots: anti-English stories became frequent, with the English merely replacing blacks as targets of xenophobia and racism, while a romantic, rebellious, tartan 'Braveheart' reading of Scottish history and identity was put forward.

The SNP's fundamentalism meant that in the 1992 election it had to avoid mentioning one of its most powerful weapons: of using the SNP as a lever for change, and against Labour conservatism and retreat: a charge that will have even more potency against new Labour. This could not be used as it would draw too much attention and scrutiny onto the SNP's internal divisions, despite it being widely acknowledged that the SNP vote is used in this way. The SNP has to develop a language and purpose of pluralism and alliance, and this involves reappraising its romantic notions of Scotland and Scottish nationalism, if it is to connect with the wider audience who sympathise with the SNP. A radical, pluralist SNP in a two-way relationship with the politics of identity and cultural nationalism might just help a radical Scottish Labour Party by aiding the demystification of Scottish politics.

Labour and the SNP have much in common: both are left of centre, social democratic with a commitment to a Scottish Parliament, while their main constituencies are the same: the Central Scotland urban working classes. This gives the rationale for their intense competition and vilification of one another – they have to differentiate themselves by insult and abuse. What this should not exclude though, is that just as there is a post-Thatcherite market economy/'One Nation' reformist consensus in Britain, in Scotland, there is a Scottish civic nationalist consensus which is based on the inter-relationship between a distinct Scottish ideal of democracy and distinctiveness and wider social democratic ideals. A radical, pluralist SNP invoking the politics of democracy, rather than independence, and creating and working in alliances and coalitions, would change the face of Scottish politics, and challenge Labour to regenerate itself. Instead two conservative parties deal in the politics of certainty and closure.

A Popular Constitutionalism?

Support for constitutional change has in some form always been with us and has also changed dramatically in the last thirty years. Support for change has nearly always been wide, but often shallow. A rudimentary straw poll in the Scottish *Daily Express* in 1932 showed majority support for home rule: 112,984 for home rule, 4,596 against,[23] while in 1945, a *News Chronicle* poll gave devolution 53 per cent support, status quo 39 per cent and independence 8 per cent.[24]

There has been a significant shift towards and within constitutional change since the SNP first turned Scottish politics upside down by winning the Hamilton by-election. The period 1965–74 saw an average: devolution 41 per cent, status quo 37 per cent, independence 22 per cent; February-March 1979, an average: devolution: 49 per cent, status quo 33 per cent, independence 18 per cent. This dramatically changed in the 1980s, so that the average for 1992 was: independence 39 per cent, devolution 36 per cent, status quo 22 per cent, but this changed again with a 1995 poll giving devolution 47 per cent, independence 31 per cent, staus quo 21 per cent.[25]. The shift towards Scottish independence from 1979-92 was in part due to Thatcherism being seen as synonymous with the British political system and the only viable road to a Parliament, independence. The decline in support post-1992 may be due to a more conciliatory Conservative stance towards Scotland, and also Labour's re-emergence as a government in waiting re-opening the British road to a Scottish Parliament. However, when the Scots arrive at seemingly decisive moments of change, the translation of this widespread support for change into action seemingly disappears: as in the 1979 referendum and 1992 Scottish election result. This is in part due to the low salience of constitutional change: in 1979 only 3 per cent ranked it an important issue, although this had risen to 12 per cent by 1992;[26] the possibility of majority support for constitutional change achieving a Scottish Parliament depends on its inter-relationship with broader economic and social issues.

One of the most important obstacles to a Scottish Parliament is the concerns of the British Parliament. Debates in Gladstone's and Asquith's time show the same terms of reference and claims of support as now, with Scottish home rule seen as a means of maintaining Scotland's Liberal strength, and home rule concerns over how a Parliamentary Bill with Scottish majority support can overcome English MPs' opposition. This is matched by Unionist anxieties over maintaining the supremacy of Westminster and whether the election of a majority of Liberal or Labour members in one part of the UK proves majority support for constitutional change.[27]

The British road to a Scottish Parliament has been tried repeatedly for over a century and failed. Since Gladstone's time, thirty-four home rule bills have been presented to the House of Commons for consideration and been blocked in one form or another, from outright resistance to contempt and dismissal.[28] The British Parliament with its obsessions over West Lothian questions and making any body subordinate to itself is ill-suited to deal with the passage of a radical home rule bill.

Hybrid Scottish-British approaches to reform have been attempted, like the 1949 National Covenant and 1989–95 Scottish Constitutional Convention. These have progressed no further, standing at a half-way house of proclaiming popular sovereignty while in reality upholding parliamentary sovereignty. Neither of these forums were abject failures, raising the Scottish dimension, and teaching participants the benefits of co-operation and dialogue; the Convention particularly was an important learning curve for Scottish Labour towards devising a radical new kind of Parliament.

The only really viable option for radical change is a Scottish-based solution, not exclusively tied to a Parliamentary strategy. This would involve cross-party co-operation, civic forums, linking constitutional change to economic and social change, and a range of mechanisms whereby Westminster was only able to indicate its opinion at the start and end of the process, with all the work taking place on a 'contracted out' basis, and the important vote being a popular referendum. This is a radical Scottish nationalist stand, one commensurate with a rolling, evolving plan which emphasises Scottish democracy as its principle, rather than the closed options of home rule or independence. All the other options for change carry with them grave and fundamental problems, and it is only with such a radical break that Labour can secure genuine majority support for its proposals and make them into a long-term sustainable settlement.

The pressures on a Blair Labour government will be immense from day one. The Scottish constitutional question will not be a top priority, but is nevertheless a pressing demand. When Labour comes to power, the parameters of the Scottish debate will change, not in the way Kim Howells suggests, but because Labour will face pressure from all sides. This will mean that Scottish Labour's agreed plans via the Convention will be inclined to get marginalised in the drawing up of details, in part because of the failure of Scottish and British Labour to find a common dialogue, but also because of the inert, top-down nature of the Convention, which makes it unlikely to be able to act as an instrument of popular mobilisation during negotiations with and within a Labour government.

There is no guarantee that British Labour will enact or honour the Convention's proposals when in government, and all that can be assured is that the Convention will provide a resource in the drawing up of Labour's home rule policies. The commitment to legislation in Labour's first year for a Scottish Parliament and a Referendum Act puts enormous pressure on the parliamentary timetable, while Labour's tax and electoral system proposals will also prove contentious, exposing sensitive faultlines in British labour. Most of these tensions will find expression in argument over the referendum. New Labour's two question plan has not closed the debate, only opened new questions: Scottish Labour home rulers will wish to reduce it to one question on a Parliament, while others will wish to increase the number of questions to include electoral reform, independence, and in Tam Dalyell's view, a post-legislative vote. A Scottish home rule referendum was always likely because of 1979. It may even occur with a resurrected 40 per cent rule.[29] The conventional wisdom is that a referendum will be easily won by the home rule forces, but that was the view in the 1970s – and in Quebec in 1908 and 1995 – substantial devolution majorities in 1976 disappeared as the reality of the Scotland Act became apparent, and the same will happen with any future home rule bill.[30] A referendum is not only welcome and potentially radical, but its result is no foregone conclusion.

DEFINING THE NEW SCOTLAND: 1997 AND AFTERWARDS

The next general election campaign provides Labour with its best opportunity to defeat the Tories in two decades. The following possible Scottish scenarios lead on from this and are based on: firstly, Labour winning the election in 1997 with an overall majority; secondly, British Labour's strategy of modernisation being qualified in Scotland by Labour traditionalism; thirdly, the Scottish/British debate continuing on separate lines resulting in problems for Labour in Government at a UK and Scottish level; and finally, Scottish Labour only cursorily addressing new groups and interests and being left in an unprepared state for the challenges leading up to a Scottish Parliament.

From past Scottish political trends and, particularly, those under post-war Labour governments, some patterns are possible to map out into the unknown contours of the first Blair Government. It is important to acknowledge the limits of Scottish Labour's appeal: its vote in a four party system does not fluctuate by that wide a margin in good or bad times, only having a margin, since 1981 when the Social

Democrats were formed, of a low of 35 per cent in 1983 and a high of 43 per cent in the 1994 Euro-elections: an 8 per cent difference; whereas English Labour's figures are a low of 27 per cent in 1983 and high of 44 per cent in the 1994 Euro-elections: a 17 per cent variance.[31] Scottish Labour seldom achieves the average national swing Labour attains when it wins power, because of the small difference between its vote in good and bad performances. The three post-war occasions when Labour was returned to power from opposition saw Scotland swing less to Labour in two: 1945 and 1974, and slightly more in one: 1964; the Scottish swings were (with UK swings in brackets): 1945: +5.8 per cent swing to Labour (+11.8 per cent), 1964: +4.3 per cent (+3.2 per cent), 1974: 1.4 per cent swing to Conservatives (+1.3 per cent).[32] It is more than probable that such a similar pattern of behaviour will happen in 1996–7 with the swing to Labour in Scotland being under the national average, with consequences for the size of the Labour vote and the possibility of winning key Scottish marginals.

The Scottish political map under a Labour government will see the Scottish Labour vote under siege from the SNP and Conservatives for most of the next Parliament due to the pressures put on a Labour government. First, the Labour vote for the first Scottish Parliamentary elections will be depressed by this, while the timing of the elections will be long after any Blair post-election 'honeymoon' has evaporated and may be at the deepest part of any mid-term troubles.

Second, the SNP vote will be on an upward trend, rising from 1992–7 and thereafter. Historically, the SNP vote has risen under both Labour and Conservatives, but risen more significantly under Labour 1964-70 and 1974–9, breaking through not just in Parliamentary by-elections, but also in local elections. In the 1968 municipal elections, the SNP won 30.1 per cent of the Scottish vote, beating Labour in popular votes in Glasgow with 36 per cent to Labour's 25.5 per cent and making 100 gains across Scotland,[33] while in 1977, the SNP on 24.2 per cent achieved 107 gains and control of half a dozen authorities.[34] This may happen again and if so, Scottish Labour is in a real crisis.

Finally, the Scottish Conservative vote post-election will rise as they regain short-term ground lost without reversing long-term decline: as happened with the Conservatives in 1964–70 and 1974–9, who increased their Parliamentary seats and popular vote under Labour governments. The Scottish Conservatives post-1997 will follow the fate of Heath and Thatcher in this respect; Heath in 1970, despite a pro-devolutionary approach, gained a mere 0.3 per cent rise in the

Scottish Tory vote and three extra seats, whereas Thatcher in 1979 saw the Tories vote rise 6.7 per cent, while they had a net gain of six seats, winning seven and losing Glasgow Cathcart.[35] The Scottish Tories will reposition themselves under Labour and a Scottish Parliament to fight those elections: and the constitutional rethinking by John Major and Michael Forsyth, Scottish Secretary, on extending the powers of the Scottish Grand Committee, has been seen by some as one more evolutionary step in the Tory tradition of administrative devolution to ease themselves back into the mainstream of Scottish majority opinion for fighting the Scottish Parliamentary elections.[36]

Labour in power will face the twin pressures of resurgent Unionism and nationalism in Scotland. Attacks from both sides of the political spectrum will make Labour's constitutional position in some ways seem more reasonable, but its popular base in the short-term more vulnerable. It would be foolish to think that the creation of a Scottish Parliament carries with it any immediate political pay-off for Labour; rather the benefits are in avoiding the debacle that would result from inaction and the long-term consequences in developing a specific Scottish political agenda.

Bernard Crick foresees problems for a Labour government no matter the political environment:

> A new Scotland Bill will have a rough passage through parliament whatever size majority Labour enjoys, even with Liberal Democrat support. It may be a boon to Britain in the long run, but its importance and complexity will be the bane of Labour's Chief Whip in the run-in of a new government's programme. If the majority is large, the unregenerate and unrewarded will feel free to amend the Bill – not to defeat it, mind, and endanger the government, but to water it down to a degree below proof tolerable in Scotland, perhaps to something as weak and uninspiring as the present proposals for Wales. And if the majority is small, a few English Labour MPs aided and abetted by the Laird o' the Bairns may try, just like the Conservative Euro-rebels, to hold the government to ransom.[37]

The different Scottish Parliamentary scenarios detailed below are based on the Scottish Constitutional Convention plans for a 129-seat Parliament. Although there are many doubts about the influence of the Convention's proposals under a Labour government, it is in most cases probable that this part will remain. This is to be elected from the existing seventy-two Westminster constituencies, with Orkney and

Shetland divided in two, plus fifty-six Additional Member Seats, allocated from the eight Euro-constituencies each returning seven MPs. This system in effect means parties only need a 6 per cent vote in a Euro-constituency to gain representation.

1. Labour Division and Delay

Labour is elected with 341 seats, a small overall majority of twenty-three after a net gain of sixty-eight seats. Labour divisions, particularly between the Scottish and North East Labour Groups of MPs, evident in the 1970s and buried in the 1980s, come to the fore with the North East Group pushing for a Scottish Parliament without tax raising powers and electoral reform, and an elected forum for the North East.

The Scottish Referendum Bill, designed as a constitutional short-cut is held up by opposition. The North East Labour rebels force through on 1970s precedent the 40 per cent rule for a Scottish referendum with Conservative support. Amendments are also carried with Labour support to increase the number of questions to include votes on electoral reform and whether a Parliament should be in the UK or independent. The bill is finally passed in 1998 and referendum scheduled for 1 March 1999. The multi-ballot referendum encourages greater cross-party co-operation across the home rule cause, but increases Labour divisions with anti-home rulers campaigning for a 'No' vote on tax, and old style labourites opposing electoral reform. The SNP, with independence on the ballot, campaign more enthusiastically than Labour for a parliament. The Conservatives dominate the 'No' campaign invoking fear of over-government and high taxes, as well as the threat to the union. Due to the unpopularity of the Labour government they find a ready response, producing a 59:41 home rule majority on a 76 per cent turnout. Tax powers are rejected 54:46, electoral reform supported 63:37, and Scotland in the Union narrowly affirmed 53:47. New Labour has won support for its proposals, but at the cost of its timetable being blown off course.

The Scotland Act is finally passed in 2000 and Scottish parliamentary elections scheduled for 2001, but before this can happen, Labour unexpectedly calls a UK election and despite leading in the polls during the campaign, loses to the Conservatives. Scottish Labour holds its vote at 41 per cent, to the SNP's 32 per cent, Conservatives 15 per cent and Lib Dems 12 per cent, with the Conservatives losing all but two of their Scottish seats. Across Britain, they are returned with a majority of forty-nine and massive swings in the South West and East; their programme 'A Free Britain' is right wing, populist and for minimal government whether in the UK or European Union. In its first year in office, Prime Minister Portillo repeals the Scotland Act 1999 and Maastricht Treaty 1993 calling them 'a threat to the British way of life and democracy'.

2. An SNP Minority Administration

Labour passes the Referendum Act 1997 and Scotland Act 1998 with breathtaking speed and ruthlessness. The first Scottish Parliamentary elections in 1999 witness the SNP fight the election as the best guardians of Scotland's interests against a Treasury-driven parsimonious Labour government with the theme: 'Scotland's Best Defence'.

The SNP breakthrough finally happens with a 35 per cent vote, outpolling Labour for the first time ever in a national election, with 32 per cent to the Conservatives 22 per cent and Liberal Democrats 11 per cent giving the SNP forty-six seats, Labour forty-one, Conservatives twenty-six, Lib Dems fourteen, others two, leaving the SNP the largest party but nineteen seats short of an overall majority.

SNP intransigence due to the strength of their fundamentalist wing means they cannot find suitable coalition or alliance partners to form a Parliamentary majority. The 'fundos' want to push ahead with a strategy for independence in one term, while the 'realos' wish the SNP to gain respectability by garnering a governing majority. Alex Salmond, SNP leader, wants to pursue the latter course, but cannot and for the sake of party unity he has to adopt a hard-line no compromise position due to the strength of the 'fundos'.

No other parliamentary majorities exist, so a nominal, minority, powerless SNP administration holds office, power resting with brokered deals in a hung Parliament between the parties. Scottish Labour leader, George Robertson, sees the situation as an ideal opportunity to put a constrained, toothless SNP into office, associating them with unpopular and tough decisions they have little say over. This is part of a long-term anti-nationalist Labour strategy which sees the SNP being sullied with the compromises and choices of power as key to reducing its appeal as a protest party. This strategy pays its dividends as Labour wins a second term in the UK with an increased majority, and wins the second Scottish Parliamentary elections with 44 per cent to the SNP's 29 per cent and decides to govern alone but with the tacit support of the Liberal Democrats.

3. Labour-Liberal Democrat Alliance

The Scottish Parliamentary elections produce a result: Labour 35 per cent, SNP 27 per cent, Conservatives 20 per cent, Lib Dems 14 per cent, others 4 per cent, giving Labour forty-five seats, SNP thirty-four, Conservative twenty-six, Lib Dems eighteen, others four.

Labour and the Liberal Democrats form a joint administration on an agreed common programme of job creation, improving public services and democratising the quango state. On most votes, they can count on the support of the one Scottish Socialist Alliance MP, Tommy Sheridan, leaving the two Orkney and Shetland Movement MPs and one Scottish Green having to vote together to defeat the Lab-Lib coalition, which seldom happens.

The Lab-Lib administration is aided by the divided nature of the opposition facing it, with the Conservatives attacking it as left-wing and extremist and making play of the influence of Militant, while the SNP attacks it for being too tame and selling out Scotland, allowing Labour and the Liberal Democrats to position themselves in the middle ground. Scottish public opinion, after years of Westminster government and impotent Scottish Labour majorities, grows accustomed to the politics of coalition and compromise with politicians being forced to listen and be flexible.

4. Conservative–SNP Alliance

The Scottish Parliamentary elections produces a three-way split: Labour 32 per cent, Conservatives 29 per cent, SNP 28 per cent, Lib Dems 11 per cent, with the number of seats: Labour forty-one, Conservative thirty-six, SNP thirty-five, Lib Dems fourteen. After negotiations lasting two weeks, and the practicalities of a Lab-Lib minority coalition and even Labour–Tory Grand Coalition, the Conservatives and SNP uneasily agree a pact based on a careful division of cabinet responsibilities and a minimal programme of a public works plan for aiding the long-term unemployed, tax cuts and incentives for businesses and a programme of open government and decentralisation at local and national level, exposing generations of Labour patronage to popular scrutiny and consumer choice: combining Thatcherite empowerment with a social conscience.

The alliance is a nervous one given its protagonists' opposing views, and several times nearly falls apart, but it holds together because of lack of an alternative and neither SNP or Conservatives having any other viable option. A rejuvenated, outraged Scottish Labour attacks the SNP and Conservatives as opportunists, seeing this as a useful strategy allowing them to portray themselves as a party of principle. Labour loses power at a UK level in 2002 to the Conservatives, but wins 42 per cent in the second Scottish elections the following year, forming a coalition with the Liberal Democrats. However, while Labour's Scottish strategy works in the short-term, the policies of the Conservative-SNP coalition have begun to sow the seeds; introducing choice, opening up and democratising Scotland, while slowly beginning to unravel Labour's natural constituency and appeal in the long-term.

These scenarios indicate not only the unlikelihood of a Labour Scottish majority, but also that the odds are stacked against a Labour-led Parliament in coalition with allies. This is because of a number of factors: a proportional electoral system, the probable balance between the parties, and the likely timing of the first Scottish elections. Scottish Labour has hardly begun the difficult journey of thinking in terms of the multi-party politics of a Scottish Parliament. Scottish Labour still sees Scotland as its own territory and from this perspective views a future Scottish Parliament which it creates as part of itself in the way it sees the NHS (despite agreeing to electoral reform): it will be a major challenge to its world view when it wakes up to find others running a Scottish Parliament.

NEW LABOUR AND A NEW UNION

The Scottish question has long proven troublesome to Labour, whether old Labour or new Labour, but also to the Conservatives.[38] Conservative and Labour notions of the United Kingdom have shifted dramatically this century. Rokkan and Urwin's typology of state-building of 'unitary' and 'union' states is relevant to this process: a unitary state being constructed 'around one unambiguous political centre ... of administrative standardisation', while a union state 'still has some pre-union rights ... and regional autonomy'.[39]

Modern Conservatism under Churchill, Macmillan and Heath conceived of the UK as a union state, celebrating localism, tradition and difference and opposing what it saw as the alien socialist notion of a unitary state of centralism and conformity. Thatcherism dramatically broke with this, perceiving the UK as a unitary state emphasising the supremacy of Westminster over diversity and negotiation, with profound consequences for Scotland. Labour's territorial approach has shifted from its original union state, decentralist and home rule origins, to the unitary state centralism of Attlee social democracy and afterwards, which has slowly unravelled since 1979 into a quasi-unitary approach. Conservatism's shift has corresponded with the longest uninterrupted reign in power of a party this century, and a blurring of party and state boundaries and interests. Labour's moves to a unitary, then quasi-union position can be traced to the party's changing electoral fortunes. As Labour became the official opposition in 1922, so it turned its back on its home rule traditions, an approach underlined by the Attlee government and Gaitskellite-Croslandite social democracy in the 1950s. This position only began to unravel, first, under electoral pressure from Scottish and, to a lesser extent, Welsh nationalism, and second, from Thatcherism's mobilisation of British nationalism and manipulation of the political system.

Labour's quasi-union approach is an uneasy compromise between old style social democratic centralism, the party's old and new local socialist traditions and the influence of liberalism and rights-based critiques of government. If Labour does not rethink and focus its position now, the temptation in office will be to fall back on big government politics, coloured in post-corporatist rhetoric. A union politics has much to offer Labour, allowing it to decentralise and respond to the different needs of the constituent parts of the UK in a strategic way; it is a politics which because of its combination of flexibility and localism is more relevant to the UK than Conservative unitary centralism or Liberal Democrat federalism.

A union politics would enable Labour to locate its approach to Scottish politics in a coherent territorial politics which acknowledged the need for a common agenda between Scottish and British Labour, and recognised that changing parts of the Scottish political system has repercussions for the English political system and British state, that cannot be met by simply brushing aside the West Lothian question or inventing and then disinventing proposals for English regional assemblies. Central to this is the Westminster question, which McCrone vividly describes as 'an imperial Parliament without an empire, and possibly without a state'.[40]

Scotland has been autonomous since the union, and is 'at least as autonomous as other small European nations, for which the reality of politics has always been the negotiation of partial independence and the rivalry of great powers.'[41] Scottish autonomy and distinctiveness have evolved and entrenched, while debates about the withering of Scottish identity and culture are predicated on notions that Scotland has been 'lost' and has to be 'rewon' under the romantic certainties of a 'Rise Now And Be a Nation Again' project. This is an essentialist 'Braveheart' nationalism of myth and folklore that is not appropriate to the modern world of negotiation and diverse, plural identities.[42] Any future Scottish settlement has to be situated in this reality of negotiated autonomy, recognising the legacy of previous settlements, rather than invoking old battles and certainties.

Recent sociological analysis has focused on Scotland as a 'stateless nation' and engaged in comparative study with similar territories such as Catalonia and Quebec, but this perspective problematises Scotland, unless it is complemented by placing it in the context of the UK as a 'nationless state': the inverse of Scotland's condition. This would demand an examination of the UK as a state that has no identity and focus on rather different comparative examples such as the Soviet Union and Yugoslavia. To achieve a new equitable, sustainable political settlement, a new notion of Britishness is needed invoking an 'imagined geography' of the UK.

The Scottish question is, irrespective of whether any constitutional settlement leads to independence or home rule, part of the wider British question. Scotland changes Britain, as Britain changes and influences Scotland. It is the challenge of new Labour to take up this historic project at a time of great change and uncertainty in the politics of nation, state and identities. This offers the potential to encourage the growth of the new Britain and new Scotland and a politics of partnership in a new Union. To attempt any less – a business as usual politics – will neither capture the political imagination or remake the political system and will be devoured by the post-Thatcherite right. The choice is between creativity and the continuation of the politics of retreat into office: new Labour has so far shown both.

REFERENCES

1 Stuart Hall, 'Parties on the Verge of a Nervous Breakdown', *Soundings*, Autumn 1995, p30.

2 James Mitchell, 'The Myth of Dependency', Scottish Centre for Economic and Social Research, Edinburgh 1990, p4.

3 H.M. Drucker, 'Breakaway: The Scottish Labour Party', Edinburgh University Student Publications Board, Edinburgh 1979. There have in fact been two Scottish Labour Parties prior to the current one: Keir Hardie formed the first Scottish Labour Party in 1888, and Jim Sillars the second in 1976, making the current SLP the third version.

4 William L. Miller, *The End of British Politics?: Scots and English Political*

Behaviour in the Seventies, Clarendon Press, Oxford 1981; 'The Scottish Dimension', in David Butler and Dennis Kavanagh, *The British General Election of 1979*, Macmillan, London 1980, p98; *The British General Election of 1987*, Macmillan, London 1988, p284; *The British General Election of 1992*, Macmillan, London 1992, p286.

5 Michael Keating and David Bleiman, *Labour and Scottish Nationalism*, Macmillan, London 1979, p167.

6 Lindsay Paterson, 'The Myth of Consensus', *The Herald*, 11 March 1995.

7 *Scotsman*, 12 September 1995.

8 *Herald*, 8 December 1995.

9 The *Independent*, 26 December 1995; 'Tartan Terrors of Mr. Blair', The *Independent*, Editorial, 27 December 1995.

10 Rosina McCrae, 'Women in the Scottish Labour Party', in *A Woman's Claim of Right in Scotland: Women, Representation and Politics*, Polygon, Edinburgh 1991, pp50-51.

11 Bob Cant, *Footsteps and Witnesses: Lesbian and Gay Lifestories from Scotland*, Polygon, Edinburgh 1993.

12 Catriona Burness, 'Drunk women don't look at thistles: women and the SNP', 1934–1994, *Scotlands*, Vol. 1 No. 2, 1994.

13 Magnus Linklater, 'Mohammed in the Dock', *Sunday Times* magazine, 29 October 1995; *Herald*, 15 December 1995; 25 June 1996.

14 Three out of Glasgow Labour's eleven MPs voted against both sixteen and eighteen years in the age of consent debate in February 1994: Jimmy Dunnachie, David Marshall and Michael Martin.

15 See: John Bochel and David Denver, 'The 1992 General Election in Scotland', *Scottish Affairs*, No. 1, Autumn 1992; James Mitchell, 'The 1992 Election in Scotland in Context', *Parliamentary Affairs*, Vol. 45 No. 4, October 1992; Lindsay Paterson, Alice Brown and David McCrone, 'Constitutional Crisis: The Causes and Consequences of the 1992 Scottish General Election Result', *Parliamentary Affairs*, op.cit. For example, Paterson *et al*, comment on the 1992 election: 'So long as the opinion polls suggested that there was a possibility of a Labour government, there was little risk of support slipping to the SNP. Although the SNP ran a triumphalist campaign, claiming it was on the verge of winning a majority of Scottish seats, and therefore of being in a position to negotiate for independence, it was continually frustrated by the prospect of a Labour government delivering a Scottish parliament shortly after coming to office.' *Parliamentary Affairs*, op.cit., p635. While not disagreeing with the broad thrust of Paterson *et al*'s comment, this is an area which has been left completely unresearched: the nature of the SNP's appeal and why it failed to electorally break through in 1992.

16 *Scotsman*, 29 February 1992.

17 David McCrone, 'Opinion Polls in Scotland', 1991–1993, *Scottish Affairs*, No. 4, Summer 1993, p129.

18 Richard J. Finlay, *Independent and Free: Scottish Politics and the Origins of the Scottish National Party 1918-1945*, John Donald, Edinburgh 1994; Jack Brand, 'SNP members: the way of the faithful', in Pippa Norris, Ivor Crewe, David Denver and David Broughton (eds), *British Elections and*

Parties Yearbook 1992, Harvester Wheatsheaf, London 1992.

19 Gavin Wallace and Randall Stevenson (eds.), *The Scottish Novel since the Seventies*, Edinburgh University Press, Edinburgh 1993, contains critical assessments of the work of Kelman, Gray, McIlvanney and many others.

20 David McCrone, *Understanding Scotland: The Sociology of a Stateless Nation*, Routledge, London 1992, p174, 175. Tartanry and Kailyardism have defined Scotland across the globe from Scots at home, to the Scots diaspora and world at large. The phenomenon of tartanry according to one observer has shaped Scottish culture and society to the present day negatively: 'Tartan's principal legacy is ... a cancerous national inferiority complex: the quite unmistakable psychological end-product of two centuries of tawdry palliatives – of escaping from social problems into wishful fantasy. It is the result of being told, and telling ourselves, that adventure is a thing only of the distant romantic past – now safely tamed on to postcards, on to football grounds, into bagpipes in the mists of wee bit hills and glens, or into impotent nostalgia for past glories (and that includes nostalgia for bygone days of Red Socialism).' Lindsay Paterson, 'Scotch Myths', *Bulletin of Scottish Politics*, No. 2, Spring 1981, p71.
   See also, I. Campbell, 'Kailyard', in David Daiches (ed), *The New Companion to Scottish Culture*, Polygon 1993, p169. For a persuasive examination of the cultural importance of tartanry and Kailyardism see: Tom Nairn, *The Break-up of Britain: Crisis and Neo-nationalism*, New Left Books, London 2nd edn. 1981.

21 Colin McArthur, 'Scotland and Cinema: The Iniquity of the Fathers', in Colin McArthur (ed), *Scotch Reels: Scotland in Cinema and Television*, British Film Institute, London 1982; John Caughie, 'Scottish Television: What Would It Look Like?', in McArthur, *op.cit.*

22 David McKie, ' "Fact is free but comment is sacred"; or, was it The Sun wot won it?', in Ivor Crewe and Brian Gosschalk (eds), *Political Communications: The General Election Campaign of 1992*, Cambridge University Press, Cambridge 1995; Martin Linton, 'Sun-powered Politics', *Guardian*, 30 October 1995.

23 Jack Brand, *The Nationalist Movement in Scotland*, Routledge and Kegan Paul, London 1978, p215.

24 Chris Harvie, 'Nationalism, Journalism and Cultural Politics', in Tom Gallacher (ed), *Nationalism in the Nineties*, Polygon, Edinburgh 1991, p31.

25 Miller, 1981, *op cit.*, pp99-101; Allan Macartney, 'Summary of Scottish Opinion Polls Relating to Voting Intentions and Constitutional Change', in H.M. Drucker and N.L. Drucker (eds), *The Scottish Government Yearbook 1980*, Paul Harris, Edinburgh 1980, p229; David McCrone, 'Opinion Polls in Scotland, July 1994 to June 1995', *Scottish Affairs*, No. 12, Summer 1995, p144.

26 Miller, 1980, *op.cit.*; The Scotsman, 29 January 1992; 8 April 1992.

27 Andrew Marr, *The Battle for Scotland*, Penguin, Harmondsworth 1992, Ch. 2.

28 Paul H. Scott, *Scotland in Europe: Dialogue with a Sceptical Friend*, Canongate, Edinburgh 1993, p50.

29 Vernon Bogdanor viewed the 40 per cent rule as having long-term

constitutional implications: 'it may be that whenever a referendum comes to be held in the future the defenders of the status quo will insist that a 40 per cent requirement be inserted so as to ensure the genuinely "full-hearted consent" of the voters. It will be a difficult demand to resist ... ' Vernon Bogdanor, *The People and the Party System: The Referendum and Electoral Reform in British Politics*, Cambridge University Press 1981, p60.

30 ORC found in October 1976 a 65:16 devolution majority, narrowing to 43:40 for System Three at the outset of the referendum campaign, finally finishing 33 per cent yes 31 per cent no (52:48). Richard Rose and Ian McAllister, *United Kingdom Facts*, Macmillan, London 1982, p117. See: John Bochel, David Denver and Allan Macartney (eds), *The Referendum Experience Scotland 1979*, Aberdeen University Press, Aberdeen 1981.

31 David and Gareth Butler, *British Political Facts 1900–1994*, Macmillan, London 1994, pp213-221; Richard Parry, *Scottish Political Facts*, T & T Clark, Edinburgh 1988, pp2-3; David Butler and Dennis Kavanagh, *The British General Election of 1983*, Macmillan, London 1984, p301.

32 *British Political Facts, op.cit.*; *Scottish Political Facts, op.cit.*

33 James G. Kellas, 'Scottish Nationalism', in David Butler and Michael Pinto-Duschinsky, *The British General Election of 1970*, Macmillan, London 1971, p455.

34 Miller, 1980, *op.cit.*, p107.

35 James Mitchell, *Conservatives and the Union: A Study of Conservative Party Attitudes to the Union*, Edinburgh University Press, Edinburgh 1990; David Seawright and John Curtice, 'The Decline of the Scottish Conservative and Unionist Party 1950-92: Religion, Ideology or Economics?', *Contemporary Record*, Vol. 9 No. 2, Autumn 1995.

36 The *Scotsman*, 17 November 1995; 1 December 1995.

37 Bernard Crick, 'Ambushes and Advances: The Scotland Act 1998', *Political Quarterly*, Vol. 66 No. 4, October–December 1995, p237.

38 Gerry Hassan, 'The Scottish Stalemate', *Renewal: A Journal of Labour Politics*, Vol. 1 No. 3, July 1993; 'Blair and the Importance of Being British', *Renewal: A Journal of Labour Politics*, Vol. 3 No. 3, July 1995.

39 Stein Rokkan and Derek W. Urwin, 'Introduction: Centres and Peripheries in Western Europe', in Stein Rokkan and Derek W. Urwin (eds), *The Politics of Territorial Identity: Studies in European Regionalism*, Sage, London 1982, p11.

40 David McCrone, 'Part of the Union: Scotland and the Constitutional Question', *Renewal: A Journal of Labour Politics*, Vol. 3 No. 3, July 1995, p41.

41 Lindsay Paterson, *The Autonomy of Modern Scotland*, Edinburgh University Press, Edinburgh 1994, p4.

42 For a recent example of reproducing and reinforcing some of the myths and symbols of Scotland from an unexpected source see some of the papers within: 'Scottish Dimensions: History, the Nation and the Schools': *Conference Papers* Vol. 1 & 2: A conference organised jointly by History Workshop and Ruskin College, 24–26 March 1995.

ONLY CONNECT: TOWARDS A NEW DEMOCRATIC SETTLEMENT

Martin Summers

> Those most in need of help deserve the truth. Hope is not born of false promises; disillusion is.
>
> They are tired of dogma. They are tired of politicians pretending to have a monopoly on the answers. They are tired of glib promises broken as readily in office as they were made on the soap box.
>
> When we make a promise, we must be sure we can keep it. That is page 1, line 1 of a new contract between Government and citizen.
>
> But we should do more. We have to change the rules of government and we will.
>
> We are putting forward the biggest programme of change to democracy ever proposed by a political party.
>
> Speech by Tony Blair MP to the 1994 Labour party conference

Much of new Labour's appeal is the hope it offers of a new political settlement – one that marks a sharp and invigorating departure from what has been, for many, over fifteen years of centralisation, de-democratisation and 'sleaze'. Moreover, new Labour's programme aims to 'reconnect' politics with the British people, to end the widespread sense that government, at all levels, has lost touch with their needs and concerns, by bringing government 'closer to the people' (through devolution and restoring 'proper democratic control' to institutions that have become quangos[1]).

There is good reason to believe that a Labour government would not be able to achieve such a transformation. This is not because its programme – a Bill of Rights, Scottish devolution, regional government and reform of the House of Lords – is either not radical enough or too limited in its likely effects. Rather, such a transformation would not be achieved because Labour's programme – like that of the other parties – simply fails to address some of the fundamental weaknesses in the British political system. Labour's programme would change the architecture of the system; that is, the way in which its elements relate to each other – but not its culture nor the dominance of traditional party political activity. More fundamentally, it does not question some of the core assumptions and beliefs upon which the system is premised. Unless Labour addresses these issues it will not be able to reconnect politics with people and achieve a new democratic settlement.

LABOUR'S DEMOCRATIC DILEMMA

The challenge for a Labour government is the same challenge faced by developed democracies throughout the world: to reconcile people's rising expectations of what governments should provide with the requirements of fiscal prudence, while also trying to counter the frustration and political antipathy that can result when these expectations are not met.

This has led to disillusion with politics and politicians, with electorates, particularly in the US, Britain, France, Italy, and the former Warsaw Pact countries looking for fresh political approaches (whether embodied by new parties or personalities) that promise a new politics which decisively breaks with the past. This sense of disillusion is not new in itself, and has led to landslide victories for political forces promising sweeping change in the past, such as Ronald Reagan in 1980 or the 1945 Labour government, and this in turn has led to disillusion as dedicated supporters and the ordinary electorate alike have been disappointed by their records in office.

This pattern of expectation and then disillusion is not surprising because political systems have not changed sufficiently to cope with the rising demands placed upon them by the electorate and organised interests – whether they be farmers, ailing industries, professional associations or public sector unions – often to the point that the democratic process can no longer function effectively (a phenomenon one American commentator has termed *demosclerosis*[2]).

One reason for this is that competing politicians try to outbid each others' promises, thus driving up voters' expectations and demands.

There are few brakes on this inflationary spiral of expectations; the only forces restraining the spiral are voters' and financial markets' assessment of the credibility of the promises made. What Robert Spero said of American political advertising, in *The Duping of the American Voter*, can be said of politics in general the world over: 'The sky is the limit, with regard to what can be said, what can be promised, what accusations can be made, what lies can be told'.[3]

The disillusionment and disappointment that voters feel when their hopes and expectations are dashed by the party they voted for is exacerbated by the frustration and impotence they feel between elections. In this period they have little or no influence or direct say in how their locality or nation is governed, and few opportunities to get involved; in this sense they are effectively disconnected from politics. The frisson of democratic excitement felt every five years is not sufficient to satisfy most people's desire to feel that they can exercise some influence or power over government.

The task then is to develop means by which people can be connected with politics, so that they have the opportunity to exercise their influence in meaningful ways, without feeling that these opportunities are merely consultation exercises or devices to lend legitimacy to decisions already taken by those in power. There is a danger that the potential of new means of democratic participation – such as citizens' juries and electronic voting from home – will not be realised if they are only used to inform established decision-making procedures and thus become regarded as ineffectual talking-shops.

A Labour government, if it is to transform politics in the way that Tony Blair envisaged in his 1994 conference speech, has a clear need to address two main issues: first, how to change the rules of government so as to reduce the possibility of disillusion and frustrated expectations; and second, how to develop the political system so that it is more open and 'connects' with ordinary people who have no inclination to get involved in party politics.

THE STATE WE'RE ALL IN

The British political system, relative to others, has been remarkably stable and robust and has not had to reconstitute itself radically in response to internal or external threats of the magnitude of revolution, civil war, or invasion. This to some extent explains the absence of soul-searching about the fundamentals of the political system, such as the primacy given to sovereignty rather than constitutional and institutional checks and balances on central and local government.

The longevity of parliamentary sovereignty has made it, by default, one of the defining characteristics of British politics – the supremacy of Parliament and the absence of constraints upon it being a focal point for discussions not only of Britain's relationship with the rest of the world, but also of any proposals to constrain Parliament's powers (such as a codified constitution or Bill of Rights). It is also the key determinant of the nature of democratic debate. For both Conservatives and many socialists, any check on parliamentary sovereignty undermines British democracy, because it is equated with Britain's ability to govern itself and make its own laws; therefore any interference in that process is by its very nature undemocratic. Labour and Liberal Democrats echo these sentiments regarding local government; that removing or restricting its powers undermines local democracy because communities cannot then govern themselves effectively.

Democratic debate is still premised on party politics as almost the sole focus for democratic life, with the units of democracy – Parliament and local councils – essentially unchanged in the way they operate and are comprised. Ideas for local referenda, citizens' juries and electronic democracy (voting from home via TV or computer links) have received little support, and most advocates want them to inform rather than challenge or replace traditional local and national politics.

There is no room for complacency. Surveys indicate widespread discontentment with conventional politics, not only with politicians but also with the political system.[4] The desire for alternative forms of political expression reflects widespread scepticism about politicians and party politics, yet the political parties are wedded to a concept of democracy that places party politics, in Parliament and local councils, as the primary vehicle of political expression. The consequence is that ordinary people have few means of direct political participation, except through public protest and through voting in national and local elections. But voting is a very limited and passive form of political expression, akin to writing a blank cheque, with the voter only having a vague idea how his or her taxes might be used and to what purpose, and with little scope for having subsequent influence or a direct say in the policies that this vote has mandated. The ballot box is, however, still seen, with little scepticism, as the main and indeed an effective source of democratic accountability.

LESSONS FROM WALSALL

The adequacy of traditional forms of democracy and electoral accountability were challenged by Walsall Council's proposals in 1995 for a radical programme to decentralise decision-making. This would shift the emphasis away from the traditional model, centred on the town hall, departmental committees and party politics, to a model based on 54 budget-holding neighbourhood councils with elected members representing hundreds rather than thousands of people.

The proposal was immediately condemned by the national Labour Party which took steps to prevent the programme from being implemented, including the suspension of the Walsall Borough Labour Party. At the 1995 Labour Party conference, the shadow environment spokesman, Frank Dobson said that Walsall's advertisement claiming that local government did not work was 'bloody stupid' and warned councils to look to other councils' experiences before embarking on radical plans to change service delivery.[5] He could only have been referring to other British councils as there are plenty of examples of decentralisation being extremely successful in other countries, not just in terms of increasing participation but also as a force for greater efficiency. Professor Patrick Dunleavy, one of the few commentators to make the case for decentralisation, has pointed out that: 'In Sweden, the authorities who were most unhappy with the service from council staffs, and hence keenest on contracting out, are the ones who have adopted radical decentralisation'.[6]

Labour's reaction to Walsall demonstrates the enormous gap between what it does in practice and the pro-experimentation/pro-decentralisation rhetoric of its consultation paper on its plans for regional government, *A Choice for England*:

> Centralisation produces a fundamental, as well as a prosaic inefficiency. It stifles debate, and reduces the opportunity for there to be a clash of ideas, of proposals which are then put to the policy test. It is by giving people responsibility, and choice that the best of government can be achieved ... Experimentation and flexibility are encouraged in a decentralised political system, but are sadly lacking from Britain's rigidly centralised one.[7]

Lessons for Labour: The Conservative Strategy for Control

Labour knows that much of its appeal rests on the promise of a new kind of politics. It also knows that it will only win office if the electorate believes Labour would be fiscally responsible when in office. A Labour government would have to demonstrate to the public and the international financial markets that it is tough on inflation, unwilling to tax significantly more and able to keep public expenditure under control.

The Conservative governments since 1979 have shown how difficult it is to keep taxes and public expenditure under control (let alone reduce them). Simon Jenkins[8] has argued that the Conservative government's desire to keep public expenditure under control is the main reason why it increasingly centralised the financial control and management of much of the public sector (though it also reflected a wider desire to achieve autonomy where possible).[9]

There are many reasons why the Conservatives have had difficulty in containing, let alone reducing, public expenditure and the overall burden of taxation; and these reasons are shared by developed democracies the world over. The dynamics of government growth, and administrations' inability to arrest it, has been analysed at length by public choice theorists.[10] They argue that one of the main reasons why public expenditure grows is that politicians, public servants and their organisations have their own interests to advance – namely votes, influence, power, bigger budgets or even personal financial gain – often to the detriment of the public interest.

The democratic process, where it allows for competition between interest groups, encourages governments to target benefits at well-organised interests, particularly industries seeking subsidies or protection, at the expense of the general populace who have to pay for these benefits through higher prices and taxes. In addition, electoral pressures – with politicians trying to outbid each others' promises to voters – can drive up government spending to unsustainable levels which are likely in the long term to be contrary to the public interest, by leading to levels of inflation, taxes and debt that are extremely economically disadvantageous (as Italy and most Latin American and African countries have found to their cost).

One way to mitigate these pressures is to have an autocratic system of government, as in Hong Kong, Chile and Singapore, but this would be politically impossible for developed democracies. Their task is more difficult: to develop a system of government that can cope with and indeed manage the short-term democratic pressures put upon it, but not at the expense of medium- and long-term goals, such as low inflation and manageable levels of national debt and spending.

What is required then is a system of government that allows for popular participation and influence but ensures that democratic activity – by politicians and ordinary people – takes place in a strong framework of strict rules and limits that ensures and indeed encourages responsible decision-taking. Such a system would be sustainable in much the same way that sustainable economic growth is said to be; that growth should not undermine the long term health of the system that generates it.

The key to achieving such a system (that could be termed sustainable government) in Britain is to recognise that strict constitutional and institutional constraints on the free and unfettered exercise of democratic power, while considered by many to be alien to the British political tradition, are essential for both a free and prosperous society and for establishing an environment for responsible political decision-making.

This is particularly important for a Labour government as it would find it politically unacceptable to pursue a centralising strategy of autocratic control, because much of its support is among people who have been particularly demoralised by this strategy, especially public sector employees. There are, however, a variety of ways in which a Labour government could restrain public expenditure without resort to the sort of command and control techniques used by the Conservatives. (These are discussed below.)

LESSONS FOR LABOUR: THE (UN)CONSERVATIVE CRACKDOWN ON LOCAL GOVERNMENT

The Conservative government has felt no constraint in removing the powers of local government and imposing strict controls on its freedom of operation. Similarly it has had no democratic qualms about placing spheres of state activity in quangos, beyond the reach of local government. This has not been the result of any principled critique of local government *per se* (indeed the Conservative Party does not assign it a distinct democratic role), but rather the cumulative impact of a series of ad hoc responses to the growth of public expenditure and Conservatives' fear of councils at a time when they were the principal sites for anti-government and anti-Conservative activity in the 1980s: such as opposition to rate-capping and the poll tax. The British Conservative approach to local government is in stark contrast to conservatives elsewhere, who regard strong, protected local forms of democracy as essential for democracy, acting as an essential check on the aggrandisement and encroachment of central government.

The Conservatives' approach to local government also runs counter to its economic principles and public choice theory.[11] In the economic sphere, it has argued for deregulation and competition as essential conditions for more innovation, greater efficiency, flexibility and responsiveness to the changing needs of customers. It has done exactly the opposite in local government; choosing to increase the regulation of councils' activity through legislation and day-to-day management from the centre. The current system of allocating funds to councils, together with capping and increased regulation, has to a great extent standardised both the level and type of service that councils can offer.

The Conservatives have taken the same approach to local government taxation and revenue-raising. Central government can choose from or invent a wide range of instruments to raise revenue, according to economic and social conditions. By contrast local government in recent years has had to rely on just one local tax for its revenue; its suitability – in terms of revenue-raising capability and administrative efficiency – being determined centrally. If local councils could choose the taxes they wished to levy, then one would expect quite different mixes throughout the country: areas with a stable population and with a history of tax-compliance could rely on a poll tax, knowing that it would stand a good chance of collecting revenue this way; while cities with highly mobile populations would stand a better chance of raising revenue through taxes on immobile items, such as property, and charges for services, such as parking, or refuse collection. Experimentation through competition in services has produced gains in efficiency and innovation; the same process should be tried for raising revenue, subject to controls by an independent regulator.

Local government in the USA has become increasingly competitive, with states and counties becoming more experienced in searching for optimum mixes of both the level and type of taxes and expenditures, in order to retain and attract people and businesses. An additional competitive force has been the emergence of thousands of self-contained 'privatised communities' in the United States, with their own schools, hospitals, roads, and fire and police services.[12] These 'opted-out' communities, with their own planning restrictions and bye-laws, are surprisingly close to the Utopia envisaged by Robert Nozick in his seminal *Anarchy, State and Utopia*, in which people can form their own self-governing communities, with their own laws and tax-raising powers.[13] (This geographic federalism has been supplemented by proposals for what Gordon Tullock calls sociological federalism[14] whereby religious and ethical communities can incorporate themselves into associations, transcending geographic communities, to govern family and marital relations or even redistribute income between association members).

A strong theme of the American right's agenda for local government is the value of competing governments and services, with the most successful states and counties reaping the rewards of attracting sources of tax revenue. While competition between national governments for internationally mobile sources of tax revenue has long been recognised in Britain (often cited as the reason why Britain has not signed up to the Social Chapter), the value of competition between local governments has not been. Indeed, the Conservatives' strategy has been one of increasing standardisation and command and control rather than deregulation and establishing the conditions for competition (the much vaunted regime of compulsory competitive tendering has only generated competition between potential suppliers of services to councils; the citizen cannot choose between competing service providers).

While the virtues of competition for goods and services – innovation, and incentives for better quality and efficiency – are widely recognised, the possibility that competition could achieve the same benefits in systems of governance and organisational forms has not been entertained. One of the most valuable benefits of opening up what have traditionally been local government domains to outside organisations – whether they be commercial organisations, quangos, charities, NHS trusts or housing associations – is that there has been the opportunity to see how different means of decision-making perform; thus presenting alternatives to the traditional monolithic, hierarchical and departmentalised local authority model.

One lesson for Labour is that effective competition between local government bodies, whereby they compete to attract residents and business by offering the most attractive mixes of taxes, charges, services and facilities, would act as a force to keep public expenditure down – as an excessively high tax and charge area would prove unattractive to current and potential sources of revenue from taxes and charges. This would be a more attractive means of controlling local government expenditure than the Conservative's strategy of ever-increasing centralisation, standardisation and top-down control. However, this would require a radical restructuring of local government (discussed later in the section *Disaggregating Democracy*) involving a dramatic reduction in the size of councils and a splitting up of their responsibilities.

Lessons for Labour: Too Conservative By Half

The Conservatives have made a tactical error in wedding themselves to the status quo position on constitutional issues. Unlike Tony Blair or Newt Gingrich, they cannot present themselves as either innovative or forward-looking on constitutional issues. The Republicans in the US and the anti-establishment nationalistic right in Italy and France have actively promoted a positive rather than reactive agenda for institutional, democratic change. Meanwhile British Conservatives have chosen, with little deliberation, to promote an extremely limited agenda for almost no change.

This Conservative opposition to constitutional reform has been subject to an excellent analysis by Ferdinand Mount, formerly a director of the No. 10 Policy Unit. He argues that Walter Bagehot was responsible for establishing the traditional view of the constitution, held dear by almost all Conservatives, that it developed organically in an evolutionary manner, with unchecked parliamentary sovereignty as its touchstone.[15] John Redwood MP articulated this position well: 'Those who seek to marginalise Parliament or ignore it, or set it under external constraint, are out to undermine the very foundations of our settled and unwritten constitution.'[16]

The strength of this view is reflected in the unwillingness of Thatcherites, so willing to challenge conventional wisdom elsewhere, to entertain the radical proposals for constitutional and institutional reform made by Friedrich Hayek, Milton Friedman and other free market thinkers whose economic views have gained a wide audience in Britain. Their work on the interplay between constitutional and institutional arrangements and the health of the economy has developed into a school of thought known as constitutional economics, which has become associated with a wide range of innovative proposals to make decision-making more transparent and thus lead to more responsible policy-making.

The American Gram-Rudman-Hollings Act is a good example of constitutional economics. The Act says that proposals for increasing expenditure have to specify both the cuts in other expenditure necessary to fund it or the taxes needed to raise the additional revenue to fund them. This makes budget decision-taking more transparent and accessible for elected representatives, interest groups and the public. It also allows them to draw close connections between expenditure and benefits, allowing them to undertake cost-benefit analysis of any proposal. A similar Act for British central and local government would not necessarily lead to better decisions, but it would allow for more informed and less secretive policy-making.

Professor John Burton[17] is one of the few British academics to have applied constitutional economics to Britain. In a seminal analysis of fiscal decision-making in central government, Professor Burton argues the case for a wide range of constitutional and institutional devices to encourage more responsible decision-taking and a strong framework of constraints to prevent public expenditure from reaching unsustainable levels. He proposes an Economic Bill of Rights that would limit government expenditure as a percentage of GDP to a specified level (most free market economists argue that it should at most be about 35 per cent; Burton suggests 25 per cent). He also suggests legislation for balanced budgets to ensure that the costs of expenditure cannot be hidden through deficit financing and are instead made plain through the imposition of higher taxes or charges.

Professor Gerard Radnitzky's[18] outline of an ideal 'constitution of liberty' shares many of the proposals put forward by constitutional economists, such as:

- the constitution should prohibit budget deficits (whether financed by borrowing or by printing money)
- taxation should be treated as a constitutional matter
- there should be constitutional limits to revenues (in times of peace revenues must not exceed a stated percentage of the national income)
- constitutional limits are required for borrowing, that is, to fund capital projects that constitute productive social investments

- the constitution should secure the free movement of goods and services, of capital and people
- the constitution should outlaw all sorts of protectionism

Most constitutional economists have a clear free market, libertarian agenda. However, their central insight, based on extensive empirical analysis – that strong frameworks are needed for governmental decision-making if an economy is to be sustainable in the long term – is one that any political party could learn from. For example, every government in Western Europe is sitting on a pensions timebomb, whereby it will be extremely difficult for governments to fund, without excessive borrowing, the pensions of those people who will retire in the next ten years or so (because the proportion of net taxpayers – i.e. working adults – to net tax beneficiaries will have shrunk considerably). The lesson here is that it is in all these governments' interests to ensure that such a scenario will not repeat itself and that state pensions should be properly funded and ring-fenced, preferably constitutionally safeguarded so that future administrations do not 'raid' the pensions kitty to support current expenditure.

Labour could gain in many ways by setting and following a constitutional economics agenda. It would fit in neatly with the rest of its agenda for constitutional reform, but would also provide substance and additional credibility for its avowed intention to be fiscally responsible when in government and to avoid repeating the tax and spend mistakes of the past. In addition it would re-enforce its analysis and criticisms of the Conservatives' inability to reduce the overall tax burden and exert strong fiscal management. In government a strong fiscal constitution would provide Labour with a set of explicit constraining conditions for policy-making, allowing it to resist more effectively pressures for more spending when it cannot be afforded.

LESSONS FOR LABOUR: EUROPE – THE CIRCLE THE CONSERVATIVES COULDN'T SQUARE

The Conservatives have clearly demonstrated their difficulty in reconciling their views on the role of the domestic state in the economy with their traditional party attachment to parliamentary sovereignty. A national government can ensure free trade within its borders but it is unable to do so beyond its borders except through bi-lateral negotiations. Such negotiations are usually successful only when a reduction in the barriers to free trade is not perceived as being significantly detrimental to politically-powerful organised interests within both countries. Where free trade cannot be negotiated it can only be imposed on nations through a supra-national body that can overturn national policies that are contrary to the goal of free trade – i.e. these supranational bodies must be able to override parliamentary sovereignty.

Samuel Brittan has pointed out, echoing Ferdinand Mount's arguments,[19] 'Free trade and the free market do not merely legitimise, but demand, some supranational constitutional framework'.[20] This is because only a supranational body, relatively free of political influences and able to act relatively autonomously in pursuit of its given goals, can act effectively in counteracting protectionism and ensuring that common principles of trade are enforced. In this sense such a body must be undemocratic and unaccountable in so far that it can only achieve its goals if it is insulated from direct political pressures.

This has been shown to be the case with current European competition policy. The mandate of DG4 (the European Commission's Competition Directorate) is to liberalise the European markets for many highly regulated industries (such as telecommunications, energy, air transport and postal services). This would exert significant downward pressures on costs, which one estimate puts at being 40 per cent higher for energy and state airlines compared to the US.[21] However, there is a tension between this mandate and the member states whose policies often go in the opposite direction (by giving state industries further subsidises). There is therefore a need to give DG4 the political independence, resources and powers it needs to do its job properly – being able to override member states where necessary.

Conservative criticisms of the European Community enforcement of a Community-wide trade policy have been misplaced. Conservatives have missed an opportunity to champion the ideal of supranational and non-political bodies as essential for achieving freer trade and thus to advance Britain's interests (as Britain's privatised utilities, the Post Office, and the financial services industry are in a strong position to take a substantial market share).

The Conservative Party's internal divisions on Europe cannot be overcome until Conservatives recognise that some form of supranational body that can override national parliaments is an essential condition for achieving free trade and open markets within the European Community. Labour does not give parliamentary sovereignty as high a priority as the Conservatives do, but it has failed to recognise that there is a conflict between trying to achieve free trade through the European Community and the claims of individual member states to protect their industries and associated special privileges. Increasing the powers of the European Parliament would not solve this problem but may in fact worsen it as it would bring more political pressures to bear.

The political horse-trading (or 'pork-barrel' politics as it is known in the United States) that plagues the European Community and prevents many useful Community policies being put into effect illustrates the need for constitutional economics to be applied in the European Community where the distance between voters, representatives and the governing bodies is far greater than at the national or local level, thus making an even greater case for clear, strictly enforced rules to govern the conduct of public bodies and institutions.

DISAGGREGATING LOCAL DEMOCRACY

It is unfortunate that local government is regarded as being synonymous with local authorities because it narrows the scope for discussing local democracy. Local government is better understood as the full range of policy-making organisations at the local level, including policy-making quangos such as TECs (Training and Enterprise Councils), local councils, police, fire and health authorities.

Broadening the conventional definition of what constitutes local government makes one realise that there are many different bodies and ways of making and implementing policy at the local level. (That the Commission for Local Democracy compared the relative merits of these models, in terms of their accountability, is one of its most important though underrated contributions to the debate on local government).[22] That there are separate authorities for health, fire and the police, each having quite distinct and separate functions and ways of taking decisions, is rarely called into question, nor is the fact that local authorities combine a wide variety of functions, professions and cultures: education, leisure, housing, planning, social services, highways and parking, trading standards, environmental health, licensing, refuse collection, street cleansing, parks, etc. To the extent that local authorities combine such a wide range of functions they are highly aggregated organisations, far more so than, say, fire authorities whose range of responsibilities is far narrower.

The high level of aggregated decision-making in local authorities has many democratic implications. The first is that decision-making is spread across several committees (a city council typically has, at the very least, separate committees for education, social services, housing, planning and transportation). The members of these committees are appointed by the political groups; voters have no direct say over the composition of these committees. This means there is a loose connection between voters and their representatives: votes are cast for councillors primarily on the basis of their political affiliations rather than on the basis of particular councillors' aims or beliefs with regard to specific areas of policy (except perhaps where a controversial issue divides political and public opinion, such as a major town centre redevelopment or road building scheme).

Another major consequence is that, in combining so many functions, local authorities are arguably far too large to function effectively at a democratic level, a point made by Anthony Jay in one of the most interesting and innovative discussions of local government in Britain. Jay, a writer on management and political issues who is best known as the co-author of the *Yes Minister* and *Yes, Prime Minister* TV series argues that:

> If local government is to learn from service industries, then the first lesson is that it should be organised in small groups placed to give the maximum convenience to the citizen, that those groups should be given as much independent authority as possible, and be given the budget and other resources to deliver those services effectively with the minimum of upward reference – but the maximum of upward and lateral communication.[24]

Jay further argues that it should be regarded as axiomatic that the lowest unit of political representation is one in which it is possible for everyone to know everyone else, for the representative to be known by, and know, all the voters he or she represents. Jay suggests that the size of these constituencies should be about 600 people – regarded as a manageable size for many democratic forums (the Commons, the ancient Athenian popular assembly) and other organisations (battalions, many schools, residents associations, neighbourhood watch schemes) – 'with significantly larger numbers you leave the region of democratic involvement and enter the realms of opinion polls'.

Jay summarises his proposals thus:

> Devolve the delivery of services to local neighbourhood offices on shopping parades, serving communities of about six thousand. Make those offices work to an elected committee of about ten people, each representing about 200 local households. Support them with four or five street representatives each. And let the chairmen of these 50-odd neighbourhood committees form the council that constitutes the next tier up, to agree policy, allocate resources, deal with Whitehall, and take the decisions and manage the services that the smaller groups are not equipped or qualified to handle.[25]

The radical democratic 'utopianism' of Jay's scheme is refreshing in a debate that is predominantly concerned with refining rather than reinventing or revolutionising local government. His central point, that for popular democratic involvement to be possible it must be based on manageable units of representation, is a vital one; more importantly, it calls into question what functions councils should have and what are the most appropriate constituencies, in terms of size and composition, for those functions.

There is, for example, an enormous difference between education and highways departments in terms of the sort of services they provide and the people affected by them. Education departments provide direct tangible services to particular individuals and families; while the benefits of the work of a highways department are less tangible and are difficult to quantify as it affects far more people, not all of them necessarily residents of the council. Housing departments, like education, have easily identifiable clients – council tenants – who also receive tangible benefits and services.

It is not clear then why all residents in a council area should have a democratic input and influence on matters, such as education or housing, which are of no concern to them and have no direct impact on them. It would make more sense – in terms of having a closer fit between client group and their representatives – to have separate authorities in these areas, albeit of a much smaller size than they are in their current departmental form (preferably closer to the 600 constituent size suggested by Jay) – at the level of council estate, street or parish.

The term authority suggests a large organisation, but what is envisaged here are relatively small organisations with official legal status, with articles of association and laws concerning their electoral processes and the composition of their governing bodies. There are many experiments in neighbourhood councils for council tenants – Southwark being particularly noteworthy – which provide possible models for separate housing authorities, for example. However, these are all determined by the local authority in question. It would be better if neighbourhoods or council estates could secede from their local authority and choose from a variety of 'off-the-shelf' models of incorporation. This would have the additional advantage of giving local authorities a powerful incentive to ensure that they provide their tenants with effective and efficient services.

This is already what is happening in respect of schools, where schools can become Grant Maintained (by central government) and secede from local authority control. It would also be better if education departments become authorities in their own right, to be elected only by families with children of school and pre-school age, thus ensuring that the constituent group had a powerful vested interest in the success of education in their area. Such authorities could have a much broader composition than education departments whose policy is determined solely by party political appointments to the education committee; instead these authorities could be composed of a combination of directly elected members and individuals randomly selected from a list of candidates that put themselves forward.

These authorities would be responsible for co-ordinating and purchasing services (the monitoring could be contracted out) rather than providing them, in much the same way that health authorities do. There are several advantages to this: the first is that it would remove the unfortunate tendency for councillors to identify too strongly with their local authority, often being more concerned with defending council jobs than improving services. The second advantage is that it would force the authority to choose a package of services from a range of providers, whether they be public, private or voluntary organisations. This would closely follow a well-established model found in the United States of 'contract cities' that buy and sell services from other cities, the private sector , or other levels of government.[26]

A 'contract city' model for separate health, housing and education authorities, etc. would also allow providers to achieve their optimum size for efficiency. The private sector is already capable of doing this, for example by providing support services (IT, finance, personnel, training) for their contracts with several authorities from just the one site. The private sector can organise its operations as it wishes, avoiding the constraints placed by the territorial boundaries and barriers to cross-boundary tendering placed on the local authority services.

Different private sector markets naturally tend to reach their optimum level of size through the competitive process leading to quite different typical organisational sizes in different sectors: for example, the success of large private sector organisations in bidding for councils' financial administrative services suggests economies of scale beyond the size of most councils, but there is no reason to suppose that this exists for all services. Indeed, the American urban economist Sam Staley argues that empirical studies have 'consistently failed to find economies of scale in city services ... According to one estimate, economies of scale may exist for communities of up to 15,000. Beyond that point, costs are either constant or rise.'[27] Economies of scale could be reached within the current system if social services, housing departments, etc could compete with each other and the private sector, leading to either mergers or, more likely, demergers to avoid diseconomies of scale. This would require a quite different system of funding and a relaxation of the rules on cross-boundary tendering.

Another advantage of having smaller, more focused authorities for local services is that they are likely to tax and spend more responsibly than larger authorities covering more functions. One reason for this is that it is easier for voters and their representatives to monitor budgets in smaller, more focused organisations, because it is easier to discern connections between expenditure and benefits. The increase in public expenditure and taxes as the units of government have grown supports Anthony Jay's contention that 'money is known to be spent better more carefully in small sums by large numbers of people at low levels than in large sums by small numbers of people at high level, and to be spent most effectively by those who will benefit directly from the goods and services it purchases.'[28]

DISAGGREGATION AS FRAGMENTATION

One familiar criticism of the government's approach to local government and the increase in the number of quangos providing local services is that it has led to fragmentation. The influential local government commentator John Stewart[29] has argued that separate elections for quangos could lead to confusion in the public's mind, making it difficult to generate interest, and worsen the already fragmented nature of the way local services are governed.

The alternative view maintains that public interest in and participation in local elections would increase. Disaggregating democracy so that people are clearly voting for competing bundles of policies in particular areas (health, education, housing, etc.) would give people a greater sense of what they are voting for and thus encourage participation.

Concerns about the fragmentation of local services can be used as a justification for having virtually all local services controlled by local authorities, but it is a fiction that even closely related services are integrated within departments, let alone between them or across committees. Education, social services and housing departments and committees have their own, often incompatible cultures and interests which would be better resolved if they were independent, forming partnerships with each other where need required. The virtues of this approach have been shown in the City Challenge urban regeneration projects that are based on explicit partnerships between local authorities, TECs, the police and the private sector, towards the achievement of specific goals within a certain time-frame.

The point about the fragmentation critique is that it reflects more fundamental assumptions about how services can be provided, whether they be in the private or public sector. Proponents of the fragmentation critique believe that services can best be provided within an established, seamless and institutionalised pattern of provision and relations between clients, providers, electors and representatives. A major argument for fragmentation and a plethora of overlapping providers, authorities and constituencies is that these patterns can and should be in constant flux and tension, mutually adjusting to new developments and changing client group needs. As Sam Staley argues: 'Destroying the complexity of local governance by replacing fragmented local governments with a larger monopoly government risks undermining the ability of the government to serve the interests of diverse communities.'[30]

TOWARDS A NEW PARLIAMENTARY SETTLEMENT

Debates on the future of both the European Community and local government have been radical compared to discussions of Parliamentary reform. Debate about the role of Parliament in the last five years has primarily been concerned with the conduct and remuneration and resources of its members. The Nolan Committee report on standards in public life focused on the integrity of MPs and possible conflicts of interests. But the Committee's remit did not allow it to ask what the role of Parliament and its members should be. It would have been better to identify the proper purposes and most appropriate role of Parliament and then ask how its members could best serve those purposes and whether there are any reasons why they don't do so now. One reason is that the resources of Parliament are over-stretched, particularly in providing support for MPs, most of whom have to work in small antiquated offices with at most a couple of staff. But calls for more resources are never accompanied by justification for what exactly these would or should be used for.

These questions have become more pertinent and in need of answers as the demands made of MPs, at Westminster and in their constituencies, have increased and as the volume of legislation has increased enormously. There is no consensus as to how Parliament should respond to these developments. More resources, in terms of administrative and research support, would undoubtedly help, but any short-term advantages this would achieve would soon be nullified as the demands of organised interests and citizens increase in response to the greater capacity of the system to absorb their demands.

As the constitutional expert Phillip Norton has said:

> In recent years it [Parliament] has shown a capacity to meet, more than before, the popular expectations held of it. By doing so it appears to have encouraged even greater expectations. To meet them, it has to strengthen the resources at its disposal. Without that will-power, Parliament is in danger of being overloaded with work and unable to meet the demands made of it. Members alone can determine whether Parliament limps into the twenty-first century or enters it as a body more responsive than ever before to the demands of a changing society.[31]

What is required then is some consensus as to what sort of institution Parliament should be and how it and its members should prioritise their tasks. There is a mismatch between MPs' understanding of what the most important part of their job is and what the public thinks.[33] Most MPs place their contribution to national debate, acting as a check on the executive, and working as a spokesperson for local interests at the top of their lists for being the most important part of their jobs. The public sees the most important aspects of MPs jobs being rooted in their constituency: expressing voters' concerns on national issues; dealing with constituents' personal problems; and attending meetings in the constituency. There is no established criteria for resolving these differences; indeed there cannot be until a debate begins within Parliament and outside it on what we want MPs and Parliament to do.

There is an urgent need to bring these tensions and differing views out into the open. One way of doing this would be to introduce Citizen's Charters for MPs (a Constituent's Charter), as Plaid Cymru and Paddy Ashdown MP have already done, and was proposed by the author in 1994.[33] Constituent's Charters would have several potential benefits, similar to those of other Citizen's Charters:

- charters would give MPs the opportunity to explain their role and aims to the public
- the public would be able to hold MPs to account on the basis of what they commit themselves to in their charters
- charters would encourage candidates to address specific tasks that lie ahead of them
- the public would know more about the activities of parliament and its members

The initial attraction of this is that it would empower constituents to hold their MPs to account, but it would also allow MPs to explain the demands made of them. A more accurate picture of the different demands made of MPs could be provided by annual surveys or even audits of Parliament which would provide information on the time and resources used by MPs in, for example, select committees, constituency work, research, business on the floor of the House, etc. The aim of this would not be to establish which MPs are 'best' in any sense but to gain a comprehensive understanding of the demands made upon MPs and how some MPs choose to spend their time and resources in contrast to others. Paddy Ashdown MP sees this as one of the most valuable aspects of a charter: 'I have to judge priorities. The Charter process is a way of explaining the demands on my time, and my decisions, to my constituents and giving them a chance to question me on those decisions'.[34]

If it is the case that most MPs spend very little of their time in acting as a check on the executive then one should ask why (and indeed whether it really matters): is it because the resources are insufficient, or is it because there are few incentives or opportunities for MPs to spend a lot of their time scrutinising legislative proposals and policies? It may also be because MPs don't have sufficient knowledge or training in the workings of Parliament to make an impact on it. The answer is a combination of these factors. MPs do not have the personnel or resources to analyse legislation and its impact, but it is also clear that many of them have neither the knowledge or inclination to do so. Training MPs in the workings of Parliament would help as would increased opportunities for backbench MPs to get involved in policy work.

Professor Patrick Dunleavy's[35] proposals for strengthening select committees – by making them more independent of the whips, paying those chairing them and making the resources of the National Audit Office available to them – would help because they would increase the status and influence of select committees. However, as Peter Riddell[36] of *The Times* has pointed out, 'The real problem with select committees is not their powers or resources but the almost invariable preference of MPs of talent to serve in frontbench posts.' This raises questions about the available career paths of politicians and their incentives for one course of action rather than another.

POLITICAL CAREER PATHS

Aspiring ministers have only two possible career paths. One is to become an MP and win sufficient favour to be promoted to a ministerial or shadow ministerial post; the other is to be rewarded with a seat in the Lords and then be given a ministerial post.

This means that the talent pool for ministers is small. Professor Richard Rose has analysed this problem at length:

> A career open to talents is the ideal of a democracy, but many occupations have restrictive qualifications for entry, and the Cabinet is

no exception. Out of a pool of 13,700,000 persons who vote for the government of the day, the 300-odd eligible for a Ministerial post because they are MPs is 0.002 per cent of government supporters.[37]

Professor Rose has proposed that civil servants and outside experts should be allowed to join what he calls a policy directorate, which would combine tasks and people that are currently divided between Ministers of State, Parliamentary Under-Secretaries and civil servants.[38] This would in effect make those civil servants in the policy directorate responsible for policy, thus opening up a new career path for people who would like to be involved in the business of government rather than simply in its administration.

This would not only improve the quality of government, but would also ensure that the business of government does not become the preserve of a narrow (party) political class, sharing similar backgrounds and political career paths. This is important because the new anti-politics has taken much of its energy from the public's perception that politics is the preserve of a narrow and increasingly careerist class of professional politicians.

TERM LIMITS

A radical idea for opening up politics, to mitigate against the formation of a narrow, entrenched political class, is term limits – whereby there are statutory or voluntary (i.e. national or local party imposed) limits on the number of terms elected representatives can serve in their posts. Term limits have won widespread support in the United States over the last five years and have been an important issue in state-level politics. It was also a key part of Newt Gingrich's Contract with America, but was eventually defeated in Congress. By 1994, voters in fifteen states had restricted their congressmen to a maximum of two to three terms in Washington.

Limiting the length of time that elected representatives can serve may seem undemocratic to the extent that voters should have a right to elect who they choose and should not be denied a popular candidate simply because he or she has served longer than the term limits say they can. The counter-argument is that while this may be true the advantages far outweigh this particular disadvantage. The advantages are that:

- term limits ensure a constant influx of new talent and fresh perspectives
- they create a specified time frame within which elected representatives must achieve their objectives, helping to focus them on the tasks ahead and plan accordingly
- they help to counter the increasing phenomenon of career politicians, who structure their lives, often from their time they leave college, around the attainment of political office (something that Professor Rose's proposals would address as well – see above). This means that national politics becomes the preserve of a highly dedicated professional class, often to the point that it is removed from the concerns of ordinary people. (In the United States this is referred to in terms of being 'inside the beltway' – the beltway being the road that encircles central Washington DC.)
- Term limits are a powerful force against creeping corruption in politics and machine politics, both of which depend on long serving and deeply entrenched politicians using their contacts and knowledge established over many years to trade favours to their own advantage or that of their political friends and associates (this being particularly true of Italy, Japan and the United States)
- term limits also mitigate against time-serving and complacency among politicians.

While the strict separation of legislature and executive in the United States does not make for any great constitutional complications in this regard, term limiting all MPs would do so as this would force ministers to relinquish their parliamentary seat after the maximum number of terms. However, Professor Richard Rose's proposals would allow for this and exceptions could be made for the Prime Minister, Secretaries of State and their shadows in opposition. There would be other complications, but term limits is an idea at least worth consideration because it asks us to address the fact that the ballot box provides no effective accountability for the 500 or so MPs who have a safe seat and who, once elected, know that they will be able to occupy their seats until they choose to leave them.

A TWENTY-FIRST CENTURY POLIS

The route to successful, sustainable government does not lie in a strategy of increasing centralisation within a highly discretionary system of command and control. Such a system lacks legitimacy, blurs responsibility and has weak lines of accountability.

There are also no grounds for supposing that such a system of government would be any more efficient than having a similar system for running the economy.

A more productive way forward, already demonstrated with varying degrees of success in the United States, Switzerland and Germany, is to have a decentralised system of government but one which operates within a tight framework of rules and procedures, perhaps enshrined in the constitution, which creates an environment for responsible decision-taking.

No democracy can be perfect. Every democratic system needs to adapt to changing circumstances and expectations. Democracies cannot hope to have viable futures on the basis of past glories and reputations made long ago. Moreover, they cannot afford to be seen by their publics as complacent and unwilling to reassess themselves fundamentally on a regular basis.

All three main parties in Britain are understandably protective of their various democratic vested interests: The Conservatives of Parliament – which remains as their only real power base in British politics; Labour of the municipal socialism and machine politics of (mainly urban) local government; and Liberal Democrats of the local community politics that have made them significant power brokers in most council chambers.

The parties are unlikely to endorse radical proposals that would directly threaten the political power and positions of their members. However, there is political advantage to be gained from promoting an agenda that would appeal to most people's increasing scepticism about politics and politicians. Moreover, the parties can stand to win support by promoting themselves as anti-establishment forces for reform; a strategy which contributed to the Conservatives' success in general elections (a point acknowledged by Tony Blair in his controversial address to Rupert Murdoch's News Corporation in 1995).[39]

If the parties are to be serious in using a new democratic agenda as a vote-winner they cannot afford to lose credibility by directing it at only those areas which pose no threat to their power base. A new, credible democratic agenda cannot pretend that there will be a cosy fit between the new and old politics, for the former came into being precisely because the latter was seen to be inadequate. The 'democratic establishment' of local and national government should recognise that it is in need of change and that continued and complacent resistance to change will ultimately undermine their legitimacy and authority.

REFERENCES

1 See speech by Tony Blair MP to the 1994 Labour Party conference.

2 See Jonathon Rauch, *Demosclerosis*, Times Books, New York 1995.

3 Quoted in David Ogilvy, *Ogilvy on Advertising*, Multimedia Publications (UK) Ltd., London 1983, p211.

4 A MORI survey in May 1995 found that only 43 per cent of the respondents think Parliament works well, down from 59 per cent in 1991, and 30 per cent think it works badly – up from 16 per cent in 1991. Another survey, by ICM in 1994, asked 1,400 people in Britain 'Does voting every four to five years give voters enough power?' 33 per cent said yes and 60 per cent said no. More details are provided by Geoff Mulgan and Andrew Adonis, 'Back to Greece: the scope for direct democracy', *Lean Democracy*, Demos Quarterly Issue 3, London 1994.

5 Reported in *Municipal Journal*, 'Labour's local blueprint', October 1995.

6 Patrick Dunleavy, 'Throw out the Bureaucrats and let the locals in', *Independent*, 10 August 1995.

7 *A choice for England – A consultation paper on Labour's plans for English regional government*, The Labour Party, London 1995, p9.

8 Simon Jenkins, *The Tory Nationalisation of Britain*, Hamish Hamilton, London 1995.

9 Privatisation and the end of direct government involvement in private sector industrial relations can be seen as elements of this strategy – both being attempts by the government to disentangle itself from areas it had little control over or chance of being successful in. The impulses behind this strategy are the same as those among many 'Eurosceptics' who wish to disentangle Britain from many aspects of the European Community.

10 A good introduction to public choice analysis is William C. Mitchell, *Government as it is*, Institute of Economic Affairs, London 1988.

11 See George Boyne, 'Local Government – from Monopoly to Competition', *Public Policy and the Impact of the New Right*, edited by G. Jordan and N. Ashford, Pinter, London 1993, pp165-192.

12 See Joel Garreau, *Edge City: Life on the New Frontier*, Doubleday, New York 1991.

13 Robert Nozick, *Anarchy, State and Utopia*, Blackwell, Oxford 1974.

14 See Gordon Tullock, 'Sociological Federalism', *Decentralization, Local Governments, and Markets – Towards a Post-Welfare Agenda*, edited by Robert J. Bennett, Clarendon Press, Oxford 1990.

15 Ferdinand Mount, *The British Constitution Now*, Mandarin, London 1995.

16 Quoted in the *Guardian*, 18 July 1995, by Hugo Young in an excellent article comparing 'sovereigntist's' views on the Nolan Committee with their views on Europe.

17 John Burton, *Why No Cuts? An Inquiry into the Fiscal Anarchy of Uncontrolled Government Expenditure*, Institute of Economic Affairs,

London 1985.

18 Gerard Radnitzky, 'The Social Market and the Constitution of Liberty', *Britain's Constitutional Future*, edited by Frank Vibert, Institute of Economic Affairs, London 1989, p11.

19 Ferdinand Mount, *op.cit.*, 1995.

20 See Samuel Brittan 'The way to recover lost traditions', *Financial Times*, 29 June 1995.

21 These estimates were quoted by Dirk Hudif, manager of EU government relations in Brussels for ICI. Quoted in 'In pursuit of a competitive edge', *Financial Times*, 30 August 1995.

22 See *The Quango State: An Alternative Approach*, by John Stewart, Alan Greer and Paul Hoggett, Commission for Local Democracy, London 1995. The Commission for Local Democracy, founded in 1993 to 'inquire into the present nature of local democracy in England and Wales and to consider its future development' constitutes one of the few attempts in the last twenty years to question established forms of local democracy, and made many interesting proposals for re-invigorating local democracy, such as electronic voting and requiring local authorities to produce an annual Democracy Plan for decentralisation and citizen involvement. However, these messages were muted by the Commission's overriding call for the powers and scope of local authorities to be extended, rather than be called further into question.

23 In the *Yes, Prime Minister* episode 'Power to the People', the Cabinet Secretary, the Prime Minister, and the radical leader of a left wing council reject an academic's plans for a Walsall-like experiment in decentralisation, on the grounds that it would mean an end to the dominance of party politics at local level and seriously weaken national parties' grip on local politics.

24 Anthony Jay, *What shall we do about local government?*, lecture to the Institute of Economic Affairs, London, June 1994 (unpublished), p10.

25 *Ibid.*, p14.

26 See Sam Staley, *Bigger is not better: the virtues of decentralised local government*, Cato Institute, Washington, DC, 1992, pp00-34.

27 *Ibid.*, p16.

28 Anthony Jay, *op.cit.*, p9.

29 See *The Quango State: An Alternative Approach*, by John Stewart, Alan Greer and Paul Hoggett, Commission for Local Democracy, London 1995, pp9-10.

30 Sam Staley, *op.cit.*, p16. Sam Staley cites a study by of St. Louis County, Missouri. The county has a population of almost 1 million people; 90 municipalities; 23 school districts; 25 fire protection districts; and numerous other organised subdivisions, county-wide associations, and special districts. According to the Advisory Commission on Intergovernmental Relations (ACIR), the provision of public services by a single unit of government would be 'suboptimal'. Each community and organisation allows for public expression of specific tastes and preferences that become part of the political process. See the ACIR report, *The Organization of Local Public Economies: A Commission Report*, ACIR, Washington, DC 1987.

31 Phillip Norton, *Does Parliament Matter?*, Harvester Wheatsheaf, Hemel Hempstead 1993.

32 See John Garrett, *Westminster: does parliament work?*, Victor Gollancz, London 1992, pp22-3.
33 Martin Summers, 'Repossessing the House: parliamentary audits and the Constituent's Charter', *Lean Democracy*, Demos Quarterly Issue 3, Demos, London 1994.
34 *MP's Charter: Notes*, 10 January 1995, available from the office of Paddy Ashdown MP.
35 Professor Patrick Dunleavy, *Reinventing Parliament: making the Commons more effective*, Charter 88, London 1995.
36 Peter Riddell, 'Worthy reforms fall short of a full solution', *The Times*, 31 October 1995.
37 Richard Rose, 'The Political Economy of Cabinet Change', Frank Vibert (ed), *Britain's Constitutional Future*, Institute of Economic Affairs, London 1991, p64.
38 See pp66-72, *Ibid*.
39 Speech to the News Corporation, 17 July 1995.

THE MAKING OF A
YOUNG COUNTRY
Helen Wilkinson

'This is a new age. To be led by a new generation.'
Tony Blair, 1995 Labour Party Conference Speech

Since Tony Blair's election as leader of the Labour Party the landscape of British politics has changed far faster and far more dramatically than anyone anticipated. There is a sense of excitement in the air, and a level of political risk taking that has not been seen for many years. It is as if a system which had begun to seem stuck, sclerotic and arthritic has been loosened up. New political alignments and new sets of ideas have at last become thinkable. At the very least British politics has become interesting again.

Of course it would be wrong to be over-optimistic or to project onto a single man or leadership too many high hopes. We live in an era that has learnt to be distrustful. There is a long history of leaders, particularly on the left, who have risen to power as the champions of great popular aspirations which have then dissipated in the face of the unhappy realities of bad administration and inexperience, currency crises and inflations. No wonder it is fashionable to be cleverly pessimistic and assume that Blair will be a resounding failure, at best a pale imitation of conservatism, at worst an innocent abroad whose inexperience with realpolitik will dash the hopes of yet another generation.

There are certainly major holes in his approach. He appears for example to have little commitment to or understanding of green issues. He is perhaps too locked into the views of a media aware metropolitan London elite. He often seems to lack sympathy for the less fortunate and does not sufficiently address the politics of exclusion. Yet despite

226

these weaknesses and to the extent that we can make any objective judgement at such an early stage, there are more grounds for optimism than for pessimism.

Certainly the charge of bland vacuity is hard to sustain. Blair has been remarkably successful in reorganising and rejuvenating the Labour Party. For the first time in a generation there is at least an effective opposition, an opposition that has learnt some tricks from the best social democratic parties on the continent; and which is no longer so tightly locked into the old, predominantly male, labourist idea of how the party should be organised. Instead Blair has moved it, albeit grudgingly, further towards an internal democracy based on One Member One Vote. He has improved the internal party communications dramatically and by the end of 1995 he had won over more than a hundred thousand new members (most notably amongst those under 40).

But even more striking has been his success in changing the overall shape of political positions. Blair has more than any other politician on the left seriously tried to grapple with Margaret Thatcher's appeal and to construct an ideological alternative to Thatcherism. He also seems to understand that Thatcher's message was as diverse – and in many ways as contradictory – as the constituencies she courted and that it was her ability to seamlessly stitch this coalition together for as long as she did that was one of her great successes.

His most visible achievement has been to make successful forays into enemy territory – taking on traditional Tory issues like the family and law and order – to the great consternation of the Conservatives. He has precisely mirrored Margaret Thatcher's success in the 1970s in winning over key groups of voters and intellectuals, by securing the apparent support of a swathe of the middle English Tory middle class, as well as the approbation of a bizarre array of Tory intellectuals, all the way from Alan Howarth, the first Conservative MP ever to defect to Labour, to Paul Johnson.

Most left intellectuals of course have been suspicious of him to the point of caricature. Trapped in the old political paradigms, many of these intellectuals give the impression of struggling to come to terms with a world post-Thatcher and a Labour party that is serious about governing the country. They self-indulgently lament our 'uncomfortable times' and stubbornly argue that: 'We need look no further than the New Labour of Tony Blair to see the profound effects on our political culture of this ideological victory of the right'.[1]

The left's critique is not wholly without substance. It is certainly the case that much of Blair's success owes more to symbolic politics, to language and rhetoric, than to substance. His first year as leader offered a new mood music rather than a detailed programme of policies, or indeed any flagship policies by which his values could be assessed. But his success goes further than symbolic politics. While the intellectual left is still broadly definable in terms of lineages of traditional social democracy, from SDP reformism through to Bennism and the strands of 1968, Blair's position, whether one agrees with it or not, is clearly distinct from all of this.

In important respects Blair has moved far ahead of the intellectuals on the left in terms of rethinking what a viable left politics might look like in the late 1990s. His agenda is distinct both in terms of content and of tone and although many of its roots can be found in older traditions of nineteenth century Christian socialism, it is better understood as a reaction to global insecurities, experienced across different classes, in the context of which the role of government becomes not one of protecting people from change, but rather providing them with the means to adapt to change.

So although the Blairite agenda includes the now familiar elements of social justice, partnership, internationalism (which is increasingly reduced to simply being strongly pro-European Union) and fairness, he has also added to this a much stronger ethical strand, emphasising personal responsibility, reciprocity between state and citizen, and the importance of community which is not reducible to the state. This attempt to forge a new synthesis which responds to the palpable insecurities of much of the electorate is also visible in areas like constitutional reform, where Blair is trying to link elements of the well-defined constitutional reform agenda – a Bill of Rights, an elected second chamber and devolution – to a renewed emphasis on what citizens owe to other citizens and to the community.

BLAIR AS A GENERATIONAL SHIFT

It remains to be seen whether Blair will be able to forge as distinctive a political programme as Thatcher. Certainly she had the benefit of a far more politically attuned and intellectually sophisticated group of intellectuals than the Labour Party or the British left can now offer. But Blair has one asset that she never had: the fact that he has the potential to represent not just a political shift but also a generational one.

He is the first post 1960s, post Beatles, party leader. He played in a rock band and even though he may not have taken drugs, he nevertheless imbibed some of the culture of liberation of those heady days that in many ways divide those brought up before and after. That may be why he seems much more modern than previous leaders, much more at ease in a range of different types of company, less straitlaced and more suited than many of his colleagues. Even though he is only a few years younger than Neil Kinnock, in important respects he comes from another era. His relationship with his young family and a successful career wife, who earns a good deal more than him, mark him out, as does the fact that his formative years were defined both by liberation and by the changing role of women. Perhaps the best indicator of this shift is the fact that but for a small twist of fate in the early 1980s his wife could have become the politician while he remained a lawyer.[2]

This generational significance may help to explain why Blair chose the theme of making Britain a young country in his speech to the 1995 Labour Party conference. He was clearly inspired by Australia – a young nation achieving success under a Labour government, at ease with the future and with new technologies, and far more classless than Britain has ever been. In a sense Blair is trying to retrieve the image that the Labour Party once had as the party of modernisation, an agent of change, and the party most able to take Britain forward out of the shadow of its history.

DISSATISFACTION, DISTRUST AND DISCONNECTION

There is an irony in using politics as the base from which to try to rejuvenate a nation. It might be more understandable to do so through popular music, fashion or business. But politics seems oddly unqualified. The House of Commons and the House of Lords are particularly archaic institutions: they look old and smell old, and their overwhelmingly male character smacks of a long-gone era.

That is why the starting point for understanding the 'young country' agenda lies with Blair's attempt to rejuvenate and reconnect politics. Blair frequently speaks of a 'new politics' to bring government 'closer to the people' and has focused in particular on changing our political culture. He has spoken of the need for politicians to regain people's trust. He frequently talks of the need for politicians to be honest and not to promise what they cannot deliver.

In many respects Blair is hitting all the right buttons. He is certainly doing more to address public dissatisfaction than other politicians, and is implicitly acknowledging that it cannot simply be ascribed to dissatisfaction with Conservative rule. Over the last twenty-five years public satisfaction with the British system of governance has steadily declined.[3] Dissatisfaction is now widespread and indeed it pervades all parts of society. For example both the elderly and Conservative supporters who are traditionally less critical of the political system show a particularly sharp increase in dissatisfaction.[4] The public also appears to have lost confidence in the ability of the political system to respond to its wishes.[5] One recent study found that whereas twenty years ago, 14 per cent of the public felt that they had no effective say in what the government does, that figure has now doubled, whilst those people believing that the 'system of governing Britain' works well has dropped steadily from 48 per cent to 29 per cent.

Similarly Blair's efforts to tackle public distrust are well placed.[6] Dissatisfaction and distrust also co-exist with high degrees of political disconnection. Attitudes to voting and participation in elections seem to symbolise this. In 1965 three-quarters of the public believed that voting in local elections mattered whereas nowadays just over half believe this.[7]

But his emphasis on political renewal is inseparable from the generational question. Blair is acutely aware that every party needs to be able to woo the young if it wants a long-term future. Yet as many as 45 per cent of under 25-year olds did not vote in the 1992 general election,[8] votes which could have been sufficient to win the election given that a study found that young people were especially volatile in their party preferences in the last election.[9] Blair knows that he needs their votes as well as the votes of Middle England if he is to win power. Moreover his attempt to appeal to them also fits with his much broader goal of reconnecting politics.

He certainly has a difficult job on his hands. If the population as a whole is distrustful of politics and politicians, there are none more so than younger generations. Their distrust and distance from conventional party politics is deep-seated.[10] Amongst younger people, especially those below 25, there is less faith in conventional party politics, with many emphasising issues which remain low on the parties' agendas: environmentalism, international campaigns, animal rights and health issues such as AIDs. There are also signs that this tendency could be deepening for the next generation. A recent survey found that only one teenager in eight is remotely interested in politics (even among adults, the figure is still an unimpressive one in three) and the same study found that a lack of political knowledge amongst these teenagers was particularly poor, with girls being considerably more likely than boys to be lacking in knowledge. The study suggested that the next generation of voters are likely to be more apathetic about politics than ever.[11] One result is that today's teenagers, far from seeing the job of Prime Minister or MP as the very summit of achievement, see politics as the least popular career choice on offer.[12]

The mainstream parties are very vulnerable to the criticism that they have not prioritised issues of concern to younger people within their own policy agenda[13] and have thus failed to channel either the energy or the commitments of young people to particular issues – such as the environment – in ways that other campaign organisations and networks have been able to.

Another area in which the parties have spectacularly failed is in the area of gender and this is inseparable from wider generational shifts. People born in 1960 and beyond are all members of the 'post-equality generation'. They have inherited a labour market with a framework of equal opportunities legislation in place and they have seen more and more women at the very pinnacles of achievement and power. Many came of age under the premiership of Britain's first female Prime Minister, others have simply assumed that women can be Prime Ministers as well as men. Younger men and women are becoming more androgynous both in their values and their modes of behaviour and poll evidence consistently shows that younger men, like their female peers, are more at ease with women's changing roles and are committed to equal opportunities.[14]

Yet it's a sad commentary upon Britain's first female Prime Minister that although she presided over an economy which was rapidly feminising itself as women entered the workforce in unprecedented numbers, she – and the other parties – followed rather than led change on this issue. The founding of the 300 Group, the cross party campaign to get more women into politics, in 1981, succeeded in sensitising the parties to the issue but in reality little was done to actively encourage women into politics or public service.

For a time the activities of the Greater London Council with its women's committees and quotas seemed to offer an alternative vision of policy making, one which better suited people's values and which promised to make the system more accountable. In the end many of their initiatives became associated with the triumph of political correctness. One consequence was that those people whom it was assumed would benefit from these initiatives – like women and ethnic minority groups – were some of the first to line up as part of the backlash against them, suspicious of a middle class elitism claiming to understand their values and to represent their interests.

Similar problems beset the national Labour Party in the 1990s which attempted to feminise itself through the introduction of a quota system for the selection of parliamentary candidates. The initiative has proved highly controversial amongst women as well as men and the spectre of one hundred female Labour MPs has in the short term at least had little effect in transforming women's views of the political process.[15] Polls consistently show that women are more likely to be disinterested in party politics than men, a trend which is repeated amongst younger generations of women, who are even more disillusioned with the parties than their male counterparts.[16] As a consequence, unlike our economy and our culture, politics has failed to feminise itself and adapt to change, confirming the impression that the parties are remote and out of touch.

But the feeling that politics has failed them goes deeper. Like other generations, today's twenty- and thirty-somethings are extremely concerned about unemployment and job insecurity. Indeed under 25-year olds are more concerned about unemployment and job insecurity than any other age group, perhaps because they are demographically the most vulnerable in this respect. But it's not just the experience or prospect of unemployment which worries today's twenty- and early thirty-somethings. Many also quite legitimately feel that they have entered the labour market at a time of unprecedented uncertainty and insecurity when many of the old rules no longer apply. Moreover they are aware more than other generations of the extent to which political leaders are failing to provide clear and decisive leadership. To many members of this generation politicians too often seem to be fighting old battles which bear little relationship to their needs now.[17]

One consequence of their overall political disconnection is that the age profile of all the parties and Parliamentarians is skewed towards older generations. This is a long term trend. For example, Conservative party membership is in historic decline, and the average age of a Conservative party member is over 61.[18] Almost half are over 66 whilst less than 5 per cent are younger than 35.[19] Moreover although the

Conservative Party has been able to take comfort from the fact that a high proportion of its activists remain female, they nevertheless are failing to recruit a younger generation of less traditionally minded female activists, and now face the danger that their numbers of women MPs could actually fall[20] as well as the long-term prospect of not sustaining their female base of electoral support.[21]

Labour too has been faced with similar pressures with the double disadvantage that it was starting from a smaller membership base than the Conservatives historically. The party is more youthful but hardly young. Research in 1992[22] found that the average age of Labour members was 48, and a 1993 report, *The New Generation*, pointed out that there were more than three times as many Labour Party members over 66 as under 25, concluding that the Labour Party 'relies heavily on older members for local campaigning and suffers from the absence at local level of active and enthusiastic young members'.[23]

Such age profiles can be self-perpetuating, since they become embedded in party cultures, thus making it ever harder for parties to reach out and appeal to younger generations. Some have tried to argue that the young are simply turning away from party politics to pioneer other forms of politics – that their underlying desire to participate is as strong as ever. They point to their commitment to 'issueism' and to campaigns such as the roads protests or animal rights to prove this. Yet for all their media visibility and the palpable successes, the numbers actually involved in these remain small by historic standards – and much smaller than previous generations when there was mass involvement in trade unions and movements like CND. Certainly the poll evidence shows that so-called Generation X and those in their early thirties – the tail end of the boomer generations for whom the materialist dream of the 1980s quickly turned sour – are on every indicator of social-political activism, even on environmental issues, less active than the old, and much less active than Blair's generation which came of age in the 1960s.[24]

Like their American counterparts, there is a real danger that they might become 'the switched off generation'. Not only are they turning off politics, they are also considerably less likely to tune into serious news and current affairs coverage on radio and TV.[25] They are reading less and less hard news, with the majority of *Sun* readers being under 25 whilst as many as 36 per cent of people aged 25–34 do not read a daily newspaper.[26]

Yet despite this unpromising outlook, Blair's new Labour has made some advances. The rapid rise in Labour membership which has occurred since his leadership is primarily amongst those under 40, and has for now reversed the trend towards a declining and ageing party membership.[27] It is of course important not to over-emphasise the shifts. Labour's membership is rising quickly but from an extremely low base. Even so, few would have expected that so much could have been achieved in such a short space of time. Certainly Blair seems to have concluded that it is the style of politics which matters most in the short term: that it is far better to only promise what he can actually deliver than to build up a groundswell of hopeful illusions only to see them shatter. There is a certain logic in his position, that only through honesty, and the moderation that honesty implies, can politicians regain a modicum of trust.

However, so far the means of restoring trust and engagement have been less clear than the analysis. It is not obvious for example that directly elected second chambers and devolution to Scotland and Wales will in themselves reverse the loss of confidence which has pervaded politics and government. A Bill of Rights is an important first step but such a procedural measure is unlikely on its own to be sufficient. Greater devolution and a Bill of Rights are important elements in framing a new contract between citizens and the state, but they do not address the extent of public dissatisfaction with our current system of governance. Growing numbers of people appear to feel that their votes do not really count and many see electoral reform through some form of proportional representation as the way to give them more power and to make their vote more relevant.[28]

Blair has said in the short term that he is unconvinced of the case for electoral reform. However he might find that in order to retain the public's confidence in party politics and in our democratic system as a whole, he needs to think much more radically about the ways in which people's views and opinions are heard and heeded in the political process.

The experience of other countries which have experimented with citizens' juries, referenda on specific issues, and electronic forms of democracy shows that these can all be effective ways of involving people in the democratic process.[29] Championing more radical forms of democracy such as the use of referenda could also institutionalise 'issueism' into the political process, with referenda on key issues acting as an alternative reference point to party politics as well as a catalyst for its transformation.

It is also clear that any politician or leader who is serious about 'reconnecting politics' will need to make it much easier for people to register and participate in the political process. The current system of registration is outdated and was designed for an era when we were less mobile. As a result it is disenfranchising many young people who are one of the most mobile groups in our society. Our method of voting itself should be reformed with a shift to week-long or weekend voting which is known to increase the participation of first time voters and more disenfranchised groups. Voting could also be made more accessible by situating polling booths in shopping centres, workplaces and DSS offices as a prelude to the use of smart cards for registration and voting.[30]

With a Bill of Rights and a Freedom of Information Act, two early candidates for legislation, a Blair government will need to think much more rigorously about matching these rights to responsibilities. A move to a system of compulsory voting will be one byproduct and whilst there will doubtless be many who instinctively resist this transition as an infringement of people's civil liberties, the socialising role it plays in the political health of the nation is likely to be a more compelling argument. Countries such as Australia which have such a system find that it serves to lock people into engaging with the political process as well as playing an important educational role, socialising people into political debate and participation from an early age. A reform of the ballot paper to include a 'None of the above' category would ensure that public dissatisfaction with the system and with the parties would not only be made more transparent but would also act as a performance indicator for government as a whole.[31]

There are other reasons why compulsory voting should be supported. Young people have throughout history been consistently less likely to vote than other age groups. But our changing demographics – in particular the aging of society combined with declining numbers of young people for the foreseeable future – means that young people's exclusion from the political process will increase. Compulsory voting will thus become an important way in which the views of young people will be heard in the political process.

THE LOGIC OF SOCIAL CONSERVATISM

Such changes are a long way off. In the short term the political challenge for Blair is to forge a coalition which enables him to win

Fig. 1- The fracturing of British values

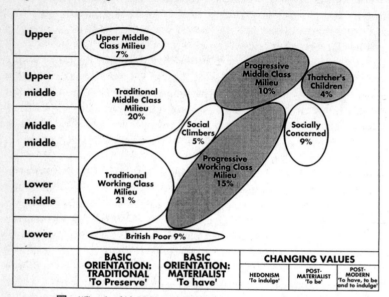

□ = Milieux in which 18-34 year olds predominate

Source: *Freedom's Children: Work, relationships and politics*
for 18-34 year olds in Britain today, Demos, 1995

power. His problem is that he is trying to do so at a time when British values are fracturing markedly. The map above illustrates the problem.

Whereas a few generations ago the values of the British population would have closely clustered together and would be broadly classified as being 'traditional' in orientation (and thus on the left hand side of the map) with distinct milieux groups defined by social class and income level, in the 1990s values have fragmented.

There is much greater diversity with milieux ranging from the traditional upper middle class, middle and working class right through to Thatcher's Children, the highly educated young who are concerned with material success and the pursuit of pleasure, the social climbers, (usually people from working-class backgrounds who are building careers) and the socially concerned in the public sector and caring professions.

As significant from Blair's point of view is the fact that the map is a snapshot of generational change. Whereas older age groups predominate on the left hand side of the map, and are more traditional in their attitudes and values, younger generations tend to be on the right hand side, more strongly attached to autonomy and to more modern progressive values – regardless of their class status. Interestingly the higher educated end of Blair's own boomer generation find themselves clustering more often than not in the socially concerned milieux, a product of their earlier 60s social consciousness.

It is not hard to see how many problems this map throws up for political parties. As values fragment it is becoming ever harder to appeal to everyone. At the same time although the demographic majority is still on the left of this map (and so long as young people don't bother to vote this skew is accentuated in the political market), the future trend seems to be away from these values and towards the modern and postmodern values.

In many ways this tension between old values and newly emerging values has always been with us. But what is different about the 1990s is the degree of fragmentation along generational lines, the greater overall diversity and the changing demographic base of the British population.

The shifting demographic base of the UK population is a useful point from which to analyse Blair's politics because it helps to explain the profound tension which underlies much of his political rhetoric. The core tension (from which many others flow) is between an essentially socially conservative philosophy which emphasises duty, family values and the need for spiritual moral guidance, and another which emphasises personal freedom, enterprise and change. The latter is clearly more at ease with modernity, and better able to appeal to younger generations whilst the former's emphasis on duty and family values more obviously appeals to older generations. In many ways the tension is between two different styles of political leadership – one is cautious, and measured, the other is risk taking and daring. One vision emphasises continuity, the other emphasises change.

This tension between young and old, between modernity and social conservatism, may well be Blair's most difficult long-term political dilemma and whilst it manifests itself most visibly in terms of words and language, it pervades the whole Blair project. For the core of the problem is that the demographic basis of the British population pulls Blair towards social conservatism.

Thus whilst modernising his own party, Blair's appeal to the public has been predicated on continuity and on our enduring social values. In this respect, Blair has deftly adapted his politics to fit a socially conservative tradition, defining what many might read as his alternative to Conservative Back to Basics. At the *Spectator*'s 1995 Annual lecture he expanded on his Clause Four declaration that 'the rights we have need to reflect the duties we owe', setting out a series of responsibilities for parents, tenants and citizens to perform as the basis of a good society.

His speech cleverly appealed to many conservatives who felt that their party had lost its way in a quagmire of sleaze, while also rooting the argument in the sacred texts of old socialists like Tawney and Robert Owen. In one stroke Blair proved himself capable of reassuring the traditional working-class base on which much of Labour's support historically lies whilst simultaneously appealing to dispirited Conservative voters through the language of duty. 'In the 1970s and 1980s', he argued, 'the Conservatives regarded the notion of duty as their own. Now, in the 1990s, they seem neither to understand it nor to act upon it. In fact, duty is an essential Labour concept. It is at the heart of creating a strong community or society. It is the only way of making sense of the rules by which people wish to lead their lives in a modern age. Without it, freedom turns to ashes'.[32]

Blair has packaged himself as a more modern type of social conservative emphasising duty, responsibility, respect and authority and predominantly directing his politics to an older generation who are still electorally and demographically in the majority. Blair's role in this respect has been that of the prodigal son, amiably reassuring older generations that the country will be safe in his hands, that there will not be too much change, and that governments can once again deliver security (albeit in a different form to that in the past). With this in mind, Blair has been careful to reposition Labour as the party of family values – most controversially by stating his own personal preference for the two-parent family. He has moved Labour away from seeing its mission as using the state to break up an oppressive patriarchal institution and instead to seeing the state's role as one of supporting society's most important social institution – the family.

In many ways Blair is absolutely right to do this. Such a politics undoubtedly appeals to more traditional Labour supporters and to those floating voters outside the party whose support he needs. It acts as a necessary antidote to the rhetoric of New Labour New Britain by reassuring insecure voters that there will not be too much under a Labour government.

Yet Blair is also politically astute. He has struggled to bridge the generation gap by emphasising the need for change. In many ways the Clause Four debate was a classic example of this. On the one hand, the rewriting of Clause Four was a metaphor for modernisation, on the other he was able to present it as a return to Labour's ethical base pre-Labourism. With one hand, he embraced change and younger generations, whilst with another he reminded the traditionalists in his party that this was not a departure from tradition.

DUTY VERSUS RESPONSIBILITY

Blair's problem is that the very phrase 'duty' seems so redolent of the past. The word is peculiarly anachronistic and outdated. The very idea that an individual should fulfil moral or legal obligations in a society where authority is so sadly lacking and where deference is on the wane feels like the last gasp of a politics which has failed to maintain social cohesion. Duty implies a consensus where one no longer exists.

Moreover the language of 'duty' also speaks only to older generations for whom 'duty' to one's country is still a meaningful concept. For those under twenty-five, many of whom are profoundly disconnected from society, Britain and their neighbourhoods, such a word is meaningless.[33] And for them politicians have lost any moral authority to assert anything as strong as 'duty'.

There is a further problem, namely that Blair's socially conservative rhetoric is all too often seized upon by a moralistic minority who see the permissiveness of the 1960s as the root cause of all contemporary problems and who hate the new found freedoms they gave women and who are fearful of diversity and difference. For them 'rebuilding the traditional family' is the panacea to society's ills whilst single parents are amoral symbols of our libertarian age. In the past many of these moralists were associated with political currents on the right. Certainly they continue to boast a number of advocates from Mary Whitehouse to Baroness Young to columnist Janet Daly, 1960s radical turned 1990s conformist. But now they are as likely to come from the left. *Observer* columnist Melanie Philipps is an articulate advocate for this new moral agenda on the left. Rightly or wrongly, Blair suffers from guilt by association and their caricature of social conservatism tarnishes his image.

This is a major problem for Blair because for all that this group are very vocal with effective access to the media, they are in fact a minority in a country where most people have rejected organised religion, and much that goes with it. The result is that many people who might otherwise be attracted to supporting the Blair project are often alienated because they assume that social conservatism is nostalgic, backward-looking and authoritarian.

Alternatively, the language of responsibility which Blair frequently uses in his speeches could prove to be much more popular and symbolic than his emphasis on duty. A politics of responsibility is interactive. There is an element of choice, and there is an assumption that respect must be earned not simply asserted. The word 'responsibility' is also a much more modern expression of the mutual obligations that we owe to each other, to the environment and to future generations.

Thus a politics of responsibility has the potential to have a much broader appeal enabling Blair to make a generational as well as an ethical appeal. After all, the young have been in the vanguard of defining a new kind of responsibility, whether it be the road protesters, the New Age travellers or the animal rights activists and in this age of 'pick and mix' politics they have been able to do so with ethics and value systems that are less bound up with orthodox religions and are instead more in tune with new forms of spirituality, the ethics of the green movement, the egalitarianism of the women's movement and the humanist tradition.

Theodore Zeldin in his wide ranging and lucid book, *An Intimate History of Humanity*, sees these movements as attempts to reclaim some of the spiritual meaning which organised religions have lost and he sees young people playing a central role in this quest to redefine ethics and responsibility. Whilst others 'scurry back to old beliefs' Zeldin talks of young people 'nibbling at new ideologies' where they can exercise personal responsibility.[34]

There certainly is a dawning realisation amongst many young people that it is they who are likely to pay the price of past profligacies as they face up to the fact that they may not be able to rely on a reasonable pension or a reliable health service, and eventually it will be them who will have to pay the costs of a deteriorating environment.

Nor does a politics of responsibility mean that Blair needs to jettison all of his social conservatism. Right across the Western world, pollsters periodically report on the 'conservatism' of today's younger people (especially those in their twenties). A range of possible explanations is offered varying from the precarious economic position which many young people find themselves in, through to the experience of having been brought up in broken homes, or having grown up in the AIDs era. Those in their early twenties certainly seem to be worried that the material successes of their parent's generation will not be handed down to them.[35] Economically insecure, many are seeking other sources of security, often through friendships and family life, for some even a revival of religious belief.

Thus Blair's concerns about safety and security on the streets are often this younger generation's concerns too. Not least because it is people in their twenties, especially men, who are most vulnerable to street crime. His desire for stable two-parent households also appeals because many have had the bitter personal experience of family breakdown and want to make their own relationships work.

But at the same time younger generations have grown up at a time of unprecedented freedom. One effect of growing up in this less deferential climate is that they are wary of any form of judgemental morality. They have, for example, a much more flexible and relaxed definition of family life than older generations. Strong families to younger generations includes cohabiting couples, single parents, gay couples as well as married couples with children. Polls repeatedly find that it is the young who are most tolerant of single parents, who believe that single parents can do as good a job as two parents and who for all their concerns about family breakdown are themselves continuing the trend to relationship breakdown which will soon make Britain compete against America on the divorce stakes.[36]

It's precisely because this generation have had both the benefits as well as some of the costs of the greater freedoms achieved since the 1960s that they can see these issues in all their complexity. They are therefore suspicious of any morality which feeds off scapegoats and stigmatises minorities.

No Turning Back?

But the tensions within social conservatism don't just revolve around issues of duty and responsibility, morality and personal ethics; they are also bound up with gender and generational shifts which have been transforming British society over the last few decades and from which our aging parties have become disconnected.

Until recently it was the Conservative party which could truly lay claim to be the party of women, pulling them in as activists and best representing their concerns for stable families, strong communities and tough policies on law and order. Labour for its part has suffered from its image as the macho labourist party. Thus historically the Conservatives have monopolised the women's vote and in the 1992 general election 43 per cent of women voted Conservative compared to just 34 per cent for the Labour Party and women over 65 were 20 per cent more likely to vote for the Conservative Party.[37]

But cultural and technological changes have transformed women's position in society over the last thirty years. The combined effect of feminism alongside rapid de-industrialisation and the shift from an economy geared to manufacturing and production towards a service sector economy geared to consumption have benefited and empowered women whilst simultaneously disenfranchising many men. The net effect of this 'genderquake' has been a shift in power from men to women which though its impact has been unevenly felt, has had a number of destabilising effects: in relationships, in family life, at work and ultimately in politics itself.[38]

The Labour Party finds itself better placed than the Conservative Party to benefit from these gender shifts which will inevitably transform the electoral map. Historically Labour has always done better with younger voters. In the 1992 general election, the only category in which Labour was more popular with women than the Conservatives was amongst under 25-year olds. Moreover Labour has more female politicians and more women in decision-making roles in the party machinery than the other parties, especially the Conservative Party. Although the culture of the femocrat – the woman friendly bureaucrat – is not as well advanced as in countries such as Australia, the party nevertheless has a well-developed set of policies and programmes to appeal to the women's vote.

Under Blair's leadership the emphasis has shifted away from mechanistic tools for bringing about equality, such as quotas or the creation of a Ministry for Women, towards a set of policies which will practically benefit the lives of ordinary working women. In this respect Blair seems to be straightforwardly copying the election strategy of President Clinton who made a direct appeal to working women in his 1992 presidential election campaign, who subsequently rewarded him with a 29 per cent lead over Bush,[39] easily enough to swing the next election.[40]

Blair's particular problem is that many of the gender shifts that have been underway in society at large are generationally specific and really only affect the lives of women in their twenties, thirties and early forties. For them there truly is 'no turning back' to the rigid gender hierarchy of the past, but amongst older generations of women, especially those in their fifties and sixties who missed the 1960s and who have not benefitted from greater opportunities for women, there are many who remain extremely traditional both in their own lives and also in their views of women's changing role in society. One study for example found that the generation gap was actually more acute between women in their sixties and women in their twenties than for parallel peer groups of men, a quite remarkable finding.[41]

For Blair such schisms in the sisterhood are inherently destabilising, not least because these divisions make it all the more difficult for him to target his appeal to women. The political paradox that he must square is that anything resembling 'feminist policies' might appeal to women in their twenties and thirties who aspire to careers and equal opportunity, as well as some women in their forties, but it will positively antagonise the majority of older women whose social conservatism extends to society's gender contract and who are ill at ease with working mothers, and uncertain about the gender shifts in society at large.

Blair is clearly trying to address the diverse needs of women in a variety of ways. Firstly he is not targeting Labour's policies for women up front. Instead, he seems to be opting for a more subtle form of niche marketing by for example announcing measures to help working mothers whilst at the same time 'feminising' the party's overall messages, which will appeal to older generations of women. So on the one hand he sells working women the policies which will benefit them whilst with the other he personalises Labour's image, thus reassuring older women voters. But he also seems to be learning the lesson that women voters of all ages are just like their male peers in seeing a party's competence to run the economy as being a crucial factor in determining their willingness to support one party versus another, and research suggests that women are even more cautious than their male peers in their belief in Labour's abilities to govern.[42]

SOCIAL CONSERVATISM AND THE FUTURE

The signs suggest that Blair is correct in his analysis that there is a new political space, a new paradigm beyond the conventional politics of left and right, which is ripe territory to be explored, but that he needs to temper this with a more libertarian and ultimately more autonomous morality.

Social conservatism has played an important role in broadening the party's appeal and in making Labour electable. But on its own it will be insufficient as the basis from which Blair can define his politics and his overall philosophy. There is also a more fundamental problem. The tensions within social conservatism which Blair is currently seeking to manage paradoxically mean that much of the energy and dynamism which flows from his one defining idea is lost, and dissipated. Precisely because he cannot and should not wholeheartedly embrace a social conservative philosophy, he is thus left without a clear defining mission with the intellectual coherence to rival Thatcherism.

SEVEN MAXIMS FOR A YOUNG COUNTRY

But there are signs that Blair has found another Big Idea. Blair has previously provided us only with a starting point for understanding what his defining idea might be. Nevertheless by the 1995 party conference there had already been discernible shifts of emphasis. Blair had courted Rupert Murdoch on the other side of the world in a speech which seemed to have been penned by a futurologist, with talk of virtual reality tourism and a world without frontiers.

Blair used the speech to place the left at the vanguard of politics in the next century by arguing that 'It is a rejuvenated and revitalised left of centre that is placed to respond to and shape this new world of change. If it can escape the constraints of its past – learning from history but not living in it – it is best equipped intellectually and philosophically for the new century'. For Blair it was now 'time to lay aside past prejudices and old ideas; to think fresh and new; to realise that the only incorrect intellectual or political thoughts are those that are pre-programmed'.[43]

At the party conference he went a step further by addressing the need for national renewal through the rhetoric of the young country. Blair's conference speech was hugely symbolic because it rooted his politics firmly in the future whilst at the same time showing respect, and to some extent nostalgia, for the country that Britain once was. But the speech also exemplified what Blair often does best: balancing two often competing messages. He is both the benevolent and sensible

prodigal son, and the young heir apparent chomping at the
to take risks and to throw caution to the wind.

The idea of national renewal and of the young country cert
the potential to resonate with a wide audience. Patriotism has always
been a populist base from which politicians can launch themselves and
Margaret Thatcher, more than any other politician, showed the way in
which it could be mobilised. Now Blair has taken the concept a step
further by directly linking nostalgia for a once great past with the
political imperative of creating a better future and by playing cleverly
with the idea that only through change can we once again become
secure.

There are seven key features which would truly define a young
country. The first defining element of a young country would be if
those in power were to be both radical and ruthless in government.
This would involve not just strong leadership but a new honesty in
government, a commitment to close things down and to be prepared to
cut back old programmes in order to create space for new ones. In
some areas, this would mean that a Blair administration should be
prepared to take on board some of Thatcher's more innovative ideas
like the introduction of market testing and competition in order to
breathe new life into the system.

The hallmarks of radical and ruthless government would be strong
leadership. Blair himself has been unequivocal in his own personal
admiration for many of the leadership qualities of Margaret Thatcher.
There are certainly indications that Blair is prepared to be as ruthless a
leader as she once was. His dealings with the unions suggest that he is a
politician who is not prepared to be hostage to the fortune of others or
in hock to special interest groups. However Blair's view that 'The
culture of politics should start to catch up with its reality'[44] needs to be
matched by a leadership style which is not only radical and ruthless but
also one which fosters a more honest, more authentic and mature style
of politics.

But fostering national renewal will involve much more than a change
of leadership style in government. Any government must also be at
ease with the cultural forces shaping the country. Thus Blair's second
challenge as the first post-Beatles politician is to show that he takes
culture seriously. In general, political parties have remained cut off
from the influences of popular culture and remarkably reluctant to
take culture seriously. We have still never had a government or a
political leadership which is truly at ease with popular culture. It is still

the norm once you reach the top to become an opera lover and for arts funding to be devoted to the high art forms – theatre, opera, and paintings. But just imagine what it would be like if we had a political leadership that was genuinely at ease with popular culture – music, dance, film and video – promoted these and gave them the same backing as other more traditional arts forms.[45] There are precedents for this. For a time the French Socialist government under the late President Mitterrand and Jacques Lang, the Minister for Culture, tried to tap into popular culture in this way and the GLC in its heyday placed great importance on having an active and effective cultural policy to create a feel good factor as well as to promote local job creation.

Third, any attempt at national renewal with the aim of creating 'a young country' must begin by defining what it means to be British in the 1990s[46] and to do so it must involve all stakeholders, however diverse their views – young and old, women and men, and, vitally important, all our diverse ethnic groups – if we are to be able as a nation to face the future with confidence about our identity and our past. But such an enterprise is inherently dangerous in a society where values have fractured so markedly. Yet we cannot move forward until this is done.

Fourth, any attempt at national renewal must also involve all those groups who have historically been absent from decision-making processes – such as women, the young, and ethnic minorities – and make their involvement the key source of rejuvenation. But acquiring a more diverse mix of decision-makers can only be a starting point for shaking up our system of governance. A young country also needs to be free of the outdated institutional legacies of the past. Constitutional and electoral reform will be inevitable as will the kind of reforms of registration, voting and participation that I have already outlined.

Fifth, a young country by definition needs to take inter-generational equity issues seriously. Blair himself has been the politician who has let the genie of generational politics out of the bottle, but he does not yet seem to have developed a coherent view of inter-generational equity issues. Dealing with these equity issues between the generations is vital if the concept of the 'young country' is to be meaningful because so many of the big political issues – from the future of the welfare state right through to the future of our planet – are concerned with the rights and responsibilities that each generation bears to the other.

Sixth, all the rhetoric of a young country will be completely meaningless if large numbers of young people still don't have any stake in the system. This is partly a product of demographic change and partly a product of disproportionately high rates of unemployment amongst today's young people. The creation of viable schemes of job creation will probably be the greatest challenge for any government of the left: in particular solving the problem of creating meaningful work and jobs for that minority of men who are not well equipped culturally or in terms of skills for the service sector jobs that are currently on offer. Nor are there any easy answers. Certainly there needs to be a cultural change on behalf of young men to recognise that their future rests upon their willingness to take up what used to be called 'women's jobs' in the service sector – like retail and catering – but it also requires at the same time a genuine commitment by government to offer young people fairer deals, whereby they are rewarded for taking on those jobs or acquiring those skills rather than being left to rot on the scrap heap. But marginalised young men are not Blair's only problem. He must also manage the anxieties of people in their twenties and thirties who are in insecure jobs and who fear that they will be the first generation in a long time whose living standards relative to their parents will decline. Managing the potent mix of their high expectations and what many fear to be a deteriorating means of fulfilling them will be a major political challenge.

Seventh and finally, Blair's politics will stand or fall by their capacity to foster a sense of social cohesion. Blair does seem to have a reasonably well developed view of how to tackle the erosion of social cohesion. Many of his solutions are drawn from his social conservatism – his commitment to being 'tough on crime, and tough on the causes of crime', his commitment to strong communities and to stable families – but he also needs to go further. The tough rhetoric of social conservatism needs to be tempered by an understanding of the much more volatile politics of exclusion that is now evident in 1990s Britain and the vicious cycle that sets in in some of these disenfranchised communities. Blair has been vulnerable to the criticism that he has not sufficiently addressed the needs of the most marginalised groups in our society and that he often does not seem to understand their needs. Yet it goes without saying that a new country cannot be born unless there is a commitment to tackle the inequities of the old.

There are signs that Blair has begun to make this next crucial rhetorical shift. His commitment to foster the trust and social cohesion necessary to build one nation through his commitment to a stakeholder economy makes explicit the connections that he is making between social cohesion, economic efficiency and the avoidance of an underclass cut off from society's mainstream, living on the fringes of the informal economy and drifting into crime.[47] His challenge will be to find workable policies which will actually achieve these goals.

BEYOND BLATCHERISM

Tony Blair has the capacity to be the most important radical leader of the left in living memory and to define a decade's political history in the way that Thatcherism defined the 1980s. The fracturing of British values will make it extremely difficult for Blair to build a coalition of support which is credible to diverse constituencies.

It is because the landscape of Britain has changed so much since World War II and because its impact has been so unevenly felt – by class, gender and generation – that Blair's image as well as his politics has to be as diverse as the constituencies he has to court. He is a child of the 1960s, and the first genuinely post-1960s political leader, and at the same time a social conservative, a practising and committed Christian with strong personal views both about the desirability of two parent families and a fervent believer in the duty we all share to one another.

For observers of the political scene the result is that it is hard to make any firm conclusions about Blair and his politics. It is already clear however that if Blair can balance the demands of the more vocal (and more numerous) social conservative lobby with the needs, aspirations and values of younger people, he may well prove himself to be a truly inspired political leader and someone who is capable of fostering a sense of social cohesion. If however he fails, if he chooses to play solely to the gallery of the social conservative voter, it is highly likely that inter-generational tensions will continue.

This is why the young country theme is potentially so important. It forces Labour to think not just about the short-term electoral benefits of appealing to the old, but also about how to connect to a generation who will in time run the country. It forces Labour to think more honestly about how to make socialist ethics both modern and relevant. It pulls Blair away from a politics which emphasises duty to one which emphasises responsibility. By doing so, Blair comes close to linking his political vision to the new ethics of personal responsibility and to connecting with a dislocated generation that still has no sense that it is yet represented in the mainstream debate.

Through his call for national renewal, Tony Blair is overtly trying to overcome the current malaise which seems to haunt all Western democracies by offering ordinary people the chance to shape their country's destiny and to participate in its rejuvenation. In this respect he has gone further than most politicians to date in tackling the causes of people's disconnection from mainstream politics. As Theodore Zeldin puts it: 'The current weariness with old-fashioned politics represents not lack of interest in the common good but near despair at the difficulty of contributing to it, and at the regularity with which idealistic leaders have made compromises with hypocrites despite themselves, or with the dogmatic, despite their principles'.[48]

REFERENCES

1 See Stuart Hall, Doreen Massey, Michael Rustin, 'Uncomfortable Times', Editorial, *Soundings*, Volume 1, Issue 1, 1995. Many of the articles in this first edition often seem content to caricature the position of new Labour whilst showing little appreciation of the forces transforming our politics and culture.

2 See John Rentoul, *Tony Blair*, Little, Brown and Company Limited, 1995, for an instructive account of the respective political fortunes of Cherie Booth and Tony Blair.

3 See 'State of the Nation' in *British Public Opinion Newsletter*, Volume XVII No 4, MORI, London, 1995, which reported on the MORI/Joseph Rowntree Reform Trust. 'Dissatisfaction has rapidly accelerated during the 1990s and by March 1991 the proportion of people expressing a positive view about the system had fallen to one in three and the number of people who express dissatisfaction with the way Parliament is working has doubled in four years since 1991.'

4 See Simon Atkinson, 'Suspicious Minds; public distrust of government' in *Demos Quarterly*, Issue 7, Demos, London, 1995, pp12-13. MORI's survey reported on in this article found that both the elderly and Conservative supporters who are traditionally less critical of the political system have shown a particularly sharp increase in dissatisfaction since 1991.

5 See John Curtice and Roger Jowell, Chapter 7: 'The sceptical electorate', in *British Social Attitude*, 12th report, Dartmouth Publishing, Aldershot, 1995. This study found that twenty years ago 14 per cent of the public felt that they had no effective say in what the government does. This figure has now doubled and those people who believe that the 'system of governing Britain' works well has dropped steadily from 48 per cent to 29 per cent during the same period.

6 See John Curtice and Roger Jowell, *loc.cit*. This study found that fewer than one in four voters believe that British governments of any party place

the national interest above their party's interests. See also *Planning for Social Change*, Volume 2: Analysis and Implications, p33, Henley Centre for Forecasting, London, 1994/1995. A poll for *The Times* in November 1994 also found that just 14 per cent of the population trusted politicians to tell the truth, whilst just 11 per cent thought that government ministers would tell the truth.

7 See Ken Young and Nirmala Rao, 'Chapter 5: Faith in Local Democracy' in *British Social Attitudes*, 12th report, Dartmouth Publishing, Aldershot, 1995. See also Elsa Ferri, *Life at 33: 5th National Child Development Study*, ESRC/City University and National Children's Bureau, London, 1993, p168. This study found that people in their early thirties thought that politicians were in politics for their own benefit and 29 per cent felt that it made no difference which party was in power.

8 See Helen Wilkinson, *No Turning Back: generations and the genderquake*, Demos, London, 1994, p43. This figure first published in this short book has been arrived at by two independent sources. Nick Sparrow, Director of ICM Research found that 43 per cent of under 25 year olds did not vote in the last election. John Curtice from the University of Strathclyde's Department of Politics and co-author of the British Election Study 1992 also comes up with a figure of between 41-45 per cent.

9 See Michael Banks, Inge Bates, Glynis Breakwell, John Bynner, Nicholas Emler, Lynn Jamieson, Kenneth Roberts, *Careers and Identities*, Open University Press, Oxford, 1992, pp128-129.

10 See Elsa Ferri, *op.cit.*, 1993; Helen Wilkinson and Geoff Mulgan, *Freedom's Children: Work, Relationships and Politics for 18–34 year olds in Britain Today*, Demos, London 1995, pp98-122.

11 See Alison Park, 'Chapter 3: Teenagers and their Politics', in *British Social Attitudes*, 12th report, Dartmouth Publishing, Aldershot, 1995.

12 See *Teenager Aspiration Survey*, MORI & City and Guilds, London, 1995.

13 See *Careers and Identities*, ESRC Research Briefing 4, ESRC, London, 1992. The authors of this study concluded that 'no existing political party has a set of ideas which fits in with those of the young people studied ... particularly the issues of concern to young people, such as equal opportunities and the environment'.

14 See Helen Wilkinson, *op.cit.*, 1994 and Helen Wilkinson and Geoff Mulgan, *op.cit.*, Both books summarise up to date research on value shifts and poll data from the perspective of different generations.

15 It is important to stress that there may well be significant medium and long term benefits to having more women in Parliament. In other countries like Norway for example the parties have taken much more active steps than in the UK to change their gender balance and to preempt rejection by a more assertive generation of women. The Norwegian Labour Party for example decided in the early 1980s that at least 40 per cent and not more than 60 per cent of their candidates should be women. The other parties followed and remarkably quickly gender issues ceased to be controversial with many observers commenting that political styles also changed with more informality and authenticity. Demos' focus groups with representative

samples of the UK population under 35 also found that women (and men) looked favourably on the Labour Party for having a greater presence of female MPs.

16 See Helen Wilkinson, *op.cit.*, 1994, p41 reporting on MORI's *Women and Politics* poll published in 1994 to accompany the 75th anniversary of women's rights and also Helen Wilkinson and Geoff Mulgan, *op.cit.*, pp98-9 which reported on a survey by MORI *Socioconsult* which found that younger women were considerably less likely than men to be interested in politics.

17 It is interesting to observe that younger generations were some of the most enthusiastic supporters of Blair's decision to rewrite Clause Four and Blair also seems to be attracting younger generations to join the party with the majority of Labour's new members reported to be under 40 in 1995.

18 'Cook claims pro Europe youth vote for Labour,' report in the *Independent*, 2 August 1995. See also Paul Whiteley, Patrick Seyd, and Jeremy Richardson, *True Blues*, Clarendon Press, Oxford, 1994. This research put the average age of a Conservative member at 62.

19 See 'Ageing Tory Membership Threat to Funding', report in the *Guardian*, 10 October 1994. Also Paul Whiteley, Patrick Seyd, Jeremy Richardson, *op.cit.*, 1994.

20 'Women Like Us don't vote Labour' report in Section Two of the *Independent*, 30 November 1995.

21 See 'Discontent in the ranks of Torywomen', the *Independent*, 15 December 1995.

22 See Paul Seyd and Peter Whiteley, *Labour's Grass Roots, the Politics of Party Membership*, Clarendon Press, Oxford, 1992.

23 See Mike Waite, 'The party with youth appeal?', *Renewal*, Volume 2, No 4, London, October 1994, p88.

24 See Helen Wilkinson and Geoff Mulgan, *op.cit.*, 1995.

25 Data provided by Bob Worcester, Chairman of MORI and presented at Demos' Generation Game Conference, London, September 1995. As many as 38 per cent of people aged between 25-34 do not read Sunday newspapers.

27 Official figures suggest that Labour has increased its membership by one third to 346,000 since Tony Blair became leader. 'Young Voters: Party people,' report in *The Economist*, London, 26 August 1995, p25. See also 'Cook claims pro Europe youth vote for Labour,' report in the *Independent*, 2 August 1995. In this article Labour's Youth Section (15-26 year olds) was reported to have increased its membership since February 1994 from 14,000 to 22,000. Within the first 12 months of New Labour under Tony Blair the average age of a Labour Party member decreased from 49 to 47, a rapid rate of change. And according to data provided by Bob Worcester, Chairman of MORI and presented at Demos' Generation Game Conference, London, September 1995, Blair was more popular with 25-34 year olds in 1995 than any other age group.

28 Bob Worcester's analysis of the *'State of the Nation'* survey found that younger generations are most supportive of some form of electoral reform

and the most dissatisfied with our system of governance. These results were presented at Demos' Generation Game Conference in September 1995.

29 See: 'Lean Democracy', *Demos Quarterly*, Issue 3, Demos, London, 1994.

30 See Helen Wilkinson and Geoff Mulgan, 'Chapter Four – Reconnecting Politics', *op.cit.*, 1995.

31 See Helen Wilkinson and Geoff Mulgan, *op.cit.*, 1995.

32 Direct quote from a Speech by the Rt Hon Tony Blair MP, Leader of the Labour Party at the *Spectator*'s Annual Lecture, 22 March 1995.

33 See Helen Wilkinson and Geoff Mulgan, *op.cit.*, 1995 for poll details and degree of social and political disconnection.

34 See Theodore Zeldin, 'Chapter 8 – How respect has become more important than power', *An Intimate History of Humanity*, Sinclair-Stevenson, London, 1994, p143.

35 *Planning for Social Change*, Henley Centre for Forecasting, London, 1995. Their survey found that only 44 per cent of under 25 year olds in Britain expect their living standards to exceed those of their parents compared to 69 per cent of 45-59 year olds.

36 See Helen Wilkinson and Geoff Mulgan, *op.cit.*, 1995 for poll details.

37 Barbara Follett, 'Closing the Gender Gap', *Fabian Review*, Volume 105, No 3, Fabian Society, London, 1993.

38 See Helen Wilkinson, *op.cit.*, 1994 for more on this theme.

39 'Why Women Must be Central to the Left', reported in the *Guardian*, London, April 1994.

40 According to figures presented by Bob Worcester at Demos' Generation Game Conference, Blair reaped the benefits in 1995 and made inroads into the women's vote with women aged 25-34 being more likely to vote Labour than Conservative.

41 Anthony Heath and Dorren McMahon, 'Chapter 1: Consensus and Dissensus' in *British Social Attitudes*, 8th report, Dartmouth Publishing, Aldershot, 1991.

42 This is according to Joni Lovenduski, Department of Politics, Southampton University, who has been conducting qualitative research on women's attitudes to Labour. This finds that women are more cautious and less likely to believe in Labour's competence to manage the economy than men are.

43 Direct quote from the Rt Hon Tony Blair MP, Leader of the British Labour Party, speaking at NewsCorp Leadership Conference, Hayman Island, Australia on Monday 17 July 1995.

44 *Ibid.*

45 See Geoff Mulgan and Ken Worpole, *Saturday Night or Sunday Morning? From Arts to Industry – New Forms of Cultural Policy*, Comedia, London, 1986.

46 See Philip Dodd, *The Battle Over Britain*, Demos, London, 1995.

47 See for example speech by the Rt Hon Tony Blair to the Singapore Business Community, 8 January 1996.

48 See Theodore Zeldin, *op.cit.*, 1995, p144.

ABOUT SIGNS OF THE TIMES

Signs of the Times was founded in early 1992 as an independent and open discussion group. Its founding statement sets out the following perspectives and aims.

We are living through New Times. Our world is being remade. A fundamental political, economic and cultural restructuring is taking place – the outcome of which remains uncertain. Through these changes, our identities, our sense of self, our subjectivities are being transformed.

Signs of the Times *is a project committed to exploring the new times analysis pioneered by* Marxism Today *in he late eighties and developing an understanding of the profound changes which are redrawing the political and cultural map. We aim to chart this new landscape and shape our agendas for the nineties.*

Signs of the Times *is independent and open. We are creating a free-thinking and participative culture sadly lacking in party politics. By this process we seek the remaking of the political.*

The group organises an autumn and spring seminar series in London each year. Apart from the contributors to this collection, others who have opened discussions at these seminars include – Ted Benton, Paul Gilroy, Ernesto Laclau, Doreen Massey, Suzanne Moore, Geoff Mulgan, Michael Rustin, Martin Shaw, Sue Slipman, Judith Squires and others. Themes for the series have ranged over the renewal of ethical politics to the rise of new protest movements and the assault on reason and rationalism.

Each summer *Signs of the Times* organises a major international, interdisciplinary conference. In 1994 the group organised 'Foucault: The Anniversary Conference'. In 1995 'Postmodern Times' and in 1996 'CityStates'.

Signs of the Times also produces a regular series of discussion papers. In 1994 the first *Signs of the Times* book was published by Lawrence & Wishart, *Altered States: Postmodernism, Politics and Culture*. Edited by Mark Perryman, contributors included Angela McRobbie, David Morley, Greg Philo and Ken Worpole.

Details on *Signs of the Times* seminars, conferences and discussion papers are available from *Signs of the Times*, PO Box 10684, London N15 6XA. Tel (0181) 809 7336.

INDEX